'Ponsonby has done it again! His new book is a timely and prophetic call to the Church today. Simon has the ability to bring Biblical truth to the centre with power, humour but also vulnerability. We need this! We cannot have more of our God's power without holy living. As Simon so brilliantly points out, it is only by the grace and goodness of our God that we see our deepest need for him! This book stirs me, and reminds me that without God we are hopeless, yet with God full redemption and restoration is found!'

Christy Wimber, author, speaker and pastor of Yorba Linda Vineyard, Southern California

'Simon's excellent book on holiness is timely and clear. We all need to share his vision for *vintage church* in the best sense of the expression. I found this treatment of an essential subject strong, compelling and convicting in equal measure. It is wide-ranging yet focused, and engaging without being holiness-lite. Read, repent, pray and share'

Adrian Reynolds, Director of Ministry, The Proclamation Trust and Associate Minister, East London Tabernacle Baptist Church

'The church today is confused about the nature of holiness. Much of our moral discourse seems to miss entirely God's call to be holy. In this context Simon's book is a welcome prophetic call for us to return to our roots. He places holiness – defined as personal and moral purity and complete devotion to Christ – front and centre of our thinking. His writing is biblically faithful and winsome, but profoundly challenging. This book will help you understand holiness, but more importantly fill you with a desire to be holy. I heartily recommend it as a spur to personal growth and challenge to mission'

Richard Jackson, Bishop of Lewes

'Simon Ponsonby is not only a first-rate theologian but a loyal and trustworthy father of the Church. No one has taught me more about God, and no book has stirred my soul more deeply to be the person I need to be for the people I love most and for the people most in need of love'

Dr Vince Vitale, Senior Tutor at the Oxford Centre for Christian Apologetics and Tutor in Philosophy and Mission at Wycliffe Hall, Oxford

'Is holiness an old-fashioned idea? Of course it is. But it is about time it became a new-fashioned inspiration, revelation and lifestyle. Simon Ponsonby writes about it well and attempts to live it well. Simon's example is not a 'hard' holiness but a warm, generous, laughter-filled and life-embracing daily living – holiness that reaches out and touches lots of lives. So read this book, as soon as you can and then get someone else to read it too. Read it and you will become a holier person'

Canon Robin Gamble, author, evangelist, Leeds Diocese Missioner and founder of Leading Your Church Into Growth

DIFFERENT

Living the Holy Life

SIMON PONSONBY

HODDER &
STOUGHTON

First published in Great Britain in 2016 by Hodder & Stoughton
An Hachette UK company

2

Copyright © Simon Ponsonby, 2016

The right of Simon Ponsonby to be identified as the Author of the Work has been
asserted by him in accordance with the Copyright, Designs and Patents Act 1988.

A CIP catalogue record for this title is available from the British Library

ISBN 978 1 473 61781 0
eBook ISBN 978 1 473 61780 3

Typeset in Sabon MT by Hewer Text UK Ltd, Edinburgh

Printed and bound in the UK by Clays Ltd, St Ives plc

Hodder & Stoughton policy is to use papers that are natural, renewable
and recyclable products and made from wood grown in sustainable
forests. The logging and manufacturing processes are expected to
conform to the environmental regulations of the country of origin.

Hodder & Stoughton Ltd
Carmelite House
50 Victoria Embankment
London EC4Y 0DZ

www.hodderfaith.com

For Harford and Jenny, Dick and Rose, Janine
and David, whose many kindnesses refreshed
the hearts of the saints   (Philemon v. 7)

Contents

Introduction

Be holy, because I am holy. (1 Peter 1:16)

This is not meant to be a rant. If it reads like one then I'm sorry. I find it easier to preach than to write and I am aware that humour and tone and expression face to face do not always translate to ink on the page. This book is meant to be a gentle provocation and an encouragement in walking with God. There's a wonderful exchange between Luke Skywalker and Yoda in a *Star Wars* spin-off[1]:

Yoda: Wake up!
Luke Skywalker: Argh! What are you doing?
Yoda: Poking you with a stick.

Think of what follows, then, as a gentle prod. I am aware that in places it is hard hitting. I hope not unreasonably nor unrelentingly so. And I trust the reader will not think me 'holier than thou'. The challenges here have been first preached to myself and continue to be worked through. The standard presented is the one I aspire to, not one that I have attained. With my namesake Simon the Fisherman, I write this as one falling on his knees before Jesus saying, 'Go away from me, Lord; I am a sinful man!' (Luke 5:8).

1

In recent years, as I have had the privilege of travelling widely and ministering in a variety of church contexts, I have met some amazing Christians and experienced some wonderful ministries. However, alongside this, I have also had a creeping concern that everything is not quite right. Despite lots of activity and enthusiasm, programme upon programme, endless conferences, a relentless pursuit of the latest claimed moves of God, a proliferation of books and ministries, and the best efforts of gifted speakers, the Western Church is rapidly declining numerically and, if my observation is right, spiritually. We have increased our time spent 'worshipping' – or at least singing – and reduced our time spent studying and applying God's word. Indeed, I often sense these two are competing with each other for prominence in church, rather than complementing each other. We have promoted revivals that have produced neither substantial conversions nor social transformation. We are always looking for the next wave of the Spirit or the next 'apostolic' superstar to lead us to some spiritual Promised Land; and some of those who made the biggest promises, who shouted the loudest and proudest about the new era the Church was about to enter into, celebrating 'new ways of doing church' and being 'missional', have left the Church with no fanfare but much fallout, and 'gone back to Egypt'.

So, this little book is my attempt to highlight some of the areas where I think we need to go back to basics, and my suggestions of what some of those basics may look like. It is not a systematic study, nor consistent in style and form. Each chapter explores a different subject, sometimes thematically, sometimes exegetically, but always biblically and hopefully applied practically. Through it all there is a call to pursue holiness, which I define as Christlikeness – and to do this through the time-tested spiritual disciplines of prayer, Bible study, fellowship, worship, obedience, giving, mission, generosity to the poor and walking in the Spirit. 'This is what the LORD says: "Stand at the crossroads and look; ask for the ancient paths, ask where the good way is, and walk in it, and you will find rest for your souls. But you said, 'We will not walk in it'"' (Jeremiah 6:16).

So what can we do? In 1952 Oxford don and Christian apologist C.S. Lewis wrote to *The Times* calling for 'Deep Church' – a rediscovery and return to the historic foundations laid by Christ and the Apostles, rather than the somewhat superficial religion he observed as characteristic of much modern Christianity. Two generation on, we still need to heed this prophetic call and return to the deep things of God. Statistics forbid self-congratulation or triumphalism, but nor is this a time to be wallowing in self-pity and self-flagellation. We cannot soothe ourselves with misty-eyed nostalgia about former golden eras of revival and evangelical advance, neither can we sit in self-pity like Job, scraping our wounds in the rubble of what once was – and we must not batten down the hatches and merely hang on in there waiting for Jesus to rapture out the few elect that remain.

There's work to be done: we need to return to first principles. We need to remember who we are and who God is. We need to put the Lord back at the centre. We need to re-point our crumbling bricks. We need to learn to pray again, and witness again, and invest in creative imagining and missioning. Yes, results do matter – the book of Acts regularly lists numbers of those who embraced the gospel: big numbers at that. Karl Barth wrote that we must 'continually begin again at the beginning'[2] – we need a reboot, we need to return to firm foundations and first principles in what we believe as Christians and how we live as Christians. We have allowed our doctrine

3

and our ethics to be eroded, whittled away, and we have conformed to non-Christian norms. It is time for Christians to believe and behave as Christians again.

For this to happen, we must build on the foundation of a holy life. The invitation to holiness is the greatest privilege offered to humanity. It is the making of us, the remaking of us in God's image. Abraham Heschel, the wise Polish rabbi who emigrated to the USA in the 1930s, reminded us 'the hidden secret of our existence is to be found in the admonition "be ye holy". Only in holiness will we *be*.'[3] Holiness begins with recognition of God's perfection but is quickly followed up with a realisation of how far short we fall from this. Again, in an essay written for Yom Kippur, the Jewish Day of Atonement, Heschel urged his fellow rabbis to teach that the book of Psalms is 'full of expressions of embarrassment', with which the writers of the Psalms freely express their shame in their worship. Heschel encourages his spiritual leaders to 'teach . . . the meaning of sin' which he complains, is 'a word that has disappeared'.[4] We must not hide from sin, far less try to hide our sin – but if we are to be the people God has called us to be, the people Jesus died for us to be, the people the Spirit was sent for us to be, then we must, with the Psalmist, ask God to search us, know us, test us and 'See if there is any offensive way in me, and lead me in the way everlasting' (139:24). To meet God is to be confronted by his holiness and in turn exposed to our sinfulness. Moses discovered this when he met God in the bush that didn't burn; he was told to take off his shoes, for he was on holy ground: encountering God exposes our sin and requires us to separate ourselves from sin.

If we say 'Come, Holy Spirit', we must be clear what we are asking. For many it is an invitation to intimacy, or a call for power, but as spiritual teacher A.W. Tozer wrote, the Holy

Spirit is 'first of all a moral flame'.[5] The gift of God's Holy Spirit first provoked us to holiness, and if received will conform us to holiness. This is a *pneumatic*, a charismatic theology. It's wonderful to receive the thrilling filling of the Spirit, to enjoy his immediacy, intimacy and ecstasies. But it's perhaps less appealing, and certainly demands more of me, to become holy as the Holy Spirit is holy. Yes, it's easier, I'm afraid, to go from conference to conference, celebration to celebration, ministry session to ministry session, seeking to be filled with the Spirit, than it is to do the work of walking in the Spirit. The Spirit is not primarily given for our amusement or entertainment or even enjoyment, but for our transformation into the likeness of Christ and the empowerment of our service for the kingdom. While joy will be part of our experience of God, so will tears of repentance, a right fear of the Lord, and a profound aware-ness that he is holy, and we are not. If Tozer was right, if it is true that the Spirit is a moral flame, then we must challenge ourselves with the searing question: what spirit have we actu-ally received? Am I more like Christ today than I was twenty years ago? If not, what spirit is it that is working in me?

John Wimber, after seeing several close friends and col-leagues in ministry crash and burn over moral issues, said,

I have seen for years where some people who experience the grace and charisma of God deceive themselves that they don't have to work on their character because God is self-evidently with them and working through them. Gifts are given to the Church because of our generous God, but gifts without character can do much damage. Therefore I've learned to look for people with character rather than people with gifting.[6]

In recent years I have watched with pain as several friends, all of them church leaders, all 'charismatic', all 'Spirit-filled', all 'tongues-speaking', all 'evangelical' in doctrine, have abandoned their wives to have affairs. One even admitted to me, 'It's all about the sex.' It seems easily done – and done all too easily. Derek Prince, one of the most distinguished Bible teachers of the twentieth century, once said, 'I've been in ministry for over 60 years, and I am well aware that in a matter of minutes I can throw everything away that I have built.'[7] And too many do.

Meanwhile the world sees and hears it all. No wonder she looks at the Church and, seeing only a mirror image of herself with a religious veneer, along with a claim to moral superiority and divine agency, dismisses our invitation to explore Christianity. The credibility gap between what we profess to represent and what we live out is a key factor, I think, in the failure of our mission. There are three key factors: personal integrity, sexual ethics and our relationship to the poor.

The man is the message. Too little about the Christian makes the non-Christian think being a Christian is worthwhile. Hans Küng, in his treatment of the Church's holiness, speaks very strongly, seeing the source of our lack of holiness not merely as weakness or lack of discipline, but as the work of the evil one: 'There is an evil at work here which is far greater than the failures of individual human beings, a force which can only be described as demonic; it is this which leads to the perversion of what is Christian.'[8] The Catholic priest, writer and spiritual director, Brennan Manning, once wrote, 'The greatest single cause of atheism in the world today is Christians who acknowledge Jesus with their lips, walk out the door and deny him by their lifestyle. This is what an unbelieving world simply finds unbelievable.'[9] There is too little of God and his gospel about us Christians. To most people we are as relevant as old Amstrad computers – amusing, archaic statues that might once have served a purpose, but that are now just quaint relics.

A friend likes to joke about how so many of us have gone on pilgrimage from renewal conference to renewal conference seeking for what he describes as 'God tickling us under the arm' – yet so often the themes of sin and salvation are all too absent. If spiritual renewal does not make us more spiritual and renewed, more Christ-like, more effective in life and witness for Jesus, then what on earth are we playing at? Another friend wrote to express her confusion. Her resolve to live a celibate life until/if she marries seems a wasted effort in the face of a recent bishop's statement abandoning scriptural sexual ethics in favour of accommodating to prevailing cultural moralities. She asks, 'I'm wondering what ethics I am supposed to live by?' The implication of the bishop's unbiblical ethic, were she to follow it, would mean that 'Saturday night might just have got more interesting', as she puts it. She's right to be confused, and not a little annoyed – what is the point in seeking to live a godly life in Christ Jesus if some of our most senior leaders, as a locus and focus for Christian truth, are busily pulling the moral ground from beneath our feet by declaring that we are free to design our own sexual ethic?

Long ago the Danish philosopher Kierkegaard wrote of attending a grand church service and being struck by the contradictions between the sermon and the sermoner, between the extravagant church trimmings and the Scripture reading that stated: 'God has chosen the lowly and despised of the earth'. Kierkegaard mused that there was nothing lowly in the pomp and splendour of the service and he wondered, 'Why does no one laugh?'[10] Today in the West, society does look, and laughs,

7

and looks away – she votes with her feet, and has rejected what the Church has to offer.

When the missionary to India, E. Stanley Jones, met the Hindu philosopher Bara Dada, he asked him about Jesus. Dada commented, 'Jesus is ideal and wonderful, but you Christians, you are not like him.'[11] Most of us are not like him. I'm not. But we should be, and we could be, if only we truly received his Spirit and walked in his Spirit, and didn't grieve his Spirit. What are we playing at? The Church in the West is sick but soldiering on. But for how long? We can believe all we like that our creative courses exploring the faith, our fresh expressions of church, or our hearty summer festivals are making a significant difference and impacting the nations, but the best of it is too little too late, and too much of what we do is just shuffling seats around. For all our prayer labyrinths, candles, pebbles and wigwams, I am not aware of any lasting wave of church renewal. Changing wallpaper in a house with rising damp isn't much of a solution.

With all these enthusiasms, why so few true conversions? I'm not talking about those who breeze in, come along to church for a while, and then move on. I'm talking radical conversion to Christ that issues in the kind of transformation that is infectious. Statistics aren't always reliable in compilation and interpretation, yet the most optimistic statistics lead to pessimistic conclusions.[12] The aggressive tide of secularism has eroded much of what former church generations have built. Since the 1960s the number of people in the UK who declare themselves as having no religion has grown from 3 per cent to almost 50 per cent of the population. Sure, a few churches are growing – the African Pentecostals, for example, and Orthodox – but not through new converts, rather as a result of immigrants from Africa and Eastern Europe respectively. Recently, Linda Woodhead, Professor of Sociology of Religion at Lancaster University, stated that the Church of England and Methodist Church are 'in a state of collapse'.[13] Every town has its former church buildings, once pulsating with Christian vitality but now turned into carpet warehouses or cocktail bars, studio flats or yoga centres. How did we lose such ground? There are no doubt many factors and exigencies, but could it be that high among these is that we forgot or forsook the basics of what we were meant to be as Christians?

One final comment as we begin. The very mention of the word 'holy' can immediately make one feel guilty, a failure, or conjure up images of priests with hair-shirts and women with hairy legs; that is so not what I want this book to promote. A return to holiness is a return to the Holy One, and there is nothing dull about God. Jesus Christ, the Holy One, is all life and in him is fullness of life. I believe holiness to be a joyful pursuit. There is nothing miserable or morose about true holiness – as Anne Lamott famously wrote, 'laughter is carbonated holiness'.[14] Holiness is happiness – the holy person should be in awe, not looking like Eeyore. The Pharisees thought they were holy yet looked as if they had drunk a pint of drain-cleaning fluid. No, we are invited to be holy as God is holy – and rejoice.

There is a wonderful scene in Nehemiah 8 as the people gather in Jerusalem to listen to God's word read and applied by the Levites. Aware of their failure to measure up to God's law, they begin to weep, but that very weeping is a sign that they get it at last, and God's word to them through Nehemiah is: 'Go and enjoy choice food and sweet drinks, and send some to those who have nothing prepared. This day is holy to our LORD. Do not grieve, for the joy of the LORD is your strength' (Nehemiah 8:10).

Chapter 1

Sindividual

...for all have sinned and fall short of the glory of God. (Romans 3:23)

For the wages of sin is death, but the gift of God is eternal life in Christ Jesus our Lord. (Romans 6:23)

Christianity rejects as a fiction the notion that humankind of its own devices can significantly improve itself without God. It lays the blame for the world's ills on what it terms sin, the universally prevalent and malevolent moral virus. Sin is anything we think, say, do or don't do that contravenes what God would have us think, say, do or not do. What God would have us say, think, do or not do is revealed to all in the conscience, in Scripture, in a general revelation in natural law, and pre-eminently in Christ. Sin is a refusal to live life God's way.

I was leading a retreat when I met Carol. A woman in her early sixties, she was effervescent with delight in Christ. There was a transparent integrity to her joy that was infectious, as she shared how she was actively and effectively involved in mission teams and evangelism. I asked her to tell me something of her journey of faith. She began by sharing how over many years, from a young lady into middle age, her life had been shrouded in clouds of dark memories because of something she had done that left deep shame and guilt. She had no Christian back-ground, but her husband was a nominal Catholic and he compounded her sense of guilt by saying that the things from her past that plagued her were in fact Mortal Sins from which there could be no forgiveness, and she was condemned to hell. (Some husbands can be less than helpful!) So she would some-times pray to the unknown god in the sky to forgive her, and occasionally would go into a church to kneel at the rail and seek to cast off her angst-ridden burden of guilt. But nothing helped and she felt emotionally, existentially and spiritually ground into the ground by it.

One day as she was driving to the supermarket, into her mind as clear as a bell dropped the words 'Romans 3 verse 23'. Having no church background, she initially had no idea where on earth these words came from or what on earth they meant. She did her shopping and returned home, but these words stayed in her mind and she wondered at last if they might be from the Bible. Rummaging around she found an old Authorised Version Family Bible, and set to searching – sure enough she soon located the verse that had echoed in her mind: 'for all have sinned and fall short of the glory of God'.

Yes! Exactly! This Scripture verse held up the mirror to her condition, making sense of her years of shame and pain – she, like all of us, had sinned, and her existential trauma was the result of being separated from God in his glory and goodness. She read on, 'and all are justified freely by his grace through the redemption that came by Christ Jesus'. Oh, the relief. The shame, judgement, guilt and dread of the years fell away as she drank in great draughts of grace. She saw it all so clearly: she was a sinner, no question about that, and so was everybody, but her sin was not the end of the matter. God, knowing her sins full well, had acted in Jesus' death to deal with her sins, to forgive her and to free her. Jesus had done what she could not do: he had purchased her forgiveness. Peace and joy flooded her – the weight of years was shed as she wept and fell into God's forgiving welcoming arms. When I met her, this revelation and liberation still seemed fresh to her and was evident to us – no wonder she was so filled with life: she knew God, she knew her sins were forgiven, she knew her glory restored.

Things can only get better . . . or maybe worse

I was invited to be part of a small panel in a public debate on the theme of 'Sin and Society' – taking part were an ordained psychologist, a university academic theologian and me, introduced as a priest practitioner. One of the panellists suggested optimistically that the world was, objectively, getting better. In some senses, of course, it certainly is. I had that week read a Grimsby synagogue Jewish burial register from the late nineteenth century (I know, I know, my reading is bizarrely eclectic). On one page, almost every entry recorded the death of a child in infancy – thankfully, things have changed and today more than a third of babies born in the West are expected to live to a hundred. Perusing statistics about numbers of deaths in war, from hunger, overall quality of life, access to education, real wealth, we can see that many things that might frame how we judge life's goodness are indeed improving. However, fresh in my mind was the last time I had been in that church, a couple of years before. Walking by one evening, a crowd had gathered and the church had been cordoned off. The policeman on duty told me that a man was at the top of the tower preparing to jump off. He seemed rather shaken and told me that it was his first day back to work after a colleague's suicide. He was disgusted that the crowd outside were cynically holding up their phones to record the event and shouting, 'Jump, jump, jump.' By the time I got to the top of the tower, two policewomen there had already succeeded in talking down the potential suicide. But I asked the debaters whether *people* – intrinsically, in their natures – are actually improving? My answer was no.

The same day as that debate on sin, I attended a seminar on pornography. In 1998 there were 28,000 X-rated porn sites on the Internet; one generation later there are upwards of 30 million. Years ago porn was for sad men tall enough to reach up to the top shelf. But we have witnessed an exponential rise in immorality as porn becomes the norm, with an estimated 68 per cent of young men and 18 per cent of young women using it weekly.[1] More worrying is the abuse and sex trafficking that walk hand in hand with the porn industry,[2] not to mention the psychological and social effects that are disastrous for everyone involved. Brave new world? More like depraved new world.

Morally we are confused: there was an international outcry a few years ago when a cat was thrown in a bin, and more recently when a big-game hunter killed a lion, yet there is silence and apparent indifference about the 200,000 unborn babies aborted each year in England. There has been a serious reattribution in our morality and of our values when cats, whether domestic or wild, are worth more than defenceless humans made in God's image; surely we have lost perspective?

The prophet Isaiah foresaw that the day would come when evil was called good and good evil. That day, I fear, has come. Professor Christina Hoff Sommers, the notable US philosopher and ethicist, claims 'We have been thrown back into a moral stone age' and illustrates this by noting that when she asks modern university students about categories of right and wrong, most react by becoming visibly 'insecure', because 'they don't believe there is such a thing, they believe each person must decide for themselves'.[3] Dostoyevsky posited – and Nietzsche et al. have built on his statement – that 'Where there is no God, everything is permissible.' When you abandon God, you abandon the only authoritative basis for defining right from wrong. Without an absolute moral reference point, a divine lawgiver, a moral arbiter, then right and wrong are merely pragmatic social constructs that blow where the wind takes them. But if there is a God, and if he indeed establishes moral commands on the basis of his moral integrity, then failure to comply is at best foolish and at worst blasphemous.

This is what we call sin. I want to explore four characteristics of sin and our relationship with it.

1. We are all sindividuals

The Bible says that 'sindividualism' is a universal problem: as Romans 3:23 says, 'all have sinned and fall short . . .' The psychiatrist Dr Karl Menninger wrote a bestseller called *Whatever Became of Sin?*[4] He recalled a sunny day in September 1972. A stern-faced, plainly dressed man stood still on a busy street corner in Chicago. As pedestrians rushed on their way to lunch or a business meeting or work, this stranger would theatrically raise his right arm, and point at a person near him and declare loudly just one word: 'GUILTY!' The effect on the passers-by was extraordinary. They would stop in their tracks, stare at him, hesitate, look away, look at each other, and then rush away. One gentleman turned to another and exclaimed: 'But how did he know?' How did he know that all were guilty of something?

Well, because it isn't rocket science that all are guilty of something. All have sinned, and not just superficially and occasionally – according to the Bible, we are all 'sindividuals' – not simply individuals who sin, but *people who are sinners*: sin is who we have become, not simply what we do.

Sir Arthur Conan Doyle, the well-known detective novelist and an astute student of human nature, was also a practical joker. In a (possibly apocryphal) story, he sent twelve pals, all establishment figures, a telegram stating succinctly: 'Flee immediately, all is discovered.' Apparently, ten of the twelve left the country that weekend. I am so curious about what it was they each feared disclosure of.

Mind you, people don't need telling that they are sinful. Their consciences tell them so. I have only met one person who claimed he had never sinned – and he was a nut job. Some, it's true, try to justify their sin as not really 'that' sinful; some try to pass the buck, or blame their environment, poor education, even their DNA. Some, while recognising sin in themselves, try to suppress it by the exercise of their will-power; while many religious types attempt to atone for their own sin, to balance the scales in their favour by doing 'good works'. Mostly, people compare themselves against others – the worst they can think of: sexual offenders, or Nazi criminals – and take comfort that by contrast they are really rather good people. Of course, by comparison to Hitler everyone comes off well, but the correct comparison is not with the worst but the best: Jesus Christ. Paul says we sin and fall short of God's glory – the beauty of his glory is moral perfection, and that is the standard. As German theologian W. Günther writes, 'Yahweh is the yardstick.'[5]

Many times when folk hear I'm a priest I've received the response, 'I'm not religious, but I keep the commandments.'

My reply is generally to ask, 'Which ones?' Which command-ments of God do you keep? All 613 precepts of the Torah? The Ten Commandments? Really?

What about Jesus' summary of the law into just two rules: 'Love the Lord your God with all your heart and with all your soul and with all your mind and with all your strength', and 'Love your neighbour as yourself' (Mark 12:30, 31). When I ask that question it generally receives a frown – but it's not intended to win a cheap point: we need to see the seriousness of our condition of sin. And yes, while some of us may keep some of God's commandments, his laws are not a multiple-choice test inviting us to attempt three questions out of ten. The fact is, all of us fail most of God's moral law, most of the time.

2. Sindividuals are miserable

The tragic irony of sin is that the little slips that may appear insignificant – or at times downright appealing – are so very costly. At creation we were clothed and crowned with glory – God's own glory, God's life-giving goodness, his radiance and divine effulgence. This was the atmosphere in which we lived and moved and had our being. But sin is a disaster, as our first parents experienced; their sin unleashed a universal apoca-lypse, but all of us have a personal responsibility in that all have sinned. Sin separates us from a Holy God – no wonder he seems like a 'pie in the sky' idea to our earthbound perception. Sin separates us from the Holy God who is the source of all life and so we forfeit life eternal and the life intended. Without God, life begins to escape from our every pore the moment we take breath. In sin we fade away: we are the grey ones, wraiths, shadows of the image of God we were destined to be. In falling away from the Holy God, the God of all glory, we forfeit our glory – everything about us is tarnished. The Danish philosopher Kierkegaard understood this, writing, 'sin alone is man's ruin'. Truly, sin is an assassin, a life-taker – nothing good ever came of it. Malcolm Muggeridge quotes St Teresa of Avila as saying 'life in this world is like a night in a second-class hotel'[6] – for some, I'd say, it is a little better than that, for some considerably worse. A few seem so numbed as to have no residue of longing for lost glory or lost God; but most of us marred God-image-bearers have a deep-down inchoate nostalgia, Pascal's 'God-shaped void', that cannot be satisfied by anything else. This is the restless heart's eternal quest for a home of which St Augustine spoke so powerfully.

Billy Graham's final sermon, a video presentation of the cross,[7] features two extraordinary testimonies of transformation, by a rapper known as Lecrae and a folk-rock singer, Lacey Sturm. They are open and honest about their lives, their pain, their failings, and their emotions before they met Jesus. Lacey recalls how 'I couldn't get away from my own depression' – searching for light and liberty she explored various therapies and philosophies but came away empty: 'a lot of nice ideas, but there wasn't any tangible healing . . . I remember thinking, "I'm tired of the pain in my heart – I'm tired of going to bed that way, I'm tired of feeling a burden, I'm tired of not knowing why I am alive."' Such was this existential wilderness, with no pain-killing palliate, that she lost all hope of ever seeing a change and spiralled into despair, firmly resolved to end it all.

The rapper, Lecrae, who tell us his nickname was 'crazy', had lost all bearings – caught up with guns, gangs, drugs, sex, he was on a trajectory that would have seen him either incarcerated for his crimes or lying dead in the street through gang violence. He recalls how he felt at that time: 'I was really hurting and I did not understand the source of all my pain and problems . . . I spent my whole life burdened for something, hungering, thirsting, chasing after this thing I could not put my finger on.' Both Lacey and Lecrae referred independently to their pain, and that's where sin and separation leaves us – all alone with our gnawing pain. The famous twentieth-century atheist philosopher, Bertrand Russell, described this well: 'the centre of me is always and eternally a terrible pain – a curious wild pain – a searching for something beyond what this world contains'.[8]

3. Sindividualism invites punishment

Our sin deserves punishment – 'the wages of sin is death'. We are made for God; created to be clothed in God's glory. But our sin has separated us from a Holy God, a life-giving God – and so we find ourselves living shrouded in death. We live and die with the consequence of our sin. The Catholic writer G.K. Chesterton said 'we sinned and grew old'.[9] Sin is a wilful 'No' to God – and we get what we act. In defining sin Paul says in Romans 1:24 that God *handed people over* to their sin (the Greek is *paradidomi*, meaning to hand over, deliver, entrust). Sin is its own reward. We reap what we sow – the bed we make, we must sleep in. In Dickens' classic psychological study, *A Christmas Carol*, Scrooge meets the ghost of Jacob Marley shaking his chains and bemoaning his condition: 'I wear the chain I forged in life – I made it link by link and yard by yard – I girded it on of my own free will and of my own free will I wore it.'[10] We bear the consequence of our own sin – and often that of others' against us. Each sin is like a link in a chain that is forged to weigh us down.

My fellow panellists in the debate on sin both claimed that God will not punish us for our sin. Nice thought, and one most hope it will prove true in their case, although they will no doubt want others to be punished for the sins they perceive themselves to have been on the receiving end of. However, I had to disagree with both the academic theologian and the psychiatrist. Our sin requires and deserves God's just wrath against it. While sin may be its own reward, while God gives us to what we choose and 'hands us over' to sin and its consequences – the biblical witness is clear that in addition to these 'natural' effects, God is active in direct and specific punishment of sin. The all-knowing God cannot simply turn a blind eye – the perfectly just judge cannot ignore wrong but must judge justly. A judge who doesn't judge is not a judge but makes himself a criminal. God cannot not judge and remain God – to not judge would be to create a black hole in God, it would be his undoing, unthinkable and impossible. Sin cannot be ignored or annulled or absorbed; it must be judged. God has set a day when he will return to judge the living and the dead. And if we die before that day, we will be called to account. The philosopher Immanuel Kant deduced the existence of a supreme divine being from his observations of the created heavens above, and the universal moral register and sense of justice within. He was aware that justice is rarely seen to be done in this life – and so he posited that there must be an absolute moral referent who would do justice after we die.

My colleague, Kate, is a keen competitive Cross-Fit athlete. Recently at the gym her fitness coach, having known she was a priest for some while but having never mentioned it or questioned Kate about her ministry, finally said: 'OK, you have three minutes to explain to me what Christians believe. I just can't get this feeling of guilt away. I'm looking for something to take my guilt away . . .' Kate did her best to share her faith in the three minutes allocated – that only the cross can make you fit for God. Sadly, the grace of Jesus that could have dealt with this woman's guilt, though it was what was needed, was not wanted. All are guilty, most know it, some suppress it, many want it removed. Every religion is predicated on the awareness of a Holy God and a sinful self, on a fear of judgement and a desire for acceptance by God. All religions put the onus on the individual to overcome their sin and make themselves acceptable to God.

Only Christianity reworks religion to actually make this possible. How so?

4. Sindividuals can be forgiven and transformed

Romans 3:24–25 says, 'and all are justified freely by his grace through the redemption that came by Christ Jesus. God pre-sented Christ as a sacrifice of atonement, through the shedding of his blood – to be received by faith.' Separation from God, dissipation in life, death and eternal judgement are the realities of the sinful condition. But they aren't God's last word on the subject. Paul states that the sindividual can be *justified* – a forensic legal term that means to be acquitted, discharged, declared innocent on all charges, standing before God as right-eous. And the sindividual, once acquitted of all sin and declared righteous, can be *redeemed*, a religious term meaning to be set free from the consequences of our sin; brought out of slavery, brought into liberty and joined to God.

And all this comes not of ourselves, by our effort or through our merit, but as a gift, *freely* by *God's grace*. Grace does not 'go Dutch' – we don't split the bill; no, Christ pays it all, covers it all, by his blood. This is truly the radical *novum*, the 'news', of

Christianity: that forgiveness costs us nothing. All we bring to God is ourselves, empty-handed, trusting, believing in and relying on nothing but God's mercy and Jesus Christ's death for us: he is our redemption. Jesus is our redeemer and his death is the price of our redemption. This is a great mystery and takes us to the edge of our human logic and language. We have already said that God cannot simply absorb sin or annul the punishment. A just judge must judge or themselves be declared guilty. A Holy God must punish human sin (the technical term is 'propitiation') and remove it from his sight ('expiation'). This is a profound mystery, and some baulk at it as being inherently unjust – how, they ask, can an innocent third party pay for the guilt of the world? But God's ways are not our ways, and his thoughts are higher than ours, and as the one offended by sin, he may choose the means to satisfy his own justice.

The cross is the criterion of everything. It shows us the seriousness of our sin – which deserves punishment at the cross – and it shows us the love of God – who gave himself as a willing sacrifice and substitute for our sin. Jesus takes our place, representative of humanity; the substitute, the sacrifice, the sin-bearer – he who knew no sin became sin for us: God laid on him the iniquity of us all. He takes our place, he receives our punishment, he dies our death, he satisfies God's just judgement. C.H. Spurgeon said, 'He saved us because he did not save himself.'[11] Indeed. And three days later, Jesus rises again by God's power: his death has settled the debt, sin is paid for, condemnation is annulled, death is defeated, life eternal and total access to God are opened up. Those who by faith, belief, trust, hold on to Christ and embrace the punishment of sin in his body on the cross for them, receive all the benefits of his death and resurrection work.

I mentioned above the stories of musicians Lecrae and Lacey Sturm, who spoke on the Billy Graham video, two people who in different ways were marred by personal and social sin, and whose lives were unravelling. Both tell how at a crisis moment in their lives, they were invited to church by a friend. They went only reluctantly. Yet they both met God. Lecrae's impression was of amazement at who was actually present in church – ex-gang members, notorious and fearsome hard-men, whose lives had evidently been turned around. And he was amazed as he heard about Jesus dying in his place, for his sins, that he might be forgiven. Lecrae knew and felt his sin only too well – he was awed at the fact that 'Jesus literally took all of this on his back for me.' The realisation was overwhelming – there was only one appropriate response: 'I remember bowing out, head on the ground, saying I'm sorry God, I'm sorry God, I'm sorry.' And he knew his many and serious sins were forgiven. So began the transformation, not without its hurdles along the way, from gangster to a rapping preacher.

Lacey Sturm, meanwhile, was dragged to church by her granny the very same evening that she had decided to kill herself. Her immediate impression on entering the service was not promising: 'I hated the church – and I really hated the preacher.' But then the preacher said something that took her breath away: he said there was someone present with a suicidal spirit. She was poleaxed – *now* God had her attention. She moved to the door, whereupon a stranger came over to her and spoke into her soul of pain and longing of things that only God could have known: 'The Lord wants me to speak to you: he wants you to know that even though you've never known an earthly father, that God will be a better father to you than any earthly father could ever be – God knows the pain in your heart, he's seen you

22

cry yourself to sleep at night.' She let this stranger pray for her – and as he did so, Lacey says, 'It was as if the God of the universe showed up right in front of me – and the first thing I realised was God is holy and good – the second thing I realised was, I am not holy or good . . . It was like God was saying: "I love you, I know you are tired of the way you've been living, and I will make you new, if you'll let me" and I said "Yes, I want that, I need that, please."' Rather than end her life that day, she entered life – she found the source of life. That night she slept the deep sleep of those who have been forgiven and freed, and woke up the next day aware of such a peace and a joy that she had never felt before. A life rescued, a life forgiven, a life transformed.

Both Lecrae and Sturm discovered what Kierkegaard found 150 years earlier. He recorded in his journal on 19 April 1848, Wednesday of Holy Week: 'My whole being is changed . . . I must speak' and 'Now with God's help I shall be myself.'

Chapter 2

New

Jesus replied, 'Very truly I tell you, no one can see the kingdom of God unless they are born again.' 'How can someone be born when they are old?' Nicodemus asked. 'Surely they cannot enter a second time into their mother's womb to be born!' Jesus answered, 'Very truly I tell you, no one can enter the kingdom of God unless they are born of water and the Spirit.' (John 3:3–5)

There is a technical term for faking your own death in order to put your past behind you – the Americans call it pseudocide. However, the British refer to it as 'Doing a Reggie Perrin'. The phrase dates from the 1970s when there was a popular sit-com, based on a series of novels, called *The Fall and Rise of Reginald Perrin* about a man having a mid-life crisis. Unable to take any more, he fakes a suicide – stripping off his clothes, leaving them with his personal effects on a beach, and thus conveying the impression he has drowned at sea. He is free to begin his life again.

There is a universal longing to begin again at the beginning; for a new birth, a fresh start in life. The specifically Christian idea of being born again may date to Jesus' conversation with Nicodemus – and has become a dismissive for enthusiastic Bible-belt evangelical types – but it expresses a deep desire in the human psyche, one that finds a wide range of expression in our culture.

Born Again is the title of a *Dr Who* episode on that theme and of an *X-Files* episode; Rudyard Kipling wrote a poem titled 'Rebirth'; T.S. Eliot wrote the famous 'in my beginning is my end . . . in my end is my beginning'. Being 'born again' is a theme found in music: there have been numerous albums entitled *Born Again*, from artists as diverse as Pat Boone and Black Sabbath, Randy Newman and the Newsboys, Mica Paris and StarSailor. 'Born Again' has been used as the title of songs sung by Oxford band Supergrass and heavy metal star Marilyn Manson. It is also a concept found in some esoteric therapies; in the 1970s the therapist Leonard Orr invented 'rebirthing therapy', a deep breathing practice, often undertaken in water tanks with the participant curled up in the foetal position, intended to simulate the pre-birth womb or birthing experience, and heal traumas and 'soul scars' received *in utero*.

(In Christian circles I have seen some similarly eccentric principles and practices in play, with candidates swamped by prayer 'ministers' pressing cushions upon them, or people shrouded in sleeping bags and told to fight their way out into new life in a psycho-spiritual ministry session, all aimed at revisiting or repeating the birth experience of the soul.)

The idea of being 'born again' is in fact a theme found within various religions – we know of its presence in Judaism and Christianity, but it was also known in ancient Greek religions, which spoke of rebirth as the cosmic renewal of all things. It was found in some mystery religions, and notably in Buddhist and Hindu thought, concerning the transmigration of the soul through successive reincarnations – although there the aim is eventually to *not* be born again but to end the cycle of rebirth and find 'oneness with the One'.

The idea of new birth, then, far from being an idiosyncratic signifier for evangelicals, is a universal register, expressing a deep longing in the human soul.

Nicodemus wanted what he saw in Jesus

In chapter 3 of John's Gospel we meet Nicodemus, expert in and devout disciple of the Torah. But Nicodemus knew he couldn't live the law of the Lord he loved and laboured over. Then, however, Jesus came on the scene. And despite what some of his colleagues thought, Nicodemus knew this man Jesus, whom some believed to be Messiah, had a power to perform miracles that he had no means to comprehend, a wisdom and authority in teaching that he couldn't match, a relationship with God that he longed to know for himself.

So he came to Jesus at night – perhaps because that was when Jesus was not too busy and he could get time to talk with him, or possibly using the cover of darkness so as to avoid being associated with Jesus – or maybe John is making a figurative point about Nicodemus being in 'spiritual darkness' and coming to the light.

We know quite a bit about Nicodemus. First, he was a spiritual person, belonging to the sect of the *Pharisees*. The first-century Jewish historian, Josephus, tells us there were only six thousand members of the Pharisees,[1] the most extremely devout religious group within Judaism. They were the religious Special Forces, meticulous in observing the law as well as the rabbinical oral regulations and religious stipulations. No one worked harder at seeking to obey the Torah than the Pharisees. Second, he was a powerful person – a member of the *Sanhedrin* – the Jewish ruling council. Seventy-one men were chosen from among all the Jews to be their political leaders and representatives to Rome, possessing power and authority. Third, Nicodemus was a *learned person* – Jesus calls him *Israel's teacher* (v. 10). This is unlikely to be hyperbole: Nicodemus was a respected rabbi, a teacher and scholar, not merely a student of the law but a professor, who instructed the people of Israel in the Torah. Fourth, Nicodemus was a *wealthy man* – his position as a senior rabbi and a member of the Sanhedrin Council would bring wealth, but probably required that he had wealth in the first place, to be considered for such a position. This wealth was displayed later when he provided embalming for Jesus' burial, seventy-five pounds of myrrh and aloes, an extravagant and costly quantity, fit for a royal burial. Nicodemus had everything the world values and more – spirituality, status, wealth and intellect; but it wasn't enough for Nicodemus, and nor, for that matter, for God.

Perhaps it was the very possession of all this good stuff that made it clear to him that something was seriously missing. Nicodemus was a good and God-fearing man, a devout, upright, orthodox Jewish leader. His religious devotion and study, far from leading to pride, had actually led to an awareness he was not all he wanted to be or that God wanted him to be. Being a devout Pharisee and a son of Abraham meant he stood inside the covenant, and was as right with God as humanly possible. But, there was the rub: he understood enough to know it was not enough. He was self-aware, and also spiritually sensitive. Though he believed that being a Jew gave him the birthright of being right with God and that being a Pharisee meant he was as faultless as a man can be by

27

tenaciously obeying the Torah, he lacked the very thing he sought and which he saw in Jesus: power over sin, fullness of life, intimacy with God, spiritual authority, and a deep assurance of entering the kingdom of God.

Nicodemus begins by telling Jesus that he recognises he is God-sent because the miracles he has seen performed witness to a divine equipping. But Jesus interrupts him in mid-flow – Jesus isn't there for dialogue, and Jesus doesn't need Nicodemus' testimony about himself. Jesus knows Nicodemus' heart, and gets to the heart of the matter, the true issue for Nicodemus – Jesus states: 'no one can see the kingdom of God unless they are born again' (v. 3). The Jews had a longing for the coming kingdom, when the Lord – through his Messiah – would rule the nations – still today, at the end of every synagogue service, they prophesy from Zechariah: 'The LORD will be king over the whole earth' (14:9). Nicodemus is looking for the coming kingdom – wondering if Jesus is the long-awaited prophet, perhaps even the king himself. Jesus repeats: 'Very truly I tell you, no one can enter the kingdom of God *unless* they are born of water and the Spirit . . . *You must* be born again' (John 3:5, 7).

Nicodemus has sought to fulfil the 613 separate laws of the Torah – which Jesus so famously summed up as loving God and loving one's neighbour as oneself – but I suspect Nicodemus is only too aware that even he, good as he is, has failed to comply fully, and he is thus concerned about his own standing with God. He sees that this Jesus has a relationship with the Father which he longs for and which his own commitment to the Torah has not brought.

Belief in Yahweh and our best attempts at obedience to obey God's laws are not enough. The Old Testament is very clear – *no one* could keep the moral law of God. Precisely because of this, God instituted the sacrificial system to enable forgiveness to be experienced and righteousness to be imputed, so as to enable the penitent to stand before God within the community of the righteous.

However, God never intended the sacrificial system to be permanent and sufficient – even as Moses instituted this system, he himself recognised that the circumcision of the flesh was not enough, declaring, among other things, that fidelity to the Torah needed to be married with a circumcision of the heart (Deuteronomy 10:12–17). The prophet Jeremiah foresaw the day when God would write his law on Israel's hearts, not simply on tablets of stone (Jeremiah 31:33); the prophet Ezekiel anticipated the arriving of the Spirit who would remove the people's hearts of stone and replace them with hearts of flesh (Ezekiel 36:26). What God required of his people, God would need to give – they could perform the outward circumcision of the body and give their best towards obeying God's righteous requirements, but God himself would need to work in their hearts by his Spirit to bring a transformation at the core of their being, truly enabling them to conform to his desires and decrees. The great Oxford apologist C.S. Lewis once wrote, 'The very activities for which we were created [loving God and neighbour] are, while we live on earth, variously impeded by evil in ourselves . . . thus the command says to us you must be born again.'[2] Being born again means to have our innermost being, our spirit – stillborn at our natural birth – awakened from lifelessness, brought back from death by God's vivifying Spirit. Being born again implies a radical end to the old and an arrival of the new. Being born again is a new start in life and a new life to start. Being born again is to come alive through the agency of the Spirit of life. This act of being born again that

Jesus speaks of is the Old Testament hope of circumcision of the heart by the Holy Spirit, enabling us to fulfil the demands of the law and fitting us for entrance into God's kingdom. This is what Nicodemus wants, what Nicodemus needs – and it is what Jesus has come to bring.

The Jewish longing for new birth

In Judaism the idea of a new birth was a very well-known metaphor employed in several ways: on a national level, metaphorically, and relating to the individual/internal life. The idea of *national rebirth* was usually associated with Israel's return from exile among all the nations, which would be accomplished by the Messiah. Isaiah prophesied, 'Can a country be born in a day, or a nation be brought forth in a moment?' (66:8). Yes, is his answer. Jews believed that it certainly could, and that it would. Some see this 'nation . . . brought forth in a moment' idea as being fulfilled in the establishment of the State of Israel in 1948. Jewish tradition teaches that when Israel offered sacrifices to God on Rosh Hashanah (the Feast of Trumpets, or Jewish New Year – see Leviticus 23:24), God considered it as though he had created Israel as a new being. But there was also a concept of *individual rebirth*, which would come at the resurrection. Job hints at his own renewal at the coming general resurrection (Job 14:14; 19:25). Jewish teaching in the Mishnah says that all Israel will share in the world to come and also that those who are Abraham's disciples will inherit it. Being descendants of Abraham and the covenant by natural birth and circumcision guaranteed being 'born again' to new life at the future resurrection. Israel thought in terms of a *metaphorical rebirth* too. Rebirth was said to occur on a man's wedding day; when he takes a wife he becomes like a new-born child (y. Bik 3:3 vii). Judaism also had the concept of *spiritual rebirth*. God told Moses, when he called him to speak as his representative, that he would create him into a new being. In 1 Samuel 13:1 the Hebrew suggests that Saul was *one year old* when he became king – later manuscripts make this thirty. However, Rabbi Manasseh Ben Israel, in discussing this, suggested the one year referred to Saul's coronation at Gilgal – one year after he received the Spirit and became a new being. In 1 Samuel 10:6 Samuel told Saul, 'The Spirit of the LORD will come powerfully upon you . . . and you will be changed into a different person.' Saul evidently calculated his new age from the time he had been born again by the Holy Spirit. The Talmud describes a convert to Judaism metaphorically as a new-born infant (b. Yeb 22a, 62a, 48b; y. Bik 3:3 vii), those circumcised as if they have been newly 'born' into the covenant.

When Jesus tells Nicodemus he must be born again, though, Nicodemus seems surprised. Or is it that he feels uncomfortable at the directness of Jesus? Whatever the motivation, in rabbinical debating mode he asks Jesus how an old man can enter into a womb again. 'Surely they cannot enter a second time into their mother's womb to be born!' (John 3:4). Nicodemus was an expert in Jewish Scripture and culture. And the concept of new birth was not a new one. Like all the others, this devout scholar of the Torah hadn't made the connection between the promises of future physical rebirth at the resurrection, and the need for a present spiritual rebirth and heart-circumcision by the Holy Spirit. Jesus responds that as Israel's teacher he should understand these things. The Old Testament is clear – *no one* can fully keep the law of God by their own effort. What is required is a circumcision of the heart, a transplant of the heart of stone with one of flesh and a writing of God's laws on the heart by the Spirit. That alone fits us for entry into the future kingdom of God – the thing that all Jews longed for. And that fitting for the kingdom cannot come except by an invasion by the Holy Spirit – being born again, being born from above, being born by the Spirit.

What does Jesus say about new birth?

Jesus says to Nicodemus, 'Very truly I tell you, no one can enter the kingdom of God *unless* they are born of water and the Spirit . . . *You must* be born again' (John 3:5, 7). Let's explore what this means.

1) New birth is personal

Jesus said, '*You* must be born again.'

The invitation and the challenge confronts us individually and personally. We need to be born again. But it is our decision as to whether we will be. You cannot enter heaven based on the faith of your father or mother or the prayers of the vicar. There is no salvation by proxy; no one can be born again for someone else. Nicodemus may be Abraham's descendant, but Nicodemus must, like Abraham, exercise his own faith and he must himself be fitted for God's kingdom. God has no spiritual grandchildren – each of us individually must experience regeneration, new birth. The well-known American spiritual guide, A.W. Tozer, wrote, 'Men do not become Christians by associating with church people nor by religious contact, nor by religious education; they become Christians *only* by invasion of their nature by the Spirit of God in the new birth.'[3]

2) New birth is imperative

'You *must* be born again.'

There are no other alternatives, there are no exceptions, no get-out clauses. There is only one way to see and enter the kingdom of God, and that is by new birth. New birth is not one among many options – one of many paths up the mountain of God to heaven. New birth is the necessary prerequisite to entering the kingdom of God.

3) New birth is passive

'You must *be* born again.'

This is not something you do to and for yourselves, not something you can work up or conjure up from within; you do not have the capacity to birth yourself – new birth comes from outside, by an invasion of the gift of God's Spirit. The Spirit is both the impregnating seed of life and the midwife. The text in 3:3 is generally translated as being born 'again or anew', meaning 'at a point in time', but the Greek *anothen* can also mean 'from a source that is above', and both these senses are implied in this deliberately ambiguous term. New birth is a rebirth, one made possible by a power that is beyond us. New Testament Professor Leon Morris wrote, 'It is the perennial heresy of the human race to think that by our own human efforts we can fit ourselves for the kingdom of God'[4] – but we cannot, we must receive it as a gift, from above, from the Spirit, from God. The answer to our problems is found outside of ourselves.

4) New birth is radical

'You must be *born again.*'

While we do not make this change happen – it is something that happens to us – it happens in the profoundest sense, at the core of our being. New birth is not a superficial moral make-over, a spiritual facelift – new birth is not like having a life-coach to help you tighten up on a few things. New birth is a radical, total, soul revolution. It is life from the dead.

5) New birth is unrepeatable

Buddhism has several rebirths, and the successful conclusion that is sought is an end to rebirth. But Christianity only has one, and we only need one. The tense of the Greek text is what is termed a 'punctiliar aorist' – an action that takes place in a moment, an event at a particular point in time. This is not repeatable; it has either happened, or not happened: you are either stillborn in sin, or born again by the Spirit. It may, and generally does, come as part of a long process of awakening and of moving towards God, but the miracle of new birth, new life, occurs in an instant, a moment. Though a woman may be in labour and the child 'coming' for hours, even days, the birth itself is an either/or moment. And spiritual rebirth is an event that cannot be undone, reversed or lost. Those who are new-born, if they have been truly reborn, cannot be unborn.

How are we to be born again?

Malcolm Muggeridge converted to Christianity after a life of enjoying all the world could offer. He realised the world was morally bankrupt, he was sinful and powerless to change himself – and he longed for the God he saw in Mother Teresa. He said,

> . . . man's efforts to make himself personally and collectively happy in earthly terms are doomed to failure. He must indeed, as Christ said, be born again, be a new man, or he's nothing. So, at least I have concluded, having failed to find in past experience, present dilemmas and future expectations any alternative proposition. As far as I am concerned, it is Christ or nothing.[5]

Believing in Jesus is the basis for new birth. This great gift of God is appropriated only by trusting in the death and resurrection of Jesus, the Son of Man, the Son of God, the king of the kingdom – who will bestow his Spirit on those who believe, who circumcises the heart and regenerates us, and fits us for the kingdom of God. Jesus tells Nicodemus: 'Just as Moses lifted up the snake in the wilderness, so the Son of Man must be lifted up' (v. 14) in order that 'everyone who believes may have eternal life in him' (v. 15). Jesus continues, 'For God so loved the world that he gave his one and only Son, that whoever believes in him shall not perish but have eternal life' (v. 16). And again: 'Whoever believes in him is not condemned, but whoever does not believe stands condemned already because they have not believed in the name of God's one and only Son' (v. 18).

Jesus is adamant that Nicodemus should not miss his emphasis – the idea of new birth is wedded to the repetition of the need to believe. Jesus is telling Nicodemus that new birth, the reception of the Spirit, the circumcision of the heart, entry into God's kingdom, comes through faith in him, through Jesus. He is the One who has come from heaven, the Son of Man as seen in Daniel's vision of God's king; like the bronze snake on a pole that Moses lifted up in the wilderness to turn away the curse, so Jesus, lifted up on the cross, would bear sin's curse and turn it away. By looking to him, by trusting in him as bearer of sin and Son of Man who will bring the kingdom, new birth is received.

Faith in Jesus' blood, not sharing in Abraham's blood, is what saves. This is totally *inclusive*: it applies for all who believe – and it is totally *exclusive*: only for those who believe. Those who do not believe are already in that place of being condemned, whether Jew or Gentile. Professor C.K. Barrett in his magisterial commentary on John stated, 'There is no neutral ground between perishing and having eternal life – they are absolute alternatives.'[6] Believing in Jesus brings new birth, disbelieving keeps one dead in one's sins. This is the Bible's binary. Believing is all that is required, but believing *is* required.

———

'Behold, I make all things new'

You really can be born again – the Spirit can make you totally new, transform you from what you were and conform you into the likeness of Jesus. On a ministry trip to New Zealand I met the remarkable Revd Dr Mick Duncan. His story was extraordinary. He had been a hippy in the early 1970s, and was expelled from university after sitting his exams while high on LSD – his efforts in the exam, unsurprisingly, did not reach the required standard. He was homeless for two years, living on

the streets, a drug user himself and a dealer, permanently
stoned. He has no memory of two whole years of his life – the
drugs have erased the record. (Occasionally he meets people
who knew him then, and they fill in some details.) He met a
Christian witnessing on the streets who cared for him and
who, incredibly, gave him his own rented room and all his own
clothes and belongings. In the room he was given, there was a
Bible on a coffee table. Mick had only encountered the Bible
once before, but began reading it, and slowly, slowly, he was
wooed to Jesus. However, Mick was very aware of the challenge in discipleship, the cost of following Jesus. He knew this
was not simply a question of a light life makeover – that Jesus
demanded all. So for nine months Mick wrestled with the
decision whether or not to follow Jesus, to accept the new life
he offered and hand over his life to Jesus. Each day he walked
round Hagley Park in Christchurch, wrestling with the cost of
discipleship. Finally, in 1976, Mick says,

> in that room given to me, I got down on my knees and said
> to king Jesus 'I now pledge my troth, my loyalty to you,
> my king and my life will now be governed by an obedience
> that will come before all other obediences, there will now
> occur an allegiance shift, in the very core of my being, and
> that no matter what it costs, my life will be governed by a
> leader.' The initial response was one of loyalty to king
> Jesus . . . there was acceptance: I could see that with Jesus
> there was pardon, to be forgiven, his Spirit could witness
> with my spirit that I was indeed the son of a king. There
> was an incredible peace . . . a strong wind came into the
> room and started blowing inside of me – I found myself
> speaking in a language I never knew before . . . a beautiful

love language – so another life, the very spirit of the king came to live inside of my life – very soon afterwards new yearnings, desires and urges began to grow inside – so there was power, a new power . . .[7]

Now *that* is what I'm talking about – being born again by receiving the Spirit, having believed and trusted Jesus as Saviour and King. Mick met and married the amazing Ruby, and together they have served God and the poor and marginalised in various contexts – as missionaries in the slums of Manila, then serving with churches in New Zealand and Australia, and now as a theologian, writer, pastor, adjunct professor for four different universities, and with three adult children all in Christian ministry. That is 'born again' if you like! If God can do that for a stoned agnostic dropout, he can do it for anyone. He can, and he does.

Chapter 3

Thy Will – My Will

. . . not my will, but yours be done.   (*Luke 22:42*)

We have all seen it – as we queue in the supermarket a toddler sees a packet of sweets and demands to have them – there and then. The mother gently refuses, telling her beloved child that she has some nice things in the shopping basket for later. Suddenly this sweet infant morphs into a maniacal monster, shrieking at the top of its voice, throwing itself to the floor, weeping inconsolably, demanding to be appeased, seen and heard by all shoppers in the vicinity – wilfully humiliating the mother until, exasperated and red-faced, she can no longer take the shame and attention, the muttering of head-shaking observers, so she grabs the sweets and puts them in the basket. We have all seen it, maybe we've been the capitulating parent – and most of us were once this demanding, temper-tantrum-throwing child. As any parent who has raised teenagers knows full well, that wilful spirit generally lies more or less dormant between the ages of three and thirteen, only to rear its ugly head once more when the child hits their teenage years and the 'terrible twos' return, this time more sophisticated, with different demands, but essentially the same independent powerful will drawn up against your own. My sons became selectively deaf when they reached their teens – suddenly they no longer seemed to hear any instruction given; they were oblivious to 'Supper's ready.', 'Tidy your bedroom', 'Don't leave the bathroom in a mess', 'Please don't arrange your weekend without involving Mum and Dad', 'Don't expect your clothes to get washed and ironed while they remain in a heap of mould in a dark recess of your bedroom' – all alike. During their children's terrible twos or terrible teens the parent is wrestling with the challenge of an independent will set up against theirs. Hopefully the child eventually grows up and grows out of both.

One of the principles James addresses in his epistle is the tension between God the Father's good will and the self-assertive independent will of his children who so often throw tantrums to get their own way. Take James 4:13: 'Come now, you who say, "Today or tomorrow we will go to such and such a city, and spend a year there and engage in business and make a profit."'[1] James uses classic rhetorical techniques for emphasis – a three-fold repetition of the word *and*, and four-fold compounded verbs in the emphatic *we will*. This kind of behaviour is the mark of persons who are acting independently, asserting their own will before that of God. They go where they want, they do what they want, when they want, for as long as they want. They themselves are the driving force in their own lives, the subject, the decision-maker. They want their wishes, their wants, their way, on their terms. Does that sound familiar? I am certainly aware of it as a constant jostling in my own life. One of the traditional texts held by rabbinical and church tradition to be a statement about Satan's fall is found in Isaiah 14:13f. The distinguishing feature of the Lucifer, as named here, is this repeated assertion: 'I will', which is stated five times in swift succession in two short verses (13–14):

I will ascend to the heavens;
I will raise my throne above the stars of God;
I will sit enthroned on the mount of assembly . . .
I will ascend above the tops of the clouds;
I will make myself like the Most High.

The seed of evil is in the self-willing against what God wills. This is clearly illustrated by our spiritual forebears, Adam and Eve, whose great fall dragged all humanity down with them into death. They asserted their will over against God's will – they willed to eat what God forbade. The German reformer Martin Luther wrote about the human will being enslaved to sin and self-willing in his famous work *The Bondage of the Will*.[2] Luther saw clearly that the will, programmed for sin as it is, can only be brought into line with God if overpowered and subdued by the greater power of God. But in Christ our will is liberated, redeemed and able to be directed to will what Christ wills. These merchant members of the Church whom James addresses have not brought their will in line with the mind of Christ, but have held on to the independent mind and will directed to the world, the flesh and the devil. They are doing what they will, not necessarily what God wills. What they plan to do may not be wrong, but the independent nature of that willing is what is wrong.

Many Christians plan their lives with no reference to God. Some Christians plan their lives, then afterwards ask God to bless their plans. The question James provokes us to is, 'Am I willing what God wills?' Note that the issue for James is not 'making money' or 'planning for the future' per se. Both are good and prudent. But it is the doing of these things with an overt disregard for God, and indeed one's neighbour, that is the problem. Merely making money is these men's prime motive here – not making money to the glory of God and good of fellow humanity. Money is neutral, it can be used for good or bad, but 'the love of money is a root of all kinds of evil' (1 Timothy 6:10); and that seems to be the driver for these merchants. God is neither mentioned in these merchants' discussions nor consulted in their minds. The merchants are doing what they want, following the dictates of 'the flesh', their independent self-will – sin. This money-making motivation of the merchant is beautifully epitomised in an article I read in the *New Statesman*, by an Oxford student who abandoned his initial thought of working for the civil service to go into finance in the city: 'It's the only chance you get to earn seriously huge money. It's far easier to get into than other professions . . . and once you're in you're pretty much guaranteed retirement at 45.' Now, that attitude is perhaps understandable in those who may not know God, but James is discerning this attitude in the Church among those who claim to be disciples of Jesus, whose value system and life goals ought to have been renewed by the indwelling Spirit and kingdom principles.

Not everyone has the capacity to earn a lot of money or create wealth. If you are able to do so then that may be your sphere of influence, contribution and indeed vocation. But the question remains the same: for whom and for what are you earning this 'seriously huge money'. If it is altruistic, if submitted to God for his kingdom, then all is well and good. But if it is the allure of the lucre that attracts, or the security for the future it gives – to be able to retire at forty-five – then that goal is the wrong one. In James's epistle, the poor are always near the front of his thought: true religion, true holiness is to remember the poor. But these merchants not only do not seem to care about God, they don't care for the poor; money is the goal, not altruism – it is not a means to the alleviation of suffering – and as New Testament professor Peter Davids says of these merchants, 'The cry of the poor will be their undoing.'[3]

The sinfulness of the independent will

'Why, you do not even know what will happen tomorrow. What is your life? You are a mist that appears for a little while and then vanishes . . . you boast in your arrogant schemes. All such boasting is evil' (James 4:14, 16).

James focuses his critique on these merchants' presumption and their pride. First, their presumption: they arrogantly presume to plan without reference to God, assuming they are lords of their own destiny. They plan as if they hold their future in their own hands. James says, no, your life is but a mist, a vapour – the Greek term is *atmo*, from which we derive our term 'atmosphere'. A human life is so fleeting – here today, gone tomorrow. I looked in the mirror recently and was shocked to see a middle-aged man, with a white beard and crinkles and creases and saggy eyelids. I stared and said to the image in the mirror, 'When did I become you?' Distinguished evangelist Billy Graham, in a sermon he gave in 2012, recalled being asked by a university student some years earlier what the greatest surprises of his life were? He answered: 'Its brevity.'[4] Indeed. Poet T.S. Eliot wrote (in the character of J. Alfred Prufrock), 'I have measured out my life with coffee spoons'.[5] Breakfast coffee and mid-morning coffee and coffee to finish the dinner, and suddenly life has run its course. When taking funerals Anglican priests always read Psalm 103:15–16: 'As for man, his days are like grass; he flourishes like a flower of the field; for the wind passes over it, and it is gone, and its place knows it no more'[6] – how fleeting our lives, how insubstantial.

Jesus told the parable about the rich fool to warn against materialistic presumptuousness. The rich fool says,

> 'This is what I'll do. I will tear down my barns and build bigger ones, and there I will store my surplus grain. And I'll say to myself, "You have plenty of grain laid up for many years. Take life easy; eat, drink and be merry."' But God said to him, "You fool! This very night your life will be demanded from you. Then who will get what you have prepared for yourself?"   (Luke 12:18–20)

Second, James highlights the merchants' pride: 'you boast in your arrogant schemes'. They are peacocks preening themselves in public about making money and the money they make. How easily boasting comes to us. You don't have to invite *Hello* magazine to photograph your house or wedding to boast. Numerous subtle social techniques are employed to tell people what you have and who you are, to compare yourself to others, to give an impression and bolster your own belief that you are somebody with something. All this is pride, the flesh, and sin. When you subtly disclose your income, the size of your bonus, the investments you hold, your property value increase, the clothing, accessories, cars and holidays you can afford – when you broadcast where you eat out, where you shop, what club you are a member of, what school you attended – you are merely trying to impress, make much of yourself, put the other down by comparison, and it is pride, the flesh, sin. By puffing ourselves up, we put others down. To boast in wealth or in our stuff is evil because it is taking glory to oneself. To boast in wealth is evil because it leads to condescension over the poor. To boast in material wealth is evil because it places absolute value in the wrong thing, and that is idolatry. James's epistle is about the 're-evaluation of values' and the people of God are to place their worth in things that God says are worthy.

Earlier in his letter James highlights the problem of greed (4:1–5) and the problem of pride (4:6), the ugly fruits of the independent will. James warns 'God opposes the proud but shows favour to the humble' (4:6) and his counter-challenge is to walk in the opposite spirit: 'Submit yourselves, then, to God' (4:7). You cannot follow the way of the cross and the way of the flesh at the same time. The way of the cross means death to the flesh.

Holiness is our will submitted to God's will

Instead, you ought to say, 'If it is the Lord's will, we will live and do this or that.' (James 4:15)

I have a great friend called Mark who served for over twenty-two years as a combat soldier in the British Army, including seventeen years in the famed Special Air Service. He is full of remarkable stories, but one was almost beyond belief. He told me of a time when he was involved in training Special Forces for a Middle Eastern regime. They were teaching underwater techniques and one of the recruits was ordered to jump into a swimming pool, laden with webbing, and swim to the end. He duly jumped in. After a minute, when this recruit failed to surface, the instructors dived in, rescued the guy from the bottom of the pool and, fortunately, were able to resuscitate him. As he came round, to everyone's surprise he admitted he could not swim. When the SAS instructors asked his commanding officer why he hadn't admitted that before, the commanding officer replied simply and with absolute sincerity: 'If God wills me to swim, I'll swim.' But actually, his was a naive and misplaced understanding of divine determinism. God wills us to will his will, but that involves responsibility and action, not just blind trust.

Holiness is doing the will of God. Holiness is willing what he wills, subsuming our will in his. Holiness is consulting God for his will and living it. Paul tells Titus that an essential quality in those appointed to be church elders, overseeing the spiritual life of the people of God, is that they are 'not self-willed' (the Greek is *authades*) (Titus 1:7).[7] Holiness involves God in the daily decisions – an attitude that recognises and defers to God's rule. It is not independent, it is never arrogant, never self-willing nor self-determining. Holiness is the self dissolved into God. That said, it is not the self paralysed into doing nothing unless prompted by God. I knew of someone who expected God to tell them what to wear each day and when they walked somewhere, whether to go to the left or right – that's not being submitted to God's will, that's neurosis. But the submitted will prayerfully anticipates the gentle current of God's Spirit to direct, and humbly agrees to obey. The submitted will offers to God both the day-to-day and the once-in-a-lifetime decisions. The submitted will is constantly attentive to the Spirit redirecting, recalibrating directions and actions. Paul writes about his ministry plans, 'After I go through Macedonia, I will come to you . . . Perhaps I will stay with you for a while, or even spend the winter . . . if the Lord permits' (1 Corinthians 16:5–7). His plans are made under God, but held open-handedly, for God to nudge or change. Those who have a submitted will recognise they do not determine their future; they are both subject to the exigencies and uncertainties of life, and held within the sovereignty and goodness of God. The submitted will neither claims to know the future nor seeks to control the future – instead life is lived with an honouring attitude towards God, a prayerful involving of God in all decisions, and a flexibility to respond to the way the Spirit leads. Through it all, there is a desire to trust and obey God, a longing to live for his glory. We are not masters of our destiny, after all: God is.

It was common in the Victorian era to express humility when speaking or writing about future plans and decisions using the Latin term *Deo Volente* – if God wills it. The initials DV became a popular signoff to letters when future plans were expressed. Judaism has a similar form, Hebrew *Im Yirtzeh Hashem*, 'If it pleases God', and there is a similarly prominent theological concept and saying in Islam: *Inshallah*, 'If Allah wills it'. Of course it's very easy to put DV at the end of your letter but still do exactly what you want. The difficulty is always *living* 'DV'.

The Danish philosopher Søren Kierkegaard wrote a tract entitled *Purity of Heart is to Will One Thing*.[8] For us as Christians, desiring to be holy and to walk with God, that all-determining 'one thing' is 'to will what God wills'. To will what God wills, to live out the submitted will, is simply another way of saying or living 'Jesus is Lord'. This, of course, is the great challenge of the Christian life. Jesus fully complied with his Father's will – even as hell crushed in on him, he conse-crated himself to his Father and declared to the principalities and powers 'not my will, but yours be done'. We still dwell in 'Adam's Tent' – our body, the flesh, is not yet resurrected and glorified, and its inherited predication is towards sin, towards self. We struggle daily against the sinfulness programmed into human nature since Adam's fall – to bring that under the

47

Lordship of Jesus. Through prayer; through studied obedience to God's word; through drinking deeply of the transforming power of the Holy Spirit; through attentive listening to God for direction; through open-handed offering to God of the decisions and actions that frame our life; through prompt repentance and renunciation of sin; and through the cultivation of holy desire, we will increasingly will the one thing that matters – to live according to God's will.

How shall we then live?

The issue of whose will we will live by on earth has eternal consequences, as two classic authors on the subject portray so clearly. First, C.S. Lewis in *The Great Divorce* writes, 'There are two kinds of people: those who say to God "Thy will be done" and those to whom God says in the end "All right, have it your way."'[9] Those who live to God's 'Thy will be done' will spend eternity with God in heaven, while those who reject God's will and live to please their own, are those who, says Lewis, get the hell they choose. Second, Dante, in his dramatic masterwork *The Divine Comedy* describing journeys through the afterlife, meets a lady named Piccarda in the lower chamber of Paradise. He asks her whether she would not have preferred to go up higher, even nearer the throne of God, and she replies:

Brother, our love has laid our wills to rest,
Making us long only for what is ours,
And by no other thirst to be possessed.
If we could wish to bide in loftier bowers,

Our wish would jangle with that will of His
Which hath assigned our proper place and powers;
And in these gyres thou'lt find no room for this,
If love is here our necessary state,
And thou bethink thee what love's nature is.
Nay, 'tis the essence of our blissful fate
To dwell in the divine will's radius,
Wherein our wills themselves are integrate;
Whose being from threshold unto threshold thus
Through all this realm doth all the realm so please,
And please the King that here in-willeth us
To His own will; and His will is our peace . . .[10]

A Scottish Covenanter's prayer

I was given the printed pledge that follows on a visit to East
Kilbride just outside Glasgow, when speaking at a conference on the themes in this book. It is part of a lengthy and
detailed solemn vow, made by a noble Scottish lady who
had been imprisoned for her faith, over three centuries ago.
The Covenanters, so named because they signed a covenant
refusing to recognise the Stuart kings as the spiritual heads
of the Scottish Presbyterian Church, suffered imprisonment, torture and execution for treason. For the Covenanter,
no man, not even a king, could be the head of the Church,
whose sole head is Jesus. While in jail, she held to her Lord
and wrote a lengthy prayer of consecration, holding nothing back. It shows an absolute willingness to hand over her
own will to Christ's will. This is the sort of commitment
owed to King Jesus, looked for by the world and feared by
the demonic.

A SCOTTISH COVENANTER'S PRAYER

I here give my full consent to you coming and taking
possession in my soul, and to your casting out all there
that stands in opposition to you. Come Lord Jesus, subdue
all my corruptions, and bring them under your feet that
I may be, through you, a conqueror over them. I desire
here to take you for my all, to be ruled and governed
by you, surrendering to whatever shall be your way of
dealing with me. Give me yourself, and this shall be all my
desire . . . O Lord I desire to close all by giving myself up
to you and all mine . . . that when you come, I may rejoice
in you, crying 'this is my God and I have waited for Him'.

Janet Hamilton, Lady Gordon of Earlstoun,
Prisoner for Christ, Blackness Castle, December 1687[11]

Chapter 4

Take Off Your Shoes

Now when Joshua was near Jericho, he looked up and saw a man standing in front of him with a drawn sword in his hand. Joshua went up to him and asked, 'Are you for us or for our enemies?' 'Neither,' he replied, 'but as commander of the army of the LORD I have now come.' Then Joshua fell face down to the ground in reverence, and asked him, 'What message does my LORD have for his servant?' The commander of the LORD's army replied, 'Take off your sandals, for the place where you are standing is holy.' And Joshua did so.   (Joshua 5:13–15)

Doing church we've tried a lot of stuff – programme upon programme – and many were pretty good. From trying out a 'Rock Mass' or 'Raves in the Nave' in the 1980s, where contemporary music was used to update the liturgy and engage the younger generation; to Taizé services where we all sat in circles around candles and sang simple Latin *a capella*; from Marches for Jesus, when we took to the streets and sang enthusiastically to the bemused onlookers on the one hand, and the principalities and powers on the other; to trying out the Orthodox focus on reciting the 'Jesus Prayer'. Evangelistic endeavours have included courses like 'Good News down your street' or 'Evangelism Explosion', and stadium-style outreach events like Billy Graham's 'Mission England',

Eric Delve's 'Down to Earth' and, more recently, J. John's 'TEN'. We've been equipped by John Wimber's *Power Evangelism* and Robin Gamble's *Lead Your Church into Growth*, and we've run enquiry courses like The Y Course, Emmaus, Start, Alpha, Christianity Explored. We've seen remodelling of church structures, with Restoration Church and House Church and Shepherding Church and New Church and Alternative Worship, Church Planting, Emergent, Fresh Expressions, Ancient Future, Liquid Church, Cell Church, Celtic Church, Messy Church, Seeker-friendly Church, Purpose-Driven Church and driven-round-the-bend church. We've had New Monasticism, Post-Evangelicalism and New Apostolic Revival. We've done Soul Survivor's NOISE, Prayer and Pilates (no, actually, I just invented that idea), Marriage courses, Discipleship programmes, Five-Fold Ministries. We've been Toronto Blessing-ed, Ghost-busted, Inner-healed, Freedom-ed in Christ, Tacoma-ed, Sozo-ed. We do Healing on the Streets; 24/7 Prayer; Soaking, Healing Rooms, 'Harp and Bowl' and David's Tabernacle. I've tried most on this list – and some have proved good and fruitful, others less so – but in the large scale of things clearly none of these has been enough. The Church in the West, for all her efforts, is still shrinking rapidly.

Maybe it's time to try something else.

Joshua is on his face. It's the right place to be – it is said the spiritual writer A.W. Tozer used to pray each morning for a few hours, lying on his face in adoration of Christ. Songwriter Matt Redman, in his book *Facedown*, wrote: 'When we truly face up to the glory of God, we soon find ourselves face down in worship. To worship face down is the ultimate outward sign of inner reverence.'[1]

Joshua had encountered a sword-drawn warrior as he went out to survey the scene of the next day's battle against the walled garrison city of Jericho – a place probably named after the word for *moon*, indicating that this ancient city's inhabitants were most likely devoted to worship of the lunar bodies that God created – rather than the God who created the lunar bodies. Joshua begins to interrogate this stranger: whose side are you on? Are you with us or with them? And no doubt Joshua has his hand on his sword hilt ready to take on this stranger if his answer goes the wrong way. This mysterious warrior figure immediately silences Joshua's presumption with one word 'No'! Not *neither* as some translations render it, but a robust rebuke – 'Stop right there, you don't get to ask the questions here.' Recently, as I was reflecting on this passage, I was having supper with evangelist Robby Dawkins, who shared an extraordinary experience with me.[2] He said he had a vision or visitation to heaven, whether in the body or spirit he knew not. But it was vivid and he approached the Lord, and a torrent of questions flowed out of him – all the theological problems and mysteries he had always wanted an answer to. And rather than answer, the Lord told him to be quiet and listen. Robby didn't tell me what God told him – you'll have to listen for yourself. Sometimes our words get in the way and don't let God get a word in edgeways. Our speech can sometimes be presumption – the Psalmist says 'be silent before the LORD' (Psalm 37:7)[3] while Zephaniah declares, 'Be silent before the Sovereign LORD! (1:7).

Holy ground

This mystery warrior then declares (depending on your translation): 'as commander/captain/prince of the army/host/angel armies of the LORD I have now come'. Joshua is leading Israel into battle in the natural or physical realm, but there is also a battle to be fought in the spiritual or heavenly realms. Joshua will be fighting the pagan Canaanites who do not worship Yahweh, but the Prince of the Angel Armies will be fighting the spiritual demonic powers behind Canaan's idols. Then Joshua is told, 'Take off your sandals, for the place where you are standing is holy.' This is not an invitation to 'make yourself comfortable', as one commentator suggested – it's not like kicking off your shoes when you get in from work. No. This command is about making the necessary response to the revelation of God. God's presence makes this place holy ground, and you cannot remain in God's presence without making a clear sign of respect. The first requirement on coming into God's presence is to be quiet and listen; the second is to take off your shoes – to remove whatever represents a barrier between you and him. This command is the same as was first given by Yahweh to Moses as he approached the burning bush that didn't burn.

Joshua falls on his face when he realises who is before him – that's good but not enough, his shoes must be removed too. A church member recently said to me: 'At St Aldates we're good on worship but poor on holiness' – I was sad, because he was probably right. Our church is widely respected for its outstandingly gifted musicians, creative song writing and production of worship CDs. But true worship always leads to holiness. Face down. Shoes off.

Why shoes matter

Shoes were powerfully symbolic in the ancient Near East. To remove your shoes before another was to acknowledge their dignity and their authority or supremacy over you. In ancient Israel the Israelites ratified a contract by taking off a shoe and handing it to the other party – it was the equivalent of signing an agreement. This was exactly what Boaz did to secure his purpose of taking Ruth as his bride. Slaves were identified by going barefoot: you gave yourself into indentured service by writing your name on your shoe and giving it to your new master; in Luke 15 the prodigal son returned and was given shoes to wear, the father rejecting his offer to be treated as a slave.

More comprehensible to our Western use, shoes provided protection from uncleanness – this was in the days before sewers, remember, and most communities were agricultural – with plenty of animals even in the city. However, by extension the shoes themselves became unclean. In a sense, they represented one's sin. Shoes were quite literally dirty. And they were made of animal skin, which to the Jew was unclean in itself, which is why priests and Levites had to serve in the temple barefoot. David danced barefoot before the Ark of Covenant. After the destruction of Jerusalem's temple in AD 70, when no sacrifices for sins could be made and new forms to express and seek holiness were developed, in an act of piety no Jewish pilgrim would wear shoes on any part of the Temple Mount. In the Jewish commentary on the Torah, *Rash Rabba*, it says 'every place where holiness is observed you shall not wear the sandal'.[4] (Interestingly, in the medieval period, in order to be prophetically distinct from Muslims, the Jewish worshippers changed the rules and you were no longer permitted to enter the synagogue barefoot.)

The command to Joshua, as to Moses, to 'take off your sandals, for the place where you are standing is holy' prefigured all of this ancient symbolism, and ancient hearers or readers of the Scriptures – and indeed many people in Eastern cultures today – would understand very well what was taking place in this drama. However, the command to 'Take off your shoes' has lost its symbolic meaning to us modern Westerners – but

Joshua knew exactly what it meant: he was faced with one who was far superior and purer to whom reverence and allegiance was due, and Joshua duly obeyed.

God's imperative is also invitation, to remain in his presence, and so we can see that this command from the Lord is all grace – God has taken the initiative to move towards Joshua – but as a practical measure it must be done for there to be sustained communion and the receiving of God's commission. God is simply stating the basis on which Joshua can be with him, in his presence.

Why it's not about shoes

I have been at several church events where someone piously suggested that we should take off our shoes, as we were on holy ground – and I found myself hoping everyone had put fresh socks on that morning. This has always seemed more weird than worshipful to this twenty-first-century Westerner and rather reminds me of the parody in Monty Python's *Life of Brian*, where the crowd, who have missed the actual Messiah, follow Brian instead, and when his shoe accidentally slips off someone says: 'Take off your shoes and follow him.' What is required of us, I believe, is not a literal taking off of our shoes, nor indeed the command to 'Take off his filthy clothes' given to those standing before Joshua in the prophecy of Zechariah 3. But when God draws near, he requires us to be holy as he is holy. He requires us to act towards him with a heart attitude that mirrors what taking their shoes off conveyed to the ancients: repentance, and reverence. In some respects the power of this symbol was picked up by the early Christian community when baptising converts, who were required to come to the baptistry and remove their clothes – then go into the waters before emerging and being re-clothed in white. Indeed, this is still practised in certain Orthodox traditions. This symbolic act must repeatedly be lived out.

To ask God, 'What do I need to remove?' is a challenging spiritual discipline. What patterns of ingrained sin remain? What defiles me? What stands between me and God? Is there pride, greed, jealousy, temper, lust, unkindness of speech, indifference to the poor, materialism? In what ways am I not loving God with all my heart, soul and strength and my neighbour as myself?

The heart of the Christian gospel, the world's greatest news, is that Jesus took the penalty for our sin, and Jesus broke the power of sin. However, we must partner with his Spirit in obeying his word and conforming to his likeness, in throwing aside the patterns of sin and the presence of sin that clings to us (Hebrews 12:1). Some tense up at the very mention of the Christian life as something we 'do'. I was amused a few years ago when a reviewer of my previous book on holiness sharply criticised it for being 'tainted by the subtle poison of works righteousness'. I wonder whether they really read my book, or indeed the Good Book, but I definitely do not subscribe to works righteousness, which historically referred to the fiction that our own works or efforts bring righteousness. They do not. But I do believe that those declared righteous through faith in Christ and the imputation of his righteousness must themselves become practically righteous, and that definitely requires that we do something – we are not made righteous by our work but by faith in Christ's work; but those made righteous do right works. The New Testament is saturated with imperatives, commands of a moral nature. The Christian is as the Christian does. We are justified by faith, but sanctified by doing something. Yes, God saves us singlehandedly – our salvation is *Sola Gratia, Sola Fidei* and *Solus*

Christus – only by grace, only in faith, and all through Christ. But an emphasis on grace and faith for salvation without also recognising a responsibility and obedience to be holy as he is holy leaves us with a justified but unsanctified Church. We are not saved by good works, but the truly saved do work out their salvation. Dallas Willard rightly reminds us: 'Grace is not opposed to effort, it is opposed to earning.' Jesus commanded his apostles to 'go and make disciples of all nations, baptising them in the name of the Father and of the Son and of the Holy Spirit, and teaching them to *obey* everything I have commanded you' (Matthew 28:19–20). There can be no evading the implication: the mark of a disciple is his (or her) union with Christ through baptism and his (or her) doing what Jesus commanded be done. To emphasise the believing and baptising without also emphasising the obeying and the keeping of the commandments is to produce half a disciple that is no disciple at all.

We need to rediscover our responsibility to be holy, to take off our unclean shoes. This takes place in the church community, but is ultimately the responsibility of the individual. No amount of prayer ministry, ecstatic experiences and expository preaching is going to do it for you. Repentance and obedience are the way of the believer. Joshua didn't get someone else to remove his shoes – it was his own responsibility.

You must take off your shoes – do not expect someone else to. When I first got married I remember getting annoyed by little things that Tiffany didn't do that I somehow expected her to – things I'd probably seen my mum do and assumed Tiff would do. We had a few sharp exchanges. 'The bathroom is rather messy, why haven't you cleaned it?' And Tiffany would say: 'It's your mess, you tidy it.' 'Tiff, my shirt I wanted to wear to preach in hasn't been ironed' – and Tiffany would respond, 'Well, why haven't you ironed it?' Generally, I had my own expectations of her that she had no intention of fulfilling. I assumed she would do certain things for me. I presumed wrongly. We often presume on God – we expect him to do what he requires us to do. But we must actively search out and destroy sin in our lives. We must not tolerate it, and we must not assume it is God's job to deal with it. We must never be on easy terms with the presence of that which nailed Jesus to the cross operating in our lives. As John Piper rightly says, 'When it comes to killing my sin, I don't wait passively for the miracle of sin-killing to be worked on me, I act the miracle.'[5]

The Corinthian church, as we saw already, were not working at holiness, by any standard – what with their pagan feasts, syncretistic devotions, their cliques and sexual immorality. St Paul writes with tenderness but robustness: 'Therefore, since we have these promises, dear friends, let *us* purify *ourselves* from everything that contaminates body and spirit, perfecting holiness out of reverence for God' (2 Corinthians 7:1). There's holy work to be done. Let us consecrate ourselves – not expecting someone else to do it for us.

Holiness begins with the house of God

Long ago God spoke to Solomon and promised: 'If my people, who are called by my name, will humble themselves and pray and seek my face and turn from their wicked ways, then I will hear from heaven, and I will forgive their sin and will heal their land' (2 Chronicles 7:14). What a promise! But what a precondition! Judgement begins at the house of the Lord. Repentance must always begin at the house of God. We want a healed land, but it begins with a holy Church. The Old Testament prophets generally went to Israel and Judah and challenged their sin. Jesus didn't initially go to the Gentiles but came first to the sons of Israel. His first exorcisms were in the synagogue, not the street. Again, Paul writing to the Corinthians is very clear on this point: 'I am writing to you that you must not associate with anyone who claims to be a brother or sister but is sexually immoral or greedy, an idolater or slanderer, a drunkard or swindler. Do not even eat with such people. What business is it of mine to judge those outside the church? Are you not to judge those inside? God will judge those outside. "Expel the wicked person from among you"' (1 Corinthians 5:11–13). Too often the Church has tolerated sin within and at the same time harangued society about her lack of holiness. Nowadays much of society dismisses the Church because of her hypocrisy. We, the Church, are called to be salt and light – yet often we've been judge and jury. Jesus warned us: salt can lose its saltiness, and if it does it's fit for nothing. God doesn't expect the world to be holy – everyone knows sinners sin. But God does expect the Church to be moving towards holiness.

In one uncomfortable Barna study comparing evangelical lifestyles in the USA with those of non-Christians, it was demonstrated that they were virtually indistinguishable. Apart from their religious faith itself, people's lifestyle, use of money, values and divorce rates were the same for believers and non-believers alike. The philosopher and spiritual director Dallas Willard bemoaned what he termed 'The Great Disparity'[6] – the inconsistency between what Christians are called to and profess, and what they actually practise. The late Victorian and Edwardian British humourist and novelist Israel Zangwill aimed his wit against Christians, observing: 'Scratch the Christian and you find the pagan – spoiled.'[7]

The infamous anti-evangelist Friedrich Nietzsche had a point: 'If that glad message of your Bible were written in your faces, you would not need to demand belief in the authority of that book in such stiff-necked fashion.'[8] And again of Christians he said, 'They would have to sing better songs to make me believe in their Redeemer; his disciples would have to look more redeemed!'[9] Nietzsche was brought up a Christian, son of a Lutheran minister. But his experience of Christians put him off Christianity – its followers looked too miserable, too unlike the Jesus they claimed to follow.

Some years ago we had our church vicarage painted by diocesan decorators, a father and son team. I decided it was my duty to witness and win them for Christ and where others had failed I felt I would succeed. When they arrived I put on my best vicar's smile and winsomely offered a coffee and cake. They were surprisingly brusque and rejected my offer. I came back down at lunch and offered them a drink or something to eat and tried making conversation but again was met by a cold wind. Such a response seemed unusual, as if I had offended them in some way. And then the son, perhaps sensing my confusion at their coolness, couldn't hold back: 'We could tell you a thing or two about what went on in this vicarage before you.' He gave no details, but it suddenly dawned on me that these guys had painted most of the vicarages in the diocese. They were familiar with the vicar behind the door, not just in the pulpit. They knew what went on behind the vicarage doors. And whatever it was that they had seen and heard over the years, far from wooing them to Jesus, it had cumulatively warned them off. They were not prepared to have even a few minutes' polite conversation or accept a cuppa from a vicar. In their mind we were all tarred with the same brush – a very dirty one indeed.

Before we can be salt and light, let us be sure that we are salty and lit! An unconverted church cannot convert an unconverted world. The blind don't want the blind to lead them astray. People won't hear the good news if we look like bad news. And tragically, we often do. The father of the seventeenth-century Evangelical Awakening in England, John Wesley, in 1734 once wrote to his father, 'My one aim in life is to secure personal holiness, for without being holy myself I cannot promote real holiness in others.'[10] Of course, by God's grace he did secure that holiness and was used to turn this nation back from the brink of a possible revolution like the French were having at the time – or perhaps another civil war – and instead to start a revival that laid the spiritual and moral foundation for the golden era of England in the nineteenth century.

It's time to try holiness. After all, we have tried everything else . . .

Holiness is a divine word. Old Testament professor Gordon Wenham has said that the biblical idea of being holy might almost be substituted for the word divine.[11] 'Holy' expresses something fundamental about everything associated with God – all his ways, words, predicates, perfections. At its most basic root, it simply refers to being separate, distinct, other – in distinction from that which is morally unclean or profane. Indeed, holiness is opposite to sinfulness and sinfulness to holiness – God's being defines holiness and its opposite, sinfulness. When used of people it speaks of those who are set apart for God, those who are becoming like God and those who are becoming further removed from sin.

The word holiness and its cognates occur about 850 times in the Old Testament and 150 times in the New Testament. So that's a thousand times in the Bible that holiness is directly referred to – and in numerous other places indirectly, of course. How often does it feature in the language and life of the Church?

I am convinced that holiness is at once the most important factor in the Church's effectiveness and also the most neglected factor in her daily life. We have replaced holiness in various ways: with hype; with the sin of spin; with the cult of personality; we have been distracted by exaggerated claims about thousands of miracles, with gnostic reaching after the bizarre, with the esoteric, with talk of angelic visitations and the like. Meanwhile foundational doctrines like the lordship of Christ, the cross of Christ, and their ethical outworking like loving our neighbour, ministry to the poor – these are often relegated. Long ago C.S. Lewis warned us in *The Screwtape Letters* about the additions we make to our church life and doctrines – 'Christianity plus' he called it – and today we are often more plus than Christianity.

There was a time when we thought we were on the edge of revival as we abandoned hymnbooks for overhead projectors and sang songs on screens. We've illustrated our sermons using flannelgraphs, visual aids, drama sketches, interactive dialogue, PowerPoint presentations and multi-media. Every church leadership I've ever been part of has raised the importance of 'Improved Communications'. We've used hand-outs and newsletters and notices, notice boards and email updates and websites, Twittering, Facebook. I mean, seriously, it's not like we haven't tried stuff – and much of it good stuff. But here's the thing. Why is it that the Church in the West, for all her 'stuff', is shrinking – while the Church in Africa or Asia, where so much of this religious activity and industry is absent, is actually growing? Despite our multifarious efforts, are we more Christ-like? Are we more effective?

In 2007 Tearfund sponsored a church attendance survey[12] and concluded depressingly, but realistically, 'So far nothing church leaders have done seems to have brought about any change in the decline that started in the 1950s.' My own denomination, the

Church of England, has declined in real terms every year for the last sixty years. The Tearfund report stated that two-thirds of Britain's population had no connection whatsoever to any religion. 'This secular majority presents a major challenge to churches. Most of them – 29.3 million – are unreceptive and closed to attending church; churchgoing is simply not on their agenda.' Our efforts have at best simply slowed the aggressive decline of the Church; we have been building sandcastles to hold back the coming tide.

So, does this mean I am pessimistic for our Church's future? Not at all. I do not believe the decline of the Church and the erosion of her influence in society is inevitable. Jesus must have the supremacy. I cannot conceive that the devil wins more for hell than Jesus for heaven – the yeast of the kingdom will work through the whole batch, the weeds will not be more numerous than the wheat. And I believe the decline is reversible. But we need to put more confidence in God than our programmes – we need to get more God into our Church. If we want to get more people to church we need to let more of Jesus into his Church – God himself must be the Church's USP. And we need to be a credible witness to Christ's transforming power. We need to be holy as he is holy. God's immanent presence is predicated on holiness: we need to take off our shoes.

We need Vintage Church – Holy Church.

Imagine what it could be like

There is a newish literary genre known as 'Alternate History', which plays with the idea of how history and culture would be different if certain events had happened differently: e.g. what if the Moors hadn't been stopped by the Frankish knights? What if Hitler had actually invaded Britain in 1940 instead of turning his focus and forces to Russia? What if Al Gore had been elected president following 9/11? What if Brazil had had their two best players on the pitch against Germany in the 2014 World Cup?

What if Joshua hadn't removed his shoes? Would the Lord have withdrawn? Would Israel have gone into battle alone – would Jericho have resisted and all Israel been enslaved? What would have been at stake by resisting this invitation to holiness on behalf of Israel? And for us? What if every Christian made holiness their goal? What would we look like, as God's people?

Mahatma Gandhi, the apostle of peace, considered Jesus as the answer to India's ills and the means to reconcile Muslims and Hindus. When a young lawyer in South Africa, he wished to attend a local church meeting in his area and find out more about Jesus. As he entered the church he was stopped by the usher. 'Where do you think you're going, kaffir?' an Englishman asked him. Gandhi replied, 'I'd like to attend worship here.' The deacon barked back, 'There's no room for kaffirs in this church. Get out of here or I'll have my assistants throw you down the steps.'[13] Gandhi left the church and left behind the idea of Jesus as the answer. What would have happened if he had received a Christ-like welcome? How would Pakistan and India look now? In an interview with the missionary E. Stanley Jones he said: 'If Christians would really live according to the teachings of Christ, as found in the Bible, all of India would be Christian today.'[14]

Take your shoes off!

Chapter 5

Religion is Nuts

Since you died with Christ to the elemental spiritual forces of this world, why, as though you still belonged to the world, do you submit to its rules: 'Do not handle! Do not taste! Do not touch!'? These rules, which have to do with things that are all destined to perish with use, are based on merely human commands and teachings. Such regulations indeed have an appearance of wisdom, with their self-imposed worship, their false humility and their harsh treatment of the body, but they lack any value in restraining sensual indulgence. (Colossians 2:20–23)

John Lennon's 'Imagine' talks of a place and time where 'there's no heaven, and no religion too'. Well, he was right on one account and wrong on the other. There will always be a heaven, as the habitat of God – but he was right that religion has no place in it. The great twentieth-century Swiss theologian Karl Barth boldly differentiates Christianity from religion per se. He regarded all religion as sin from the bottom up – a human construct, human effort, human merit, human striving for God, all done on human terms rather than in response to divine revelation. For Barth, religion was a 'Tower of Babel'-style enterprise: humans building their way to God. Christianity, he claimed, was the polar opposite – the direction and action being that of

God, coming down to meet humankind in Christ. We are not to reach but to receive, not to build but to believe. Religion leads to pride in one's deluded sense of spiritual and moral achievement or idolatry, constructing a god in the image of creation, not the true Creator. For Barth, religion fails fundamentally in the very thing it seeks to do – bring us to God. Dietrich Bonhoeffer, imprisoned and executed for his association with those in the plot to assassinate Hitler, penned various letters and papers from prison while awaiting execution. In one he wrote that what was needed was Religionless Christianity. It is not clear what he meant by this, as his thoughts were not systematic, but it seems he believed that what was needed was for the act of following Jesus to be stripped of all external forms – and get back to pure faith and obedience to Jesus. Certainly Bonhoeffer had witnessed the formal State Church in Germany in large part acquiesce to Hitler, and the so-called German Christian Movement enthusiastically endorse Nazism – and from this he realised that much of the Protestant and Catholic Church was so encumbered by centuries of religion-baptised culture that it was rendered incapable of discerning the way of Christ and the word of Christ in the day of trouble. The world at war had exposed what was known as Christianity as little more than religion, a human construct, with no divine prophetic power within. Thus Bonhoeffer espoused a Christianity stripped bare of the religious and cultural accretions that had buried its true apostolic authority and muffled its prophetic voice – returning to Christ, with a new, unreligious language, and a life marked by prayer and doing what was right in the world.

God's 'Amazing Grace', revealed to us in Christ, is perhaps the unique and central message of Christianity – but when it becomes the name of a brand of perfume and deodorant or a

New Age book on naturalistic magic, it's clear the Church has lost its voice. On BBC Radio 4 I heard a fascinating discussion about the popularity of science fiction as a form of literature. The host observed that science fiction took off as institutional religion declined, suggesting that we are all basically religious animals, but having rejected the religions, we need other texts, themes and grand stories to help us work out our ethics and eschatologies. Science fiction can be a new religion.

The need to strip back Christianity from religious accretions is nothing new, mind you – and nor is science fiction. Paul, in his letter to the Colossians, is doing just that: seeking to restore the Church to her pure form, and to put down the science-fiction notions they had fallen for. Paul had a nose for religion; he had been an expert in it after all: he could smell it a mile off – and he smelled it at Colossae. Not content with '*Sola Christus, Sola Fidei*' (One Christ, One Faith), they had bolted on some added extras, gilding the gospel as once delivered, creating a mishmash of science-fictional worldviews and practices.

The heart of the so-called 'Colossian heresy' is the replacement of a relationship with Jesus based on faith with a religion of esoteric beliefs and legalistic actions (2:16–23). Paul reminds them of the core of the Christian faith:

- Submission to the Lordship of Jesus Christ (2:6–7)
- Reception of the Spirit's fullness through Jesus' divine fullness (2:9–10)
- Trust in and union with Jesus Christ (2:11–12)
- Acquittal and deliverance by Jesus Christ (2:14–15)

These are the basic tenets that the religious in Colossae have dismissed. The target of Paul's attack is summed up in 2:23 – the

NIV speaks of their 'self-imposed worship'. Paul employs a rare Greek term, *ethelo-threskia*, which translates as 'self-made religion, do-it-yourself-religion, idiosyncratic religion, would-be religion'.[1] So, what are the features of the Colossian DIY religion which so obfuscated an authentic relationship with God?

Despotic dictators

Paul writes in verse 16 'do not let anyone judge you'; and in verse 18, 'do not let anyone . . . disqualify you': the Greek is *brabuo*, and referred to an umpire awarding prizes or sanctions. These religious leaders were setting themselves up as divine umpires, dispensing divine prizes and pardons based on terms they set. The mark of religion was the *manner* of the false religious teachers: authoritarian, controlling and repressive. They were sitting in the judgement seat and their words determined who was in or out, what was right or wrong. Paul writes of the Colossian believers submitting to rules (vv. 20–22) – the Greek term is *dogmatizesthe*, literally meaning 'being dictated to' (see also 3:18). False teachers in Colossae were laying down the law and throwing their weight around. True Christianity, true life in Christ, is liberating and enables flourishing. The Spirit brings freedom but religion dominates and dictates, it makes decrees and imposes rules, and causes adherents to be bowed and cowed in fear of whether they are in or out, qualified or disqualified. The religious spirit is quick to sit in judgement. It is a bullying spirit that inculcates fear – not righteous fear of God, but fear of men who claim God-given authority to open or shut the heavens and qualify or disqualify us before God. Jesus invited us from grace, saying 'Follow me' – he summed up the law as loving God and loving our neighbour as ourselves. Of course, that would need some expansion, and Jesus taught and showed us what that might look like – but the whole tone and tenor of his approach was to act from grace to call us to grace. These gnostic nutters in the Colossae church were setting themselves up as absolute authorities, arbiters, divine gatekeepers. But it is before God that we will one day stand, not men; it is Christ who will judge the living and the dead, and the basis of judgement is whether we have lived out faith in Christ, revelling in his grace.

We have a long way to go. I read an article in a Catholic journal which boldly declared, 'Only when there is greater equality among all members of the church can we hope to prevent the sexual abuse and abuse of power that characterise this moment in the life of the church.'[2] And I once heard of a well-known evangelical charismatic leader who was reputed to punch his staff. Bullying, intimidating or 'fleecing' the flock is regrettably not rare among the clergy. But our Lord Jesus showed us how to lead – he took a towel and washed his disciples' feet! Jesus served, whereas religion bullies.

Dodgy diets

> Do not let anyone judge you by what you eat or drink. (Colossians 2:16)

One area in which the religious bullies were sitting in judgement was over dietary matters – possibly the influence of Old Testament kosher Jewish food laws which had been abolished in Christ, who declared all foods clean (Mark 7:19) and commanded Peter to eat what was formerly prohibited (Acts 10). It may be that 'meat' was prohibited for a variety of reasons, whether because they were holding on to Jewish laws about not handling dead carcasses and becoming unclean, or possibly the influence of a Greek notion of 'metempsychosis', the 'transmigration of soul through body' (similar to the concept of reincarnation in Hindu thought), thus leading people not to want to desecrate another soul by eating its temple. Judaism had no specific prohibitions on any drink (except blood) but perhaps a quasi-Nazirite anti-alcohol attitude was being prescribed to all. The mark of religion is often to control what is eaten or drunk, as the basic actions and demands of human nature. These controls also function as nice clear indicators of who is in and who isn't.

Certain Christian traditions have made much of 'teetotalism' – indeed one could not be a Methodist or in the Salvation Army if one took the 'demon drink'. This was a pastorally grounded and pragmatic ruling seeking to help people fight their addictions by removing temptation at a time when alcoholism was endemic in British society. However, teetotalism was often therefore elevated to a religious virtue, and those who drank even in moderation and celebration were deemed as sinful for doing so. Jesus turned water into wine – and the religious wanted to reverse the miracle. I occasionally meet sincere, good, godly folk, who tell me they have renounced certain foods prohibited in the Torah for Jews under the old covenant. Shellfish and pork are the main two that get quoted. Invariably they pick and mix which rules from the Torah they take, but they clearly feel they are closer to God, more faithful to his word and in better standing than others who imbibe such non-kosher food. The fact is that this is theologically unjustifiable – they have put themselves under a yoke that cannot be carried and which Christ annulled anyway. Paul discussed the role food plays in the faith in Romans 14 and 1 Corinthians 8. While leaving such matters to the conscience of the individual, he is clear that the imposition of food laws is wrong – and he states unequivocally, 'food does not bring us near to God' (1 Corinthians 8:8).[3] Laying down the law on diet is the sign of a religious spirit – it inculcates spiritual pride, puffing up the legalist and putting down those who do not comply – it needs renouncing and resisting.

John Wimber was the founder of the Vineyard, a church-planting movement which now numbers over one and a half thousand churches worldwide, and one of the late twentieth century's outstanding global church leaders. He was a man who desired all that God had for him. His wife Carol recalls how one day John decided to get really holy. He packed his bag and rented a cabin in the mountains. He told his wife he didn't know how long he would be gone – he intended to fast and seek the face of the Lord until he had found that place of holiness. It might take weeks! Smiling, she kissed him goodbye and off he went. Later that day his resolve to fast for several weeks began to wobble as he started to feel the pinch of missing lunch. Sheepishly, he arrived back at home, with his arms full of pizza. It's not easy being holy if holiness is a fortnight praying in a shack in the hills, far from family and food. But is that holiness? Certainly John, confronted with his own frailty and beaten by the dictates of his appetite, was a little wiser and a little meeker and a little more aware of his demanding flesh – and holiness always grows from a recognition of our own weakness. I like the story told to me by one of his close friends in Anaheim. John was once asked what he did to prepare for a conference. They expected him to say he fasted and prayed to gain spiritual power. He replied that he watched (American) football on TV, ate cheese sandwiches and drank Coke!

Divine days

. . . do not let anyone judge you . . . with regard to a religious festival, a New Moon celebration or a Sabbath day.   (Colossians 2:16)

The Colossians were being encouraged to mark out certain days as if they were specially blessed by God, and observance of such days would give them better spiritual standing – no doubt about it, this was religion at its worst. The Colossian church was perhaps influenced here by a mishmash of Judaism and paganism that invested special spiritual value in certain days. The Greco-Roman culture was much taken with the heavenly bodies, the location, movement and alignment of the stars and moon. They believed that special days were framed by special heavenly body configurations and were touched by the divine. To the Jew, meanwhile, the Sabbath day was all-important. But they had lost sight of it as 'God's gift', a day to enjoy rest and celebrate God's goodness, and instead had framed it with numerous rules of what was permissible and what was prohibited. Jesus rebuked the Pharisees, saying, 'The Sabbath was made for man, not man for the Sabbath' (Mark 2:27) – they had made the day to lay down your burdens *into* a burden. Paul was clear in Romans 14:5 that no one day is better than any other – that those who wanted to celebrate one day over another were free to, but should not impose it on anyone else.

While respecting those who want to honour the Sabbath, and believing in the principle of a day of rest from work, I do not subscribe to the theology of a 'sacred' seventh day. Of all the Ten Commandments, this is the only one not repeated or mandated in any form in the New Testament. The fact that the first

73

Jewish Christians abandoned the Sabbath as their day of worship shows a radical rethinking of how Sabbath functioned in their spiritual life. The early church in the ensuing centuries, in developing the architecture of worship, designed baptistries with eight sides, octagonal. This was because they believed – profoundly, and prophetically I believe – that baptism is into the life of God, such that the cycle of six days' labour and a seventh for rest had been transcended and that now we live in the eighth day, permanently resting in God, rather than repeating the work cycle back to workday one. This is not to say that in the rhythm of life days of rest and play are not essential, nor that holidays – 'holy days' – and festivals are not important spiritual markers and memorials. As Christians we helpfully set apart special days to focus on the day Christ was born, the day he died, the day he rose from the dead, the day he ascended, the day he sent his Spirit and so on. Though we do not know exactly the historic date of most of these days, they are rightly celebrated and appropriated. However, this is our choice to deepen our faith by a focused remembrance – what we do not do is impart an intrinsic special spiritual weight to one day over another.

Dos and Don'ts

> *Do not handle! Do not taste! Do not touch!* (*Colossians 2:21*)

Of course Scripture presents us with numerous prohibitions and exhortations, imperatives to live and act in ways that are righteous. Christianity is not antinomian, a spiritual 'free-for-all'. However, a mark of the religious spirit is its focus on petty rules and regulations rather than on relationship with God – in religion the laws become the very core of the religion, rather than the framework which demonstrates the covenant we have entered into with God. Often in religion the nature of these laws involves pedantic prohibitions on handling or tasting and even touching certain things. Again, the specific purity laws being imposed on the Colossian church may relate to Jewish Old Testament holiness rules about not touching or handling the dead, or dead animals, thus making oneself unclean. Paul is clear that these Jewish-specific, context-specific, old-covenant-specific laws have no further place in the church of Jesus Christ.

I have an American pal who quotes a Bible-belt slogan: 'Don't drink, smoke or chew [tobacco], or go out with girls who do' – there may be wisdom in this, or there may not, but such a legalistic rule-based approach to life with God is not the way of Christ; it cannot describe life in the Spirit. Jesus said 'Greater love has no one than this: to lay down one's life for one's friends' (John 15:13) – he did not come to *lay down petty laws*. Interestingly, twice Paul says 'do not': do not let anyone judge you – do not accept such arbitrary religious-minded 'do-nots'!

My mum grew up in the Christian sect of the Exclusive Brethren. My ancestors were well-known and respected Brethren elders, teachers and evangelists in the West Country. The expression of her faith was framed tightly by rules, and particularly prohibitions – 'what not to dos'. In the 1950s my mother sat the '11 Plus' exam to determine whether her education path would lie either in the vocational 'secondary modern' for those who 'failed' the test, or in the academic 'grammar' stream, for those who passed. My mother failed the exam, went to a secondary modern, and left school at fifteen. Now I have always been surprised that my mum failed this 11 Plus exam, as she is so successful in all she does – a popular local and county politician, a councillor, and mayor of the town twice. Prior to this political career she was a top-level manager and business-woman, responsible for contracts worth millions of pounds with hundreds of staff working for her. Was it just that she was a late starter? No, in fact religion had interfered. She recently told me she had failed the 11 Plus exam because she got 0 per cent in the English paper – because she couldn't even attempt an answer. The exam question was 'Who is your favourite TV/radio personality and why?' She had never heard a radio nor watched a TV – they were banned by her Brethren religion as being worldly and dangerous demonic portals. So she left the exam sheet blank, except for her name/number. And she failed. Some years later her father, my granddad Bob Stuckes, a well-respected teacher in the Exclusives, was 'silenced' and cut off from contact with his children (my mum, and her brother my uncle) who remained in the Brethren. The reason for his being 'disciplined' was that he had said it was OK for the housemaid of an Exclusive sister to own a radio. But this con-cession seemed like worldliness to his other Brethren elders, and compromise with sin, and he was evicted from the fellow-ship. It was not until some months later, when my granny was involved in a car crash, that my mother was rightly restored to relationship with her parents and they all left the cult of Exclusives. This illustrates a key component of the spirit of religion: defined and articulated as often pedantic rules and prohibitions, not directly decreed in Scripture, and placed above or obscuring the primary law to love God and love one's neighbour, and indeed leading to judgement of others and bul-lying. That was the sort of thing occurring in Colossae.

Drubbings

These rules, which have to do with things that are all destined to perish with use, are based on merely human commands and teachings. Such regulations indeed have an appearance of wisdom, with their self-imposed worship, their false humility and their harsh treatment of the body. (Colossians 2:22–23)

It is possible the church in Colossae was influenced by Greek gnostic philosophy – dualism, the belief in a radical divide between spirit and matter. God was spirit and thus qualitatively distinct and separate from matter. Matter didn't matter. Value was placed on the intellectual and spiritual, and the physicality of the body was not celebrated but subjugated. This led to two opposing responses to how one treated the body; for some it led to an Epicurean indulgence of the flesh – what did it matter what you did with it? For others, the response was a Stoic suppression of the body, suppressing its drives and desires to attune to the spiritual or psychical. In the Colossian church it would seem the latter Stoic idea was adopted, and the body battered into submission.

The religious-inspired fiction that God being spirit means the body is of no worth has sadly crept into the Church, under the guise of our wanting to be 'spiritual', and has led to great harm. Rather than celebrating the physical as a gift of God, historically the Church has often negated what God made good. It has led to a fear or rejection of all things physical – rather than celebrate our God-created bodies and physical pleasures like sex and good food and healthy sporting expression, the gnostic religious crowd have negated the body and even punished the body with excessive fasting, purging and flogging, and hair-shirts and celibacy.

As a young monk, desperate to know peace from the fear of condemnation, Martin Luther flogged himself 'till he ran with blood', he fasted in total for a third of the year, and he climbed the steps of Santa Scala in Rome on bloody knees as if to impress God with his pain and suffering. Religion is a hard taskmaster. Yet God isn't impressed by your blood – Jesus' was sufficient.

God created the body as good; God incarnated himself in human flesh, Christ rose bodily – a transformed and imperishable resurrection body, yes, but recognisable as his human body nonetheless, with its nail scars showing – Jesus ascended into heaven bodily and in a human body is seated at the right hand of the Father; he will return again, in a body, to reign in the New Jerusalem. There's no getting away from it, Christology is a profound affirmation of the body. The Christian's body is the temple of the Holy Spirit. We must have a robust theology and spirituality that celebrates our physicality, or we will find ourselves disrespecting it either through abuse, neglect and indulgence or through negation and suppression.

Many years ago, I got trapped in a religious spirit – it began well and the desire was good, to seek God for intimacy, to experience his anointing on my ministry and service. I had developed the discipline of always fasting before preaching. As a young evangelist in ministry, I was preaching most days, on the streets, in schools, in church etc. This meant I was fasting a lot. It became obsessive – what began as a sincere desire for God to bless me, became a rod to beat myself. I somehow imbibed the notion that God would withhold his blessing from me if I did eat before speaking. Having previously had a strong and muscular physique, I lost several stone in a year and went down to under eleven stone (I acknowledge that I may have swung the opposite way now, at over eighteen stone). I was unhealthily thin, and I am now unrecognisable to how I appeared during this period. This disciplinarian notion of a God who would only bless a fasted body led to a punishment of my body. My understanding of God's ways and my understanding of the body were both seriously flawed.

Demonic devotions

. . . worship of angels . . . such a person goes into great detail about what they have seen.   (Colossians 2:18)

Both the Jews and the Greek Gnostics believed that angels were intermediaries of God. Jews believed angels gave the law to Moses; the Gnostics believed angels gave secret keys of knowledge that enabled the enlightened to access the next rung up the spiritual staircase to God. While angels are certainly biblical and appear at crucial moments, interest in them is prohibited, worship of them is demonic, because it turns people away from God. To focus one's attention on angels is like being more interested in the book cover than the book, or the dinner plate than the meal.

That was the problem here. God, revealed in Christ, was not the centre of the Colossian worship – they were off with the fairies, dabbling in esoteric mysteries. The role of angels is to serve Jesus; the mark of fallen angels is to serve the demonic. Whenever angels rather than Jesus become the focus, it is a fallen angel conducting proceedings. I once heard a popular US charismatic preacher recount an alleged conversation he had with God about the emphasis of his ministry. He asked God, 'Isn't it about getting the people to believe in Jesus?' God, he claimed, replied, 'You gotta get people believing in the angel . . . the people already believe in Jesus, but the Church doesn't believe in the supernatural.' The preacher then addressed his audience: 'The Church has no problem believing in Jesus but we don't believe in the supernatural, the angels, the prophetic, and some of what's going on . . . maybe the world is looking for something new – how many of you believe the world needs something new?' Well, I don't, for one. I don't believe God said this, and it came as no surprise when shortly after this nonsense, this man walked out on his marriage and ministry. Gnostic nonsense – just the sort of claptrap the Colossians had to endure.

Someone sent me an article which excited them, but worried me – it was from a chap in ministry who on Yom Kippur, the Jewish Day of Atonement, claimed to have had a visitation from an angel (whom, incidentally, he also claimed to have met before), who explained all that was happening in the turmoil of Middle Eastern politics in relation to Old Testament prophecy. It sounded amazing, spiritual, full of Bible references, but in fact it was religious mumbo jumbo, speculation and fabrication. The angel Gabriel is not in the habit of visiting preachers to give them special revelation, help them with textual exposition and download the whole end-times timetable to their iPad. It was the same kind of thing as the Colossian heresy – seductive, but ultimately illusory and destructive.

There is a well-known theory called 'Six degrees of separation'. Its principle is that you are never more than six people away from anyone else. For example: I know a Rhodes scholar (degree 1) who knows a US senator (degree 2) who knows the Secretary of State (degree 3), who knows the US president (degree 4) – thus there are only four steps of separation between me and the President of America! The idea of degrees of separation is not about hierarchy per se, but in the Church we have our own special version, which certainly is. The religious spirit separates people by degrees of perceived righteousness, based on how well someone follows the rules. It feeds on the pride inherent in being nearer the 'top' than the 'bottom'. Even some forms of church architecture have modelled and promoted this distinction by placing the 'spiritual' people in special seats, with special clothes, in special areas at the front, performing special jobs. This becomes more than merely functional, it conveys and enforces an ontological spiritual hierarchy. The Colossian heresy distanced God from man in such a way that numerous interme-diaries were needed – angels and those enlightened. Paul had to remind them that they had direct access to the fullness of God in Christ: one degree of separation, not six or even two. The Colossians were being led away down a demonic cul-de-sac, reinventing layers of separation that Christ at Calvary tore down. When angels, or enlightened mystics or charismatic stars, anointed priests or prophets subtly become the object and focus for our spirituality and receiving of divine insight then we are stepping away from the gospel and stepping into religion. Jesus is not accessed by proxy through the mediation of priestly powers, or someone else's intercessory prayers or prophetic insight – these can too easily become a barrier not a bridge to God. C.S. Lewis, in a lecture titled 'Inner Ring',[4] spoke of the human desire to be on the *'inside'*, in that elite place of power, privilege. There are many inner rings – the old school tie, the country club, exclusive societies, the golf club, Oxbridge, Freemasonry etc. Religion always seeks to form rings inside rings, and define who is in and who is out on the basis of degrees of conformity and subscription to its particular rules and regu-lations. But to be a Christian baptised into Christ and into his Church *is* to be inside, to be in the circle of the Trinity – and

81

Jesus invites the whole world to come inside. Paul exposes these religion-based extra layers – despotic dictators, dodgy diets, divine days, dos and don'ts, drubbings and demonic devotions – and says a spirituality built on these is dangerous and unchristian. A religion predicated on such rules actually does the opposite of what it promises – these rules obfuscate rather than facilitate worship and encounter with God. They do not help our relationship with God – they ruin it.

True discipleship is disciplined not disciplinarian. Christianity is not without rules and forms, but like vows made at a wedding, they come from love, they frame the relationship of love. G.K. Chesterton said true religion should be 'more of a love affair'. Jesus in the Gospels and all the apostles in their epistles present us with clear imperatives that frame and form the Christian life. Christianity is free for all but not a free-for-all. There are indeed hundreds of instructions, imperatives that are given, all reflecting what it means to love God and love our neighbour. But the spirit of religion that Paul is opposing is one that has added to the apostolic tradition to increase the burden and demands made on people, and indeed has elevated such rules to being the very basis for righteousness, rather than taking apostolic instructions as the expression of life lived by the righteous.

Before we leave this theme, let us note that Paul does not simply denigrate religion, he also explains why he does so: because it is futile and impotent. The very thing it offers is the very thing on which it cannot deliver. Indeed, it actually keeps God at arm's length. At its root 'religion' is self-justifying and ultimately refuses grace. It is a refugee from the grace offered in Christ, instead attempting to 'go it alone'; religiosity supplements Jesus and the sufficiency of his work and our dependency on that alone, and therefore utterly denies it. It sets up the religious man as the 'subject' who saves or sanctifies himself, rather than being a starving beggar receiving the bread he needs as a free hand-out. Christ at the cross needs no help to save us! Only those who know that they are spiritually bankrupt and are willing to kneel at the blood-stained foot of the cross, empty-handed and desperate, receive grace and find salvation.

Paul levels several criticisms against religion – first, it produces spiritual *pygmies*: 'They have lost connection with the head, from whom the whole body, supported and held together by its ligaments and sinews, grows as God causes it to grow' (Colossians 2:19). Religion cannot bring spiritual growth and maturity because there is no life in it. For all the appearance it gives of superiority and insight, of great depth in spirituality, the religious spirit actually keeps one in spiritual infancy. Farmers castrate young male lambs that will not be bred from. To do this they place a tight rubber band round their family jewels – this stops the blood flow, whereupon the testicles rot and fall off. The religious spirit is exactly like that, a castrating rubber band – stopping the life-flow of God's blood to his sheep, rendering them impotent and infertile.

Second, the spirit of religion is *passing*: 'These are a shadow of the things that were to come; the reality, however, is found in Christ' (2:17). Plato taught that the true substance or actuality belonged to the realm of ideas, of which the world was just a shadow. But Paul says that the substance has already come in Christ and these religious rules, laws, festivals, holy days, even where they were once prophetic and proleptic, are now a mere shadow that has passed; they have served their purpose, left behind with the old transitory order. Any attempt to pursue God on the basis of the forms of religion is a retrograde step.

Third, the spirit of religion leads to *pride* – 'puffed up with idle notions' (v. 18) – and this is perhaps the greatest sin that keeps us at arm's length from God. The hallmark of a religious spirit is spiritual arrogance with a hypocritical appearance of *humility* (v. 23). This was the mark of the Pharisees, the pre-eminent religious sect among the Jews, who upheld a total devotion to external forms, leading to a smug self-righteousness. Jesus called them whitewashed sepulchres, possessing scrubbed-clean exteriors but with their souls full of uncleanness. If you believe your religious actions or devotions impress God, then the more you do it, the more you will swagger. Just as in Jesus' parable of the Pharisee and tax collector (Luke 18:9–14), the religious spirit boldly enters the temple, looks up to heaven and thanks God he is not like the tax collector, who is so conscious of his sin that he refuses to even cross the threshold of the temple and who keeps his head bowed as he prays. Christ pronounces that it is the broken and self-abasing tax collector who goes away justified, not the spiritually self-assured Pharisee.

Fourth, the religious spirit is *powerless*: 'they lack any value in restraining sensual indulgence' (v. 23). Some of the most outwardly religious folk I know are trapped in sin. In chapter 3 of this letter, Paul will address a whole catalogue of sins of the flesh, ranging from sexual immorality to greed to aggressive outbursts. Despite their religiousness, the deeds of the flesh are very much in evidence. The same is seen in the letter to the Galatians where, despite the Galatian Christians' religiousness, their circumcision and their embrace of the Torah, they have all manner of wickedness in their midst, from sexual immorality to witchcraft. The religious spirit cannot cleanse and deliver us from the power of the sinful nature. Ironically, the religious spirit actually feeds their appetites. The prophet

Isaiah tells us that 'by his wounds we are healed' (53:5) – not our own! It is only as we hide in Jesus' wounds, and are filled with his Resurrection Spirit's power, that we can know his forgiving power to free us from sin. If our religious efforts amount to anything, Christ died unnecessarily.

Leave it to the nutters

I have struggled much of my Christian life to live by grace rather than by the law, and have too often followed a religious spirit rather than keep in step with the liberating Holy Spirit. I have struggled with being petty-minded and inflexible, both with myself and with others. My long-suffering wife and teenage sons have to repeatedly chip away at this and teach me to 'chillax'. It was more than a week until Christmas Day but Tiffany had decorated the house and various festive niceties like pomegranates and nuts were laid out. My youngest son came into the sitting room, saw the dish of nuts and picked one up with the nutcrackers. I told him it wasn't Christmas and he needed to put it back – puzzled, he walked away. Then my older teenage son came in, saw the newly placed nuts, picked one up and immediately cracked it open. I told him off – it was not Christmas, and he shouldn't have started on the Christmas rations. Tiffany raised her eyebrow at me. My sons thought me a nutter. Yes, Christmas presents are opened on Christmas Day but nuts put out in a bowl are surely meant to be eaten in the season of Christmas? The next day I was sitting in a coffee shop when a Catholic monk I knew came in. I asked what he was doing for Christmas and if he was going home to his family and he said he and his monastic brothers were celebrating 'The Octave', the eight days of Christmas. He said he didn't want to miss these joyful festivities, worshipping together and partying together every day for eight days, with fine meals and wine in the evening – not just Christmas Day! For him, the birth of Christ deserved an eight-day celebration! They were sucking the very marrow out of the bone of the goodness of God. I immediately thought of my prohibition on eating Brazil nuts before Christmas Day and thought how ridiculously pedantic, narrow and legalistic I had been.

Religion is nuts. Let's leave it for the nutters.

Chapter 6

Even Tigger Needs a Hug

. . . the Lord's servant . . . must be kind to everyone.
(2 Timothy 2:24)

I was once preaching at a conference on the theme of holiness. I could feel the auditorium tense as I thundered away. In an attempt to let some of the pressure out I said, 'I know some of you are thinking, "This is a bit heavy – pity he didn't talk on kindness – even Tigger needs a hug."' It brought a laugh and people relaxed a little more into the talk.

Now, that's all very well, but it is actually a kindness to address the subject of holiness – what could be kinder than seeking to encourage people to be conformed to Christlikeness? However, it is also the case that to speak on holiness must involve speaking on kindness, for kindness is Christlikeness, it is evidence of holiness. Kindness and holiness walk hand in hand. Any religious expression that makes its devotees harsh and brittle, withdrawn, cold, closed-fisted, purse-lipped and looking like they've drunk half a litre of malt vinegar, is not holy. It may be very religious and unquestionably sincere, but holiness has an altogether different appearance. Holiness is Christlikeness. Christ was kindness incarnate to those in need – so yes, I say: holiness is kindness. American writer and theologian, Frederick Buechner, understood this and expressed it beautifully: 'Be kind, because although kindness is not by a long shot the same as holiness, kindness is one of the doors that holiness enters the world through, enters us through.'[1]

The father of Greek philosophy, Plato, is often quoted as saying 'Be kind – everyone you meet is fighting a hard battle.' I can find no evidence Plato ever said anything like this, nor does it fit with his other writings, but whoever did first say it was right. It's true. Tigger's creator, the twentieth-century author A.A. Milne, taught us that: 'Just because an animal is large, it doesn't mean he doesn't want kindness; however big Tigger seems to be, remember that he wants as much kindness as Roo.'[2] The words kind/kindness are related to the Old German word *kin-der* meaning children, from which we also get our English term *kin/kindred*. So the word kindness originally referred to a right acting towards your kith and kin, your children, your family, your close community. Kindness is treating someone as you should your family – although of course sometimes our families can be the most unkind! The term *kindness* may sound a bit weak, conjuring images of warm fluffy towels washed in fabric conditioner. However, it is not a limp word or action in its origin – kindness is energetic, energising, life-giving: it causes the person on the receiving end to flourish. Kindness is to be the hallmark of those who follow Jesus, for his is a kingdom of kindness. St Paul said 'the Lord's servant . . . must be kind to everyone' (2 Timothy 2:24).

Jesus was kindness incarnate

In the Old Testament Hebrew, *chesed* – translated as mercy, loving-kindness, covenant faithfulness – is a pre-eminent virtue, a primary characteristic of Yahweh. The famed twentieth-century Lubavitcher Rabbi, Menachem Schneerson, was interviewed by a CNN reporter as he handed out money to members of his synagogue to be given away to charity, blessing them with 'a double portion'. The rabbi replied that the Messiah was ready to come but to hasten his appearance we must all 'do something additional in the realm of goodness and kindness'.[3] God is kind, his kingdom is a kingdom of kindness. But we must remember that it was not kindness that brought the Messiah, but the Messiah who brought kindness – who was, in the words of the beautiful revelation to Corrie Ten Boom while in Ravensbrück concentration camp, the God *'remplis de tendresse'*.[4] Paul writes: 'when the kindness and love of God our Saviour appeared, he saved us, not because of righteous things we had done, but because of his mercy. He saved us through the washing of rebirth and renewal by the Holy Spirit' (Titus 3:4–5). Humankind cries out for kindness. Every tender touch, sensitive word, generous gesture, warm look echoes the kindness of God. Kindness has to be experienced to be known – and the little we know makes us crave for more. We are wired to receive the kindness of the God who is all kindness. Jesus, God with us, was kindness personified – kindness expressed in love and mercy in saving us and transforming us by his Spirit.

Let us consider this kind King of the Jews and the kingdom of kindness he established. Matthew shows how his Galilean ministry fulfilled prophetic expectation:

Aware of this, Jesus withdrew from that place. A large crowd followed him, and he healed all who were ill. He warned them not to tell others about him. This was to fulfil what was spoken through the prophet Isaiah:
'Here is my servant whom I have chosen,
the one I love, in whom I delight;

I will put my Spirit on him,
and he will proclaim justice to the nations.
He will not quarrel or cry out;
no one will hear his voice in the streets.
A bruised reed he will not break,
and a smouldering wick he will not snuff out,
till he has brought justice through to victory.
In his name the nations will put their hope.'

(Matthew 12:15–21)

Why did 'many' follow him? Because they were drawn by his irresistible, his tangible kindness. He did not merely throw words at people, he tenderly met the needs and transformed the lives of all he met. He did not simply walk past people in pain – he felt their pain with them and he reached out in divine love to transform it. And he healed all who came to him believing in his power and love.

We see kindness in Jesus' miracles

Jesus' miracles were never merely displays of power or divinity. Indeed, when asked for signs to prove he was God's Messiah he always refused. But moved with compassion he fed the hungry crowd of five thousand plus. Moved with compassion he healed the sick who came or were brought to him. Moved with compassion he raised the widow's dead son. Moved with compassion he set free those oppressed by demonic shadows. Moved with compassion he reached out and touched the leper, and his tender touch brought transformation. Perhaps the paucity of miracles today reflects an absence not of faith in God but of the kindness of God in us.

We see kindness in Jesus' associations

The holiness of the Pharisees led to a distancing from and even the stoning of those deemed to be sinful. But Jesus' holiness moved in kindness towards the sinner. Presented with a woman caught in adultery, Jesus said to the woman, 'Neither do I condemn you . . . Go now and leave your life of sin' (John 8:11). The Pharisees' version of holiness stoned sinners, whereas God's true holiness met sinners in transforming grace. Jesus rebuked the Pharisees, who prided themselves on holiness but who neglected the weightier matters of justice, kindness and faithfulness. That's what true holiness looks like. Jesus' kindness meant he was 'friends with tax collectors and sinners'. Friends. Not merely an acquaintance, not simply on speaking terms or even on first-name terms, but *friends*. It has always been the desire of God to be friends with humankind.

We see kindness in Jesus' teaching

Consider the extent of Jesus' kindness as shown in his famous parable of the Good Samaritan. Not simply is it a commendation of practical kindness to those suffering; it compels kindness to the Samaritans, the people group most despised in the world by Orthodox Jews as having been defiled by intermarrying with pagans. Consider the kindness shown by the father in the parable of the Prodigal Father – this is what God is like: against all cultural norms, despite the shame his son has brought on him, he welcomes back his wayward child with open arms, with a warm embrace, and treats him like a prince. Consider the kindness in Jesus' instruction to forgive 'seventy times seven' – kindness keeps forgiving; after all, it's what Jesus does.

91

Consider how Jesus makes kindness the criterion for entrance into the kingdom: on judgement day, he says, the question will not be 'are you born again?' but 'have you lived like those who are born again? Did you feed the hungry, welcome the stranger, clothe the naked, visit the prisoner?' (Matthew 25:31–46). Heaven is a holy place, it's a kind place – it's for God's kind of people, the kind. God doesn't want to spend forever with unkind people. Of course it is God's kindness, his unconditional grace, which saves us, but those who are truly saved by grace become gracious. Where someone evidences no grace one must question if they have experienced God's grace.[5]

We see kindness at Jesus' death

We see kindness shown even at the moment of Jesus' betrayal. Judas kissed him and Jesus called him '*friend*'. We see kindness as the loveliest life the world has ever known nears its end and Jesus hangs upon the cross, and in the throes of agony he still considers others: 'Dear woman, here is your son. Disciple, here is your mother' (John 19:26–27; own paraphrase). We see kindness in Jesus' extraordinary grace towards his killers, of whom, even as some of them stand at the foot of the cross, having played their part in securing his death, or even having been the ones who physically nailed him there, Jesus prays, 'Father forgive them.' Of course, we see kindness in Jesus pre-eminently in his laying down his life for others, taking their place, dying their death, suffering their condemnation, enduring their god-forsakenness in order that they might not get their just deserts but be justified and restored to right relationship with God. We see kindness at the resurrection when Jesus forgives those who denied him, and recommissions them. We see the kindness of Jesus when he confronts Saul, the great assassin on his way to kill Christians, and Jesus forgives and restores and makes this man Paul, the apostle to the Gentiles. This is godly kindness at its most unfathomably generous.

Atheistic evolution says you've got to look out for yourself in this dog-eat-dog, law-of-the-jungle world society – that's how survival of the fittest works, that's the selfish gene. Darwin's and Dawkins' view of the world is 'red in tooth and claw' and cruel to the core. Philip Kitcher is a professor in the Philosophy of Science at Columbia University in New York. In his book *Living with Darwin* he observes that there is nothing kind in evolutionism, which is inherently self-serving and violent. He claims that if there were a God presiding over life, 'it is extremely hard to equip the face with a kindly expression'.[6] The mechanics of evolution exclude altruism. This, then, throws up a conundrum, given the desire to give and receive kindness that we all feel. Indeed, some leading universities are investing in research on the apparent problem of kindness in a post-Darwinian world. It doesn't easily fit in with an aggressive, hostile and atheistic model of how life works. The research that has come out is more guesswork- than evidence-based, but posits that perhaps kindness is a developmental form of self-preservation – if I'm nice to you then you will be nice to me and it's in both our interests therefore to be kind – not for general application but in a personally beneficial way. Thus, kindness in an atheistic evolutionary world is either an aberration or an ultimately developed form of self-interest.

The problem with this idea of the universe is that the facts don't support this – some people are genuinely altruistic and self-sacrificial, pouring out their lives for the needy. Can that really just be an aberration? People across most cultures have an inbuilt moral register that would be appalled at the indiscriminate murder of babies for selfish ends (although most fail to make this connection with abortion). Almost everyone would object in principle to the self-advancement of one person, people or nation achieved via the oppression or annihilation of another people group.

The basic mechanics and philosophy of an atheistic, ethics-free evolutionary view of the world do not in reality fit with how almost all people actually feel life should be lived.

Recently a member of our church, a medical doctor, left to join a special task force working with those suffering from the Ebola virus in Sierra Leone. As we know, this is one of the most contagious viruses known to man, and a killer. She went because the love of Christ compels her, because she cares more for the wellbeing of others than her own. Unless you believe she is merely doing it out of some twisted sense of selfish ambition, or a martyr complex, an atheistic evolutionary worldview cannot make sense of this. But you might argue that her faith has skewed her thinking. Even more antithetical to an atheistic evolutionary worldview, then, is the fact that plenty of non-Christians, without this Christian moral mandate, have also been willing to go to care for others at such great risk. Our natural compassion makes no sense if there is no God in whose image we are made and by whose Spirit we are led.

Jesus was kind – Jesus people should be kind

'Remind the people to be subject to rulers and authorities, to be obedient, to be ready to do whatever is good, to slander no one, to be peaceable and considerate, and always to be gentle towards everyone . . . And I want you to stress these things, so that those who have trusted in God may be careful to devote themselves to doing what is good' (Titus 3:1, 2, 8).

The Greek word *epieikeis*, translated 'gentle' here, can be more fully understood as 'kind, courteous, tolerant'. Those who follow the Kind One are kind. The kindness Jesus modelled is the kindness God looks for in us. Kindness is not an optional extra in the Christian life, like whether you prefer choral music to charismatic celebration, clerical robes over shorts and a T-shirt. Kindness is commanded. The imitation of Christ is commanded. But, as always, God gives what he commands, and kindness is a fruit of the Spirit: graced by divine kindness, we produce the grace of kindness as a virtue, grown in our soul and harvested in our good works. Among the fruits of the Spirit are love, joy, peace, forbearance and kindness (Galatians 5:22). If Jesus was kindness incarnate then the Spirit of Jesus incarnated in us transforms our nature, our selfish flesh, and conforms us to the divine nature. Kindness is not a gift given in an instant anointing – it is a command to obey that becomes a character we display, cultivated through our walking in the Spirit.

Three standout features of the early church

In the early centuries, under Roman rule, and subsequently down the ages, whenever they are true to Christ, Christians have been distinct from others in belief and practice. Three things stand out.

1. *Rejection of idolatry.* Indeed, somewhat ironically given where we find ourselves now, the term 'atheist' (from the ancient Greek *a* = 'against' and *theos* = 'god')

was levelled as an accusation against the early church for their rejection of the plurality of gods commonly accepted and worshipped in the Roman Empire. The Romans, whenever they conquered a people group, co-opted that people's gods into their pantheon. The Romans had numerous gods to choose from, and yet Christians rejected them all! That Christians only accepted Israel's One God revealed in three persons was rightly perceived as a negation of their pantheon of gods, and an invitation for persecution.

2. *Sexual purity*. In the culture of the Roman Empire in which Christianity grew, virginity until marriage and life-long heterosexual monogamy was ridiculous. Our modern culture is obsessed with sex, but pagan Roman society was on a whole different level. Christians were markedly different in their sexual belief and practice. One ancient Roman letter, addressed to Diognetus, said of Christians: 'They marry like everyone else, and have children – but do not destroy their offspring [this refers to the Roman custom of discarding their unwanted new-born babies on rubbish dumps]. They share a common table but not a common bed.'[7]

3. *Selfless altruism*. The Church was seen and known for its genuine concern for others. In an era when it was perfectly common to turn old slaves out into streets, the Church took them in and provided for them. It was customary to literally 'throw out' unwanted babies, especially girls, leaving them at the rubbish dump to die. Again, the Church rescued and adopted these babies. Christians gave dignity to what the world discarded.

The pagan Roman Emperor Julian tried to promote paganism over Christianity in the middle of the fourth century, but failed. He could not compete with what the Christians had. He wrote to the pagan priest Arsacius: 'The religion of the Greeks does not yet prosper as I would wish, on account of those who profess it . . . [why not?] . . . observe how the kindness of Christians to strangers, their care for the burial of their dead, and the sobriety of their lifestyle has done the most to advance their cause . . . The impious Galileans support our poor in addition to their own.'[8]

My friend Dr Stephen Backhouse – a tutor in social and political theology at St Mellitus College – expanded on this for me:

In AD 165 a plague swept through the mighty Roman Empire, wiping out a third of the population. It happened again in 251, when five thousand people a day were dying in the city of Rome alone. Those infected were abandoned by their families to die in the streets. The government was helpless; the Emperor died of plague. Pagan priests fled their temples where people had flocked for comfort and explanation. Yet following the plagues the good reputation of Christianity was confirmed and its population grew exponentially. Why is this? Christians did not come armed with intellectual answers to the problem of evil. They did not enjoy a supernatural ability to avoid pain and suffering. What they did have was water and food and their presence. In short, if you knew a Christian, you were statistically more likely to survive, and if you survived it was the church that offered you the most loving, stable and social environment. It was not clever apologetics, strategic

97

political organisation or the witness of martyrdom which converted an empire, so much as it was the simple conviction of normal men and women that what they did for the least of their neighbours they did for Christ.

One wonders what record of the Church is being written in our day. Thank God there are great models of Christian kindness – ministries that advance the cause of justice and mercy. One thinks of the Samaritans, Barnardo's, Tearfund, Oxfam, the Red Cross, Christian Aid, World Vision, Leprosy Society, Amnesty International (which was set up by Peter Benenson, a Catholic convert), Betel, the environmental work of A Rocha, the Viva Network, International Justice Mission, NSPCC, Habitat for Humanity, Christians Against Poverty, Compassion, Just Love – to name but a few, all of them begun by Christians led by the Spirit of God.

Holiness is seen in kindness. But sadly, it must also be said that some of the most unpleasant people I have ever met were Christians, some of them Christian leaders! The Church often has a rotten reputation – rarely is it the scandal of the cross that offends, often it is the long history of seeking and abusing power. The Catholic Church has been rocked and her reputation shredded in recent years by revelations of systemic problems – sexual abuse by priests on the one hand, and the physical and mental abuse by nuns of those in their pastoral and educational charge. With the accumulation of power there has historically also been an accumulation of wealth – what of the billions in Vatican vaults? Should the Church of England really be the largest landowner in the UK? No doubt investments are needed to fund ministries, and no doubt charities benefit from the dividends – but what does Christ think? If we were to truly apply the criteria of kingdom kindness, what would we do differently?

The Church in every generation is mandated to display the radical kindness of Christ's kingdom. Christians, above all others, should excel at kindness. The great twentieth-century prophet and Hasidic scholar Abraham Heschel once wrote that when he was young he admired *intelligent* people, but as he grew old what impressed him most was meeting *kind* people. What a profound insight. And what a pity so many of us learn it late in life, if at all. Yes, I admit that in my childhood I was impressed by *Scooby-Doo*; in my teens I was impressed by physical and sporting prowess; in my twenties, the student years, I was impressed by intellectual and academic credentials; in my thirties, as an ordained priest, I was impressed by people with charismatic anointing and powerful, successful leadership. But now, a reluctantly middle-aged man with over half my life behind me, I am with Heschel: I am impressed by kindness. It is rarer than it should be. And yet, when found, it is all the more beautiful for it. Perhaps because I discover too little of it in myself – perhaps because I am aware of how much my soul and body longs for its tender touch.

Kindness is at one and the same time much rarer to find yet much easier to cultivate than these other impressive features of physical prowess, intellectual ability, dynamic leadership. For they are gifts that God gives to whom he wills, and we have little say in the matter – but kindness is a fruit he wills all of us to have. Kindness, not charisms, is the mark of a Spirit-filled person and a Spirit-filled church.

There is an intriguing movement that has popped up in recent years, encouraging 'random acts of kindness'.[9] I think everyone deep down loves to be on the receiving end of such kindnesses, and many likewise long to give such kindnesses. I read of a man in Canada – in London, Ontario, to be precise – who walked into a coffee shop and offered to pay for the next 500 coffees ordered that week. It cost him eight hundred Canadian dollars. He paid and walked out, remaining anonymous. For that day, there was a free coffee for 500 folk, but more than that, there was kindness received and a momentary flourishing of human generosity. The world was a better place for that man's gesture.

Kindness, of course, looks different to different people. So generally, while we should all be open to the prompting to a sudden random gesture, what is needed is thought-through acts targeted to the need. Most people, as a matter of fact, don't want a hug on the high street from a student in a polyester 'onesie'; for a homeless person, kindness may simply be not walking by but offering a smile, a cigarette(!),[10] a moment of human interaction, or a couple of quid. For your elderly housebound neighbour it might mean offering to go to the shops for them or mow their lawn or paint their fence, or just to sit and listen to their memories. I heard of a priest for whom one major act of kindness in his parish was standing in for the village Post Office owners, so they could have their first holiday in years. Kindness looks for the specific need of this one particular person and finds a way to help. Let us ask God to show us who we can be kind towards and how in the name of Jesus.

Try a focused act of kindness every day

Let us try being kind with a smile. My wife Tiffany often says I look grizzly and attract a frown from others. I have observed countless times as we are out walking, others approaching us suddenly look and smile and I know it's because Tiffany has smiled at them, blessing them.

Let us try being kind with our words. The character Oddball in the classic old movie *Kelly's Heroes* says to someone who has just spoken harshly, 'Why don't you say something righteous and beautiful for a change?' Ask God to give you something kind, encouraging, up-building, life-giving to say to everyone you meet each day. Too many people go their whole week seeing nothing but frowns and hearing nothing but put-downs.

Let us try being kind in our actions. Do a kind act for someone each day, not to gain your Brownie Badge for helping an old person across the road, but to make someone's life flourish for a moment.

Try to be kind in your prayers. I am so conscious my prayers are selfish. The weight of them are for me and my needs, or for things that directly impact on me. A while ago at a conference, a stranger came and asked me to pray for his girlfriend. I had just finished preaching, I felt exhausted and I said brusquely, 'No, I can't promise to.' He looked disappointed but handed me a card: it was about a girl, his girlfriend, who had a rare bone cancer, and was off to hospital for three months, for bone marrow transfusions and chemotherapy. Obviously I immediately felt very small, and I agreed to pray, and did so for some time, but tragically this girl did not recover. Let us be quick to pray for others – not wait to be asked, not refuse a request, but offer and pray.

Let us be kind in sharing the gospel. This is the greatest kindness – the greatest gift we have to share. The greatest unkindness is to keep it to yourself. Let us hold out the words to eternal life.

Go on – be nice

Rikk Watts is a theologian at Regent College, Vancouver, who, like me, often writes his lectures in a coffee shop (or perhaps, being in North America, a diner). He befriended one of the waitresses and felt a real compassion for her – she had obviously had a tough few years and, as he said, 'What young girl growing up has the ambition to be working as a waitress in a coffee bar when they're fifty?' So he consciously tried to be kind, engaging her in conversation, speaking warmly to her, showing genuine interest in her. Once she realised he wasn't hitting on her, she began to open up to him. When Christmas came around, as he was paying for his lunch and adding the 'tip', he felt God say, 'Not enough.' So he increased it and God said again, 'Not enough.' Finally he got in step with the Spirit and wrote an extravagantly generous tip for the lady. The next time he saw her after the Christmas vacation, she said: 'Rikk, I'm reading the Bible.' Later that term he walked in with a friend, and the waitress came over and in serious sincerity said to Rikk's friend: 'I want to tell you about this man: whenever he comes here he fills this place with light.' Now that's what kindness does. That is Christlikeness; that is holiness.

Abraham Heschel wrote: 'And I with stubborn boldness, have promised that I will increase tenderness in this world.'[11] Let us likewise covenant to be kind.

Chapter 7

Baal and Asherah

The Israelites did evil in the eyes of the LORD; they forgot the LORD their God and served the Baals and the Asherahs. The anger of the LORD burned against Israel so that he sold them into the hands of Cushan-Rishathaim king of Aram Naharaim, to whom the Israelites were subject for eight years. But when they cried out to the LORD, he raised up for them a deliverer, Othniel son of Kenaz, Caleb's younger brother, who saved them. The Spirit of the LORD came on him, so that he became Israel's judge and went to war. The LORD gave Cushan-Rishathaim king of Aram into the hands of Othniel, who overpowered him. So the land had peace for forty years, until Othniel son of Kenaz died.   (Judges 3:7–11)

In his signature sermon on church and culture,[1] New York church planter Jon Tyson asks rhetorically: 'What is it people want today?' and offers up an answer to his own question: 'They want to rule the world and be naked in an amazing setting with someone they love.' Adam and Eve had it all – that was God's plan, his design, and it was perfect. But the demonic has a way of ruining everything – the devil cannot create, he can only un-create, undo, spoil and mar. And he sowed the seed in Adam and Eve's mind that God was holding out on them – that God had withheld what they really needed and what would really satisfy. They fell for it, they ate the forbidden fruit, they sinned – they opened Pandora's Box, they made a covenant with evil – and all hell broke loose. The universe has groaned ever since with their great falling.

Our culture is cursed by 'the Hex of Sex', claimed American academic Robert Fuller. Certainly one area the demonic has sought to un-create is one of God's first and best ideas – sexual union. Adam and Eve, the two becoming one flesh, whole in the holy beauty of sexual union. Sexual union and delight was God's gift, to be treasured within the parameters of heterosexual, monogamous marriage. This was among the first of God's designs to be besmirched, dragged through the mud by the snake, and it has remained an area where God's intention in creation has been challenged ever since. Sexual promiscuity and experimentation has always been a mark of paganism, as we will consider – but as Malcolm Muggeridge observed, sex is also the home of mysticism in a materialistic society.[2] When we don't worship the God who gave us sex, we can end up worshipping sex itself. Raquel Welch, 1960s sex symbol, said recently that today we are living in an 'era of porn' where 'everyone is a sex addict'.[3] Certainly in the West the cultural shift of the 1960s which challenged all the social norms that had been handed down the generations, accompanied by consequence-free sex as a result of readily available contraceptives, led to a sexual revolution. Today, every form of entertainment is immersed in sexual imagery: comedy, sit-coms, movies, fashion, pop music, news, advertising, magazines, the Internet; sex sells, and we've bought it. And the subject matter has become more explicit and extreme. What was deemed 'hard-core' twenty years ago is fairly *de rigeur* today, when sadomasochistic porn novels become bestsellers read on the bus without anyone blinking an eye. As I prepared this chapter, a mainstream TV channel was advertising a documentary to be shown at peak viewing time, focusing on esoteric sex acts performed in public. And, of course, the Internet's highways are clogged with porn.[4] A character in the popular sit-com *Scrubs* said: 'I'm fairly sure that if they took porn off the Internet, there would be only one website left and it would be called "bring back the porn".'

We live at a time of unprecedented sexual liberties, where almost every fantasy and indeed every sexual atrocity can be indulged in, literally or in cyberspace. The only limit to our consumption is our capacity. The Internet and social media have created unimaginable opportunities for exploration and experiment. Many see this as a freedom from outdated and inherited moral repressions – a good thing, liberation even. Too few equate this with the exponential rise in STDs, date rape, sex trafficking or the problems caused by abortion on demand. The rise in pornography fuels a rise in sexual demand and activity; this inevitably produces a rise in unwanted children conceived out of covenant faithful union, thousands of lives aborted as if just a waste product. I recently read of a case of alleged rape where the accused seemed genuinely shocked to be accused – he was simply enacting what he'd seen on the screen and had been programmed to believe was the *modus operandi* in relationships, however nascent. Despite this libertinism in culture, some close observers question how free this sexual freedom really is. Michel Foucault, the foremost twentieth-century philosopher on the themes of sex and power, whose name is almost synonymous with experimentation in the sexually bizarre, could speak of the 'exploitation of eroticism [in which we are] no longer control[led] by repression [but you are nevertheless controlled] by stimulation'.[5] Make no mistake, controlled we are, only in a different way. Similarly, All Souls Fellow and Oxford Professor of Ethics and Philosophy, Charles Taylor, writes:

> We may think we are gaining some freedom when we throw off sexual prohibitions, but in fact we are dominated by certain images of what it is to be a full, healthy, fulfilled sexual being. And these images are in fact very powerful instruments of control. We may think of the contemporary wave of sexual permissiveness as a kind of 'revolt of the sexual body' [but] the ruse is diabolic . . . In going for liberation, we see ourselves as escaping a power understood on the old model. But in fact we live under a power of the new kind, and this we are not escaping; far from it, we are playing its game, we are assuming the shape it has moulded for us. It keeps us tied to the whole 'dispositif [power structure] de sexualite'.[6]

What looks like freedom is only a new type of being controlled – and we are willing slaves of the powers who use sex as control. We march to the beat of the market, of our passions, of darker powers.

The main trunk roads into Oxford city centre were brought to a standstill. A so-called 'fat-berg' had grown in the sewers under Park End Street – years of cooking fat poured down the sink, together with nappies and wet-wipes flushed down toilets, had coagulated into a filthy fat mountain, backing up the flow of effluent down the sewer and causing the drains to collapse by its sheer weight. A similar fat-berg was found in Kingston upon Thames in 2013 – that one weighed fifteen tonnes, and in volume was the size of a bus! Industrial jet-hoses were required to pump thousands of gallons of water under high pressure to break down the mass and disperse it. What a metaphor for our sex-hexed society. So many lives are clogged up by sin and dehumanising sexual immorality that the whole system is in danger of collapse. For many Christians their soul is collapsing under the weight of accumulated filth, the flow of God's life in them is at a standstill. The stronghold of sexual sin needs breaking down and flushing out.

A 'biblical chronicle of failure' is how Old Testament Professor Donald Wiseman described the oscillating relationship of the Israelites with Yahweh in his commentary on Judges. At Sinai, God instructed the people he had recently redeemed from slavery about how they were to live in the land of promise he would bring them into. Speaking of the pagan peoples currently occupying the land, he says, 'you will drive them out before you. Do not make a covenant with them or with their gods. Do not let them live in your land or they will cause you to sin against me, because the worship of their gods will certainly be a snare to you' (Exodus 23:31–32) (We should note that those Canaanites who recognised the God of Israel and who were willing to embrace Yahweh were not displaced.) Tragically, we read of a catalogue of disobedience against God and compliance with the evil religions of the land's residents – in Judges we learn that the tribe of Judah did not drive out the valley folk (1:19); the tribe of Benjamin did not drive out the Jebusites (1:21); the tribe of Joseph did not drive out the Hittites (1:24f); the tribe of Manasseh did not drive out the Canaanites (1:27) nor did Ephraim (1:29), nor Zebulun (1:30), nor Asher (1:31), nor Naphtali (1:33) nor Dan (1:34f). The tribes of Reuben and Gad chose to reside in Gilead and not across the Jordan in Canaan; the tribe of the

Levites had no lands – so out of nine tribes actually apportioned land in Canaan, not one fully fulfilled the command of God – all, against God's decree, coexisted with Canaanites and accommodated themselves over time to the Canaanites' religious culture – and their sexual habits. Why were they reluctant to obey God in this? Clearly, no one wants a fight if they can possibly avoid it. To remove these Canaanites would have involved further warfare, and perhaps they were weary of this. It may be they had a sense of altruistic conscience, and felt bad about displacing this people group, preferring to attempt a peaceful coexistence. That's a positive take, but does Scripture hint at another selfish motive in not displacing the Canaanites – were the Israelites willing victims of their sexual snares?

Baal and Asherah

My good pal David White decided for his sabbatical to read the whole Bible through, standing up and speaking aloud. He felt this change in posture coupled with the 'heard' word rather than merely the read word might give him a fresh encounter with the text. When I asked him the major impression he gained from this, I was very much surprised – he replied: 'That God hates idolatry – it makes him angry.' Idolatry is worship stolen from God and given to demons (Deuteronomy 32:17). Behind every idol is a demon, according to Paul (1 Corinthians 10:20). No wonder it arouses the wrath of God. Judah abandoned Yahweh – the God of their fathers Abraham, Isaac and Jacob – and they worshipped the Canaanite gods, demons associated with power, prosperity and sexual promiscuity – Baal, and his consort, Asherah.

The Canaanites were defined by their obsession with idolatry and immorality. Sex and fertility were the centre around which the Canaanite universe spun. Now the Old Testament does not give great detail about what took place in Baal and Asherah worship, but hints in the Scriptures and wider studies enable us to construct a fairly clear idea. Canaanite worship was practised through mimetic ritual – heterosexual and homosexual sex with temple prostitutes was understood to reunite Baal and Asherah, and their union energised the forces of nature, leading to fertility – in crops, herds and humans.[7] The *Encyclopaedia Judaica* states: 'The pagan world worshipped and deified sex. It reserved the term "holy ones" for its cult prostitutes.'[8]

It was specifically because of these evil ways that God said he was going to evict them from the land. Indeed, God said the very land itself was going to *vomit* them out (Leviticus 18:28). And it was these Canaanite sex gods, Baal and Asherah, who seduced the Israelites with their promise of promiscuity. Instead of driving out the Canaanites, Israel coexisted with them, and too often they kept the Canaanite gods, and adopted the Canaanite sexual practices. These sexual sins of the Canaanites became a snare to the Israelites. The Israelites were given laws in Leviticus specifically commanding them not to act as the Canaanites did: child sacrifice, bestiality, incest, adultery, polygamy, rape and prostitution, all common practice within Canaan, were all expressly forbidden – rather they were to live according to God's foundational design revealed by Adam and Eve's creation in Genesis 2:24: monogamous heterosexual marriage. 'The Israelites did evil in the eyes of the LORD; they forgot the LORD their God and served the Baals and the Asherahs' (Judges 3:7) – and such 'service' was indubitably accompanied by the litany of sexual sin mentioned above. At the high places, sacred shrines on hilltops or in tree groves (Hosea 4:13) self-styled worship was accompanied by sexual orgies, often with the male prostitutes of the shrine – this was the order of the day. The grove itself symbolised the Asherah or female deity and a stone pillar at its centre symbolised the male phallus and thus the male deity or Baal. Leanne Payne not unreasonably describes Baal and Asherah as 'the gods of sexual orgy'.[9]

That was three thousand years ago – but the ancient Canaanite sex gods Baal and Asherah are very much still with us. Repackaged in Western guise, they are the forces behind our insatiable sexual obsession and addiction. Just as Paul teaches us that behind every idol is a demon, so we can be certain that behind our idols of sex, lie ancient spiritual principalities and powers. Just as the Israelites three thousand years ago were enticed by the Canaanite sex gods and failed to remove them and their worshippers from their midst, so today many in the Church have been seduced and snared by the same sex gods who are so venerated in our promiscuous society. You name it, there is a hardly a sexual sin prohibited in Leviticus that I have not heard confessed to me by churchgoers. Be aware, Baal is awake and at work.

In Tolkien's *The Fellowship of the Ring,* Gandalf explains to Frodo how the power of the ring had degraded Gollum. Frodo asks: 'But if he hated it, why didn't he get rid of it, or go away and leave it?' Gandalf replies: '. . . he hated it and loved it, as he hated and loved himself. He could not get rid of it. He had no will left in the matter.' Many of you reading this understand that struggle. You have a love/hate relationship with your sin – you don't know which you want more: God and his freedom or your sexual sin. Only when you want God more than your sin can freedom be experienced. The remarkable ministry of Alcoholics Anonymous has helped hundreds of thousands of people find freedom from addiction. The core component is the first three steps of their 'twelve-step recovery' programme.

1) Admit you are powerless over alcohol.
2) Believe that a power greater than ours can restore us.
3) Decide to turn your will over to that power.

This is the framework we need to put in place if we are to walk in freedom from sexual control – repentance of sin, belief in and dependence on a greater power, leading to deliverance. Though Judges 3:7 speaks of the Israelites doing evil against the Lord in serving images of Baal and Asherah, and bringing judgement on themselves, the story fortunately does not end there. The writer goes on to say, 'when they cried out to the LORD, he raised up for them a deliverer' (3:9). Repentance of sin and dependence on God brings deliverance.

'A hard-core problem needs a hard-core solution'

These words come from addiction counsellor David Partington, who wrote a book on sexual intimacy. The problem we are faced with is indeed hard-core – and the solution we have is likewise hard-core. AA rightly emphasises handing yourself over to a greater power – and we have assurance that a great power is at hand. No wonder the great French reformer John Calvin could state: 'Before God's immeasurable power, I am struck dumb. It makes me ecstatic.' The power of God flows from the cross and resurrection.

I wrote and preached this material at an Easter Day service at St Aldates. There were a few raised eyebrows when I announced the topic, and for his part my father had said to me earlier in the week that such a theme was not appropriate on Easter Day. But I disagreed. Easter Day is the most suitable point of all from which to view our corruption and our liberation from sin – all sin, of which sexual sin is not the worst but which, as we have seen, is a besetting problem. Easter Day is where we find forgiveness and freedom and also the fulfilment of God to replace the desires of the flesh. Easter tells us that Christ had to suffer and die for our sin – our addictions have consequences, and they cost Christ dear. Easter tells us that only Christ's death could satisfy God's just judgement on sin. Easter tells us that Christ's shed blood can fully cleanse us of every sin. And Easter tells us that Christ's resurrection power can restore and transform all things.

There is full forgiveness where there is true repentance

Telling someone of your struggles may be a start – but it is not repentance. A problem shared is not a problem forgiven. It just means someone else knows about your problem. I have heard many people tell me they have addictions to sex, but not all were repenting; many were simply sharing. They perhaps wanted me to pray for them, but they were not prepared to pray for themselves, do the hard work themselves, or go to war against their sin. They wanted me to fight for them in prayer, but they weren't willing to fight for themselves. True repentance takes personal responsibility for sin and brings it to God for forgiveness and freedom. C.S. Lewis wrote, 'Now repentance is no fun at all. It is something much harder than merely eating humble pie. It means unlearning all the self-conceit and self-will that we have been training ourselves into for thousands of years. It means killing part of yourself, undergoing a kind of death.'[10]

Now, psychologists and therapists have demonstrated that

people may be predisposed to sexual addiction if they have suffered emotional trauma or privation when young. And we know that sexual addiction can lead to a neurological formatting which drives desire, an addictive determination, almost a chemical need. Of course we must be sensitive to these insights.

And we know that Jesus can heal the cause and consequence of sin – the presenting issue and the emotional, neurochemical drivers. But let these not be an excuse, an evasion of our own responsibility. Sexual sin is sin, not a medical illness or psychological condition. If we fail to treat it as a sin we will not be treating it at its source, only its effect. Full deliverance requires true repentance.

There is deliverance when there is dependence on God's power

We need Yahweh to set us free from Baal and Asherah – he can, and he will, if we will choose him and renounce sin. The Israelites cried out to God and he sent them a deliverer, whose name was Othniel. In Hebrew this means 'God is Power' – and it is God's power we need to break the power of sin and the flesh and evil. I told a non-Christian friend that I was writing about freedom from sexual addiction and porn – he immediately replied: 'Yeah right, as if that's gonna happen.' Interestingly, he didn't object to the principle that there is a need for deliverance, he just did not believe deliverance was possible. To be freed from a great power we need to experience an even greater power and as Psalm 49:15 (here taken from the metric Psalms) celebrates, there is such a power: 'God will yet redeem my soul – his greater power shall set me free.' That 'greater power' that reversed the curse of sin, that greater power that shrugged off death, is the power of the Spirit that raised Jesus from death, and that power can break every chain. St Paul's passionate prayer was for the Church to experience the reality of God's 'incomparably great power for us who believe . . . power [that] is the same as the mighty strength he exerted when he raised Christ from the dead and seated him at his right hand in the heavenly realms, far above all rule and authority, power and dominion' (Ephesians 1:19–21). Many are in the grip of the principalities and powers, might and dominion of darkness – but God can enable us to surmount them. We have a great need for God's power, and God's great power is available to us in our need.

A committed young student and small group leader in our church, recently told how he had been part of an accountability group for a couple of years. Whenever they met, others confessed their various temptations and struggles with lust and porn. He would pray for them, but never shared any struggle with sin in this area, and they considered him free and pure. For two years he kept his sin secret and gave the impression all was fine, while continuing in the grip of moral darkness. Then he had an amazing encounter with God after one service and the Spirit of God fell on him. He was deeply convicted of his hidden sin – he had been addicted to pornography and masturbation for ten years. As he met God, he sincerely repented, calling on God in desperation and brokenness. Wave after wave of divine grace and power flooded him and, in that encounter, not only did he know his sin was forgiven but he knew its power was broken. The vice of vice was shattered and he was fully delivered and has not returned to his sin.

Free at last

This may have been uncomfortable reading – but we must expose the structures and powers behind the sexual sin that affects and afflicts so many. And if you remember nothing else from this, I want you to know that the dark powers that often afflict you are inferior to the great power of Jesus Christ; revealed by his resurrection and available to you by his Spirit. And the stains that sexual sin tattoo into our soul are not permanent but can be fully dissolved by Jesus' blood when we turn from sin and turn to him for forgiveness. We can walk free, without sin, stain, shame.

There is hope – there is a future.

Chapter 8

Porn Free

But I tell you that anyone who looks at a woman lustfully has already committed adultery with her in his heart.   (Matthew 5:28)

For my eyes have seen your salvation.   (Luke 2:30)

The orgasm did not originate with the fall of Adam and Eve, but with God's creation of Adam and Eve. God gave us the gift of sex. Sexual attraction, sexual delight, sexual release, sexual fulfilment is wonderful – God made it so. God gave us sexual desire, he gave us eyes to drink in the beauty of our partner's curves and creases and form, he gave us sexual organs and sexual release so that we can achieve pure pleasure – not simply procreation but joyful recreation. Joyce Huggett, a well-known spiritual writer who has written much in this area, helpfully states: 'the ability to feel drawn to a magnet was dreamed up by God, created by him. Sexual magnetism was dreamed up and created by God. Sexual excitation, like the sex drive, was God's idea. Hormones and erections, tender breasts and ejaculations and the stomach somersaulting with desire, were God's brain-children.'[1]

But for many, this gift has been dragged through the mud and today pornography is the prevailing besmircher of souls. Pornography was once the preserve of the 'perv', available only at seedy sex shops in rundown districts of town or to those tall enough to reach the top shelf in their newsagent and brave enough to endure the sneering scorn of the cashier. But we have seen fulfilled John Wesley's old adage 'What one generation tolerates the next generation will embrace.' The 'sexual revolution' that was much vaunted in the 1960s led to a permissiveness that has become a tidal wave fifty years later. In the past few decades, two major factors have sent porn viral: first, the decline in a common moral standard, and second, the advance in technology. The decline in morality accompanies the exorcism of God from the public arena and the ensuing lack of any basis on which to ground a sound moral ethic – relativism reigns where there are no foundations. Indeed, ethical and moral relativism is not simply the result, it has become the foundation of our culture. We have no moral basis to determine right from wrong and we don't want one – indeed, we are not far from the stage where the only wrong thing is for you to tell me that what I am doing is wrong. Increasingly we are living in a morally topsy-turvy world. A Canadian friend told me that Canada Radio and the Canadian TV Commission requires that 35 per cent of media output must be Canadian in content: Canadian actors, Canadian location, Canadian news, etc. Not an unreasonable ruling to promote one's own culture, perhaps. However, recently three TV porn channels were rebuked for not showing enough Canadian-filmed porn. Not too long ago laws existed to curb indecency; now they defend it. The prophet Isaiah foresaw a time would come when evil was called good and good evil (5:20) – such times may be coming close when people forsake God and his word.

Second, the rise of pornography has come on the back of exponential advances in technology. It's hard to conceive but the

Internet, such an invaluable extension of all our lives, has been in popular use for less than twenty years. Until the 1990s the information superhighway was used only by computer nerds and techno geeks – but in the late 1990s the web went world-wide, available to the masses, with the ubiquitous portal to its delights that is Google coming online in 1998. Pornographers were among the first adopters, seeing its wide-reaching potential, and they flooded the web – Pandora's Box was wide open and all manner of evil things released. Ten years after Google, in 2008, smartphones adopted 3G technology and access to online porn was made possible anytime, anyplace, anywhere. The day I bought my sons their first smartphones in their mid-teens, I was chatting with a friend later that day, celebrating this rite of passage. One post-doc scholar, overhearing me in a coffee shop, simply blurted out: 'You know what that means: porn, porn, porn.' I was shocked. 'No it doesn't,' I responded – and by God's grace, no, it hasn't – but for many it does. The word pornography comes from a conjunction of two Greek terms: *porne* meaning prostitute and *graphein* meaning to write. Its initial use referred to written material describing sexual acts; however, as the *Oxford Dictionary* dispassionately notes, its usage has been widened to cover 'printed or visual material containing the explicit description or display of sexual organs or activity, intended to stimulate sexual excitement'.[2]

Let's talk porn

How prevalent is porn?

The rise is so exponential that by the time you read this, the statistics I cite will no doubt be redundant – but here goes.

There are 68 million search engine requests for porn daily. Twelve per cent of all Internet sites, approximately 30 million sites or 420 million pages in all, are pornographic. Indeed, I have heard it claimed that 'Sex' is the number one word typed into search engines. Porn is a $97 billion industry, which is more than the annual GDP of two-thirds of the world's countries.[3]

So who uses porn?

Surveys suggest that 90 per cent of eight- to sixteen-year-olds have viewed porn; 87 per cent of US college males and 31 per cent of college females regularly use porn; 70 per cent of porn access occurs during nine-to-five office hours; 70 per cent of Christian men in one survey said they struggled with Internet porn. In the TED talk 'The Demise of Guys', it is claimed the average young man watches fifty porn clips a week.[4] Clearly, then, a significant percentage of men and women, the old and young, at work and at play, are viewing pornography. And it's not just a male thing. One young friend told me he shared a house with young ladies who found a box of old porn magazines in the attic. So they wallpapered the whole sitting room with the centrefold. There were a few gaps and they actually went shopping to buy a few more magazines to cover the spaces. A theology post-grad at Oxford once told me that a female friend (with whom he was not romantically involved) asked him if he'd like to come back to her house to watch pornography. I can report that he declined. I asked three of our female church interns whether porn was a problem with women of their age and all three immediately said no! I then asked the interns if their friends send 'sexts' – suggestive sexual texts or mobile photos of themselves naked, or if they received them from boys – and all said it was normal! I then asked whether their friends would have read the recent best-selling pornographic sadomasochistic novel, and they said 'all of them'.

Porn is very often vile and violent, rarely a celebration of 'love making' – it is the taking out of lust on another human being. Pope John Paul II said, 'The opposite of love is not hate, the opposite of love is use.'[5] Porn is incapable of kindling love – only lust that uses the other for oneself. Porn drives criminal activity – sex trafficking is inextricably linked with the porn industry.[6] And one study showed that twenty-nine out of thirty young sex offenders had been watching X-rated porn from the age of seven.[7] Porn destroys marriages – in a 2004 study Dr Jill Manning informed the US Senate that 56 per cent of all divorce submissions claimed one partner had an obsessive involvement in pornography.[8] Porn encourages cyber-affairs, cyber-adultery, it pushes couples towards divorce. Porn debases and disintegrates the personality of the user of it – I read of a worship pastor who confessed, 'It began to eat away at who I was . . . it began to rot me away.' Porn depersonalises us, and robs us of the ability to relate properly to others. What spouse wants their partner's mind filled with intimate images of another? What spouse wants their partner to mentally honour another with their body, give all they have to an image?

Jesus said, 'The eye is the lamp of the body . . . But if your eyes are unhealthy, your whole body will be full of darkness. If then the light within you is darkness, how great is that darkness' (Matthew 6:22–23). I believe people who watch porn have 'unhealthy eyes' in exactly the sense Jesus says here – and welcome within them a very great darkness. Society has relativised and normalised porn, but we need to recognise it for what it is – darkness, the power of the demonic. I believe Satan is the great pornographer – it is he who is aroused by porn and who is excited to know that God's beautiful creation is being debased and defiled. Porn objectifies persons made in God's image – it makes them less than the divine image-bearers they were made to be, less than the sum of their parts – in fact it regards them only as body parts, for the stimulation and gratification of others. C.S. Lewis insightfully observed that the lustful man does not want a woman. In fact a woman is what he does not want. 'He wants a pleasure for which a woman happens to be the necessary apparatus.'[9]

I was recently at a shopping centre and walked past a shop known for its sexually provocative clothing. Outside was a middle-aged man taking photos of the window display of mannequins in skimpy underwear and set in seductive poses, oblivious or indifferent to all around – his flesh unrestrained, his sensitivities without shame, his lust craving images on his phone of plastic models in pseudo-sexual posture.

A minister told me of a group he runs offering Christian life-skills for young men from troubled backgrounds. The young men are asked not to use their phones. However, they take that to mean not making a phone call – the phone has become an extension of their being and they cannot imagine ceasing other activities on this all-absorbing device. So it is normal for them to disregard this request and to sit watching porn movies on their phones even as they are half-listening, half-engaging with the course input. All this is done in public, without a trace of shame or embarrassment; they have no sense that what they are doing is inappropriate in such a context. As they see it, they are complying with the leader's request – they are not 'using their phones', they are not making calls – they are passing the time watching porn. They cannot see that they are being robbed of their personhood, and robbing others in the group of their mutual potential of being persons in relationship.

Porn is a thief. It robs its user, it robs the one used to make it, it robs others of the user's full engagement with them. Whether the persons being consumed by it are photographed or filmed freely, taking part of their own volition – nevertheless they are being dehumanised, demonically influenced. One great irony of sustained pornographic use is the potential side-effect of erectile dysfunction.[10] There is growing anecdotal evidence that young men are rendered impotent through habitual pornographic usage.[11] Psychological rather than physiological, the sex receptors in the brain no longer light up and stimulate arousal at the prospect or image of the human body. Studies suggest this effect is reversible and time away from porn will return things to normal function. But what an irony, that porn should rob you of exactly the thing it promises! Pornography abuses the viewer and the person being viewed – it invites a family of demonic shadows – it addicts, it is violent and dishonest. Anne Layden, co-director of Sexual Trauma and Psychopathology at the University of Pennsylvania, spoke before the US Senate and called pornography, 'The most concerning thing to psychological health that I know of existing today.'[12] And let me add to that, that its effect on spiritual health is just as severe.

We need to see porn through the eyes of Jesus

Jesus said, 'You have heard that it was said, "You shall not commit adultery." But I tell you that anyone who looks at a woman lustfully has already committed adultery with her in his heart' (Matthew 5:27–28). Porn is adultery. Jesus raises Moses' moral bar, the willed thought is judged the same as the act. A student came to tell me that he had an issue with porn and masturbation. He then said something that shocked me, showing the confusion of the pornography user's thought patterns. What he said was, 'At least I'm not sleeping with my fiancée.' What muddled moral reasoning. I told him that watching porn was far more sinful than having sex with his fiancée; that would be the right thing at the wrong time – whereas porn is always wrong, period!

Often people's consciences have become so seared, so numbed by repeated sin, that they no longer register shame. Research suggests there may be a process of neurological formatting in which the brain functions and structure are so programmed to be stimulated by pornography that the demand for such overrides any trace of consideration of ethical or moral factors. That is certainly true for the non-Christian. However, the born-again believer has the Holy Spirit within – and when that Spirit is being joined to sin in the body of the believer, it will be grieved and will register protest (Psalm 51; 1 Corinthians 6:15f). Minister and blogger Tim Challies writes on this theme, saying, 'Every Christian . . . who looks at porn wants to stop, but many of them want to stop just a little bit less than they want to keep going. And so sin prevails. The only way you will stop is if you begin to see the monstrous nature of the sin you are committing.'[13] This was Ruth's experience. A children's and youth minister in the inner city, she was addicted to pornography, fantasy and masturbation. What broke her free from this destructive cocktail was a revelation through a dream in which she saw herself in the bath, when a man walked into the bathroom and stood in the corner masturbating while watching her. In the dream she screamed at him to stop but he continued satisfying himself and defiling her. It was then that the Spirit of God showed her: *what this man is doing is no different to what you do when you watch or read porn and masturbate* – her porn use, like the man's in the dream, was self-gratifying, voyeuristic, sinful. She repented, and was set free. True repentance comes only after true revelation of the nature of our sin – if you are in the grip of this sin, you need to ask God for such a revelation of the wickedness of it. To fully grasp that your porn use is like a thorn pressed into Christ's head. Yet Jesus paid in pain the price for your sin (and porn is always sin). I read of someone who justified their porn addiction by saying: 'porn is my medicine'. No – it's your sin. Porn is your enemy. Like heroin, it promises much but will ultimately destroy you.

Don't expect God to do what he expects you to do

Many do recognise that their preoccupation with porn is sin, but they are trapped in a sin–shame–confess, sin–shame–confess cycle. Now, the more sin, often the less shame and the less confession. It can just become a sin–sin–sin cycle. But even if this is avoided, the reality is that many do not seriously address what they confess. They come forward in ministry for prayer, but they do not choose to walk in and work out their freedom. The problem is not that the prayer didn't work out, but that they did not work out the prayer. How do we need to respond? What does God expect us to do?

Take radical action to remove sin at its source

Jesus said, 'If your . . . eye causes you to stumble, gouge it out and throw it away. It is better for you to lose one part of your body than for your whole body to be thrown into hell' (Matthew 5:29). He was certainly employing hyperbole – a rhetorical device to increase the shock factor through exaggeration, and thus provoke a heightened awareness that we must take sin seriously, and take serious steps to remove it. Some, however, actually took Jesus at his words and one ancient church tradition claims the second-century theologian Origen actually cut off his sexual member in an attempt to curb temptation and sin. Saint Francis apparently would throw himself into a thorn bush when he was tempted – an unusual but probably effective form of aversion therapy.

I recall one dear student, when I was an Oxford chaplain, telling me that he would tie his hands in Sellotape at night so as not to fantasise and masturbate. Was this legalism? I certainly would not advocate such an approach but it highlighted to me his tenacious self-discipline. It arose out of his love for Christ and I have no doubt God honoured this in him.

Jesus understood that the eye is often at the source of sin, and his teaching here demonstrates that he believed those he addressed had the capacity to recognise and defeat this sin at its source. How much more should it be so for us, who now have the Spirit of God within and know the power of sin to be broken. But we must take radical and tenacious action to prevent sin. Having a smartphone is not smart, it's stupid if you are struggling with porn – get rid of your smartphone, stop spending time Internet surfing, set up 'parental controls' on Google, don't hang around with others who encourage porn use, throw out any indecent printed material, unsubscribe from unhelpful TV channels or magazines, delete all your porn clips, images, links on your hard-drive. You won't die – indeed, you will begin to live.

I was discussing with Paul Brodersen, an Oxford neuroscientist, recent studies that show how porn addiction trains the brain to demand more and more stimulus, to release enough dopamine in the pleasure centres of the brain and elicit the emotion of pleasure. I asked him whether this programming of the brain's demands was reversible. He was immediate and emphatic in answering that it is. 'Like a spoiled child that demands sweets all the time – you can retrain it.'

'How?' I asked.

'Stop giving in to its demands – sooner or later it will stop demanding.'

Take up the fight

John Wesley, that great eighteenth-century apostle of holiness, once said, 'How can we win if we don't fight?' The fact is, we cannot – if we don't fight, we will lose. And the Church is full of losers who have given up, given in to sin. Paul wrote, 'I strike a blow to my body and make it my slave so that after I have preached to others, I myself will not be disqualified for the prize' (1 Corinthians 9:27). We cannot be passive where sin is concerned – we dare not take it lying down – we must get angry, go to war, stand against this, resist it, fight it. Do not be a victim.

I have already mentioned my chum in the British Special Air Service. On becoming a Christian, he remained in the military but found some aspects of the army life hugely demanding, in particular the widespread use and sharing of pornography by the soldiers. Mark told me that on one occasion he was travelling on a coach to a training event – a journey from Hereford to London that took four hours. As soon as they were aboard the coach, some porn tapes were handed to the driver – hard-core pornography was being watched by these elite soldiers for the whole journey. As a new Christian, who knew God had called him to a holy life, Mark forced himself not to watch but to look at the coach floor – and there he fixed his gaze, praying for strength – and for the video machine to malfunction (which it didn't) – for four hours. The problem was that while he could avert his eyes, he couldn't turn off the sound-track coming through the main speakers. And with no ear-plugs or head phones, he said the sounds were like a powerful magnet trying to draw his head upwards, and he had to battle not to visualise or watch what he couldn't block out from hearing. Mark told me he has fought in many battles but none was as severe as that, when his whole flesh was crying out to participate in this vented lust, but his spirit desired God. And he won that battle. Winning one battle does not mean you win the war, however. On the completion of the training event it was time to go back. He was the last to put his gear on the coach and as he was putting his foot on the first step of the coach he looked up and saw that the porn was on again, and in a quick silent prayer he told God that he could not take another four hours of this. In one of the quickest answers to prayer I have ever heard of, one of the instructors who had travelled up in his own vehicle shouted out that there was room for one more in his car – upon which Mark immediately shouted, 'I'll take it.' Paul says in 1 Corinthians 10:13: 'No temptation has overtaken you except what is common to mankind. And God is faithful; he will not let you be tempted beyond what you can bear. But when you are tempted, he will also provide a way out so that you can endure it.' Porn can only have a hold over you if you permit it to do so – if you resist then God will honour that.

General, later President, Eisenhower, in a letter to his troops prior to D-Day, wrote: 'Your task will not be an easy one. Your enemy is well-trained, well-equipped and battle-hardened. He will fight savagely. But this is the year . . . The tide has turned! We will accept nothing less than full victory! Good luck! And let us beseech the blessing of Almighty God upon this great and noble undertaking.'[14] This is the year to conquer that besetting sin, to fight, to accept nothing less than full victory from its oppression and seek God for his blessing on it.

Get accountable

Saint James wrote in his letter, 'confess your sins to each other and pray for each other so that you may be healed' (James 5:16). Sin makes us sick – in our soul, our mind and sometimes even our bodies. Confession of sin and eradication of sin is a step towards '*sozo*', as the Greek puts it – our healing, wholeness, salvation. Like mould, sin thrives in shadows, it festers in secret. Bring it into light. Expose it, confess, get real with others, and be healed. Make yourself accountable to someone else, your spouse or pastor or a mature Christian leader, and not someone battling with the same issue or your meetings will become ones of mutual self-wallowing – a slave can't help a slave out of slavery. Find someone who will challenge you, who won't let you get away with stuff. If you need a computer for work purposes, there are some excellent accountability software programmes that will inform others what you are watching, among them: XXX Church, Covenant Eyes, Exit.

But seeking accountability must not become passing the buck – telling someone is not enough, it is not repentance per se; if you do not address what you confess, it's simply information.

A man once told me that he had been addicted to porn for several years – and he would watch porn on his phone in order to get aroused enough to have relations with his wife, no doubt replaying with her what he had watched others do. He was ashamed, he knew this was wrong and he came to me for ministry. I asked him if his wife knew of his addiction and he responded with a shocked 'No!' – although I bet she had sensed something was wrong. But for years he had deceived her, sinned against her, lied to her, committed repeated cyber-adultery. I didn't want to pray for him – I told him to go home, tell his wife and receive her forgiveness. He was horrified at the prospect – I guess he just hoped I would lay hands on him and pray. But I do not believe my prayers for him would have had any effect – not until he did the right thing. I did not think he could get free without confessing to his wife. Jesus said that if anyone has anything against you, you should stop making your offering to God and go and be reconciled with that person (Matthew 5:23–25). One testimony I read of a husband who confessed his porn addiction to his wife said, 'The more I told her, the closer we got.' Recently I received a letter from someone training for the ordained ministry. In his search for more of God, he was challenged about a former moral sin. The hand of the Lord was heavy upon him in conviction and finally he plucked up the courage to confess the moral sin to his wife. He later wrote: 'We had a tough few days and weeks. But the quality of our relationship now soars above where it was, which was already good . . . I'll happily accept the reinvigoration, reanimation, enhanced intimacy and closer bond that we will now enjoy for life!'

This is an axiom of the Christian life: true repentance is not merely saying or being sorry, but showing you are sorry by walking in the opposite direction: 'Anyone who has been stealing must steal no longer, but must work, doing something useful with their own hands' (Ephesians 4:28) – whoever used to fill their eyes, or mouth or mind with filth must fill them with good things. 'Finally, brothers and sisters, whatever is true, whatever is noble, whatever is right, whatever is pure, whatever is lovely, whatever is admirable – if anything is excellent or praiseworthy – think about such things' (Philippians 4:8). Repentance means we change our thinking, change our direction, change the screen. Again, we must take responsibility and act with tenacity on this. Find a new focus, take up a new hobby, learn a new language, start a degree, take up a new sport – find an alternative, an opposite good to replace the sinful mode of operation. And it's crucial that we know ourselves – that we come to understand when we are vulnerable to temptation and sins of the flesh. There is a handy acronym which warns us when we may be susceptible to the demands of our flesh: HALT = Hungry, Angry, Lonely, Tired. At such times, we need to consciously put things in place or put people in place so that we do not head back into the rut of sin.

Walking in the opposite spirit is achievable, and will bear fruit.

One young man sighed reluctantly, 'I'll never be free, I just have to manage the porn use, and limit it to once every few weeks.' He was wrong: total freedom is possible. I believe no addictions are permanent. Indeed, as an aside, some studies of the brain have demonstrated that the area aroused by sexual pleasure is the same as the area stimulated by spiritual experiences and release through worship.

Choose the better way.

Be filled with the Holy Spirit

'Now the Lord is the Spirit, and where the Spirit of the Lord is, there is freedom' (2 Corinthians 3:17). If we are gripped by a great power, we need delivering by a greater power. That power is available to us – the power that raised Jesus from the dead (Ephesians 1:19–20); a power to enable us to walk in a manner worthy of the Lord, fully pleasing him in every way, bearing fruit in every good work (Colossians 1:10–11).

We need to do what only we can do: obey Christ, be filled with the Spirit, obey and walk in the Spirit – this is our discipleship; but God will do what only he can do, forgiving our sin and freeing us from every power that binds. The promise is written in blood – Jesus' blood: 'if the Son sets you free, you will be free indeed' (John 8:36) – not free only in part. The Holy Spirit transforms us from one degree of glory, into the likeness of Jesus (2 Corinthians 3:18). And it is the Spirit who truly satisfies – he is the one who fills us with joy unspeakable and with his glory – if we drink deeply of him, we will never thirst again, and the pleasures of this world will fade. The Spirit of God sanctifies and satisfies. We must seek more of the Spirit. The sin and shame of porn use often causes people to withdraw from God – but they must do the very opposite, they need more not less of God, they must press into God for freedom and fullness.

Walk free

Steve McQueens's powerful movie *12 Years a Slave* follows the true story of a black man, Solomon Northup, who, though a free man, is press-ganged and sold into slavery. He and his friends never give up hope of justice and liberty and finally, after twelve gruelling years, a US marshal and a lawyer come to the plantation where Solomon is enslaved to set him free. But the slave-master protests and refuses to give up what he possesses, grabbing Solomon and shouting at him 'I own you. I own you. You belong to me. You hear me!' But the lawyer pulls the slave-master away and demands 'Unhand him!' The lawyer then guides Solomon to the horse and buggy that will take him home. But Solomon has a choice, to stay a slave or walk free, and walk free he does.

Porn, like all sin, enslaves. Porn lays claim to you, saying, 'I own you, you belong to me.' Porn won't let you go without a fight, without protesting in all sorts of ways. But Christ and the Spirit come to declare your freedom and to lead you away into that freedom.

Chapter 9

Idols or Bibles

Then the king called together all the elders of Judah and Jerusalem. He went up to the temple of the LORD with the people of Judah, the inhabitants of Jerusalem, the priests and the prophets – all the people from the least to the greatest. He read in their hearing all the words of the Book of the Covenant, which had been found in the temple of the LORD . . . He took the Asherah pole from the temple of the LORD to the Kidron Valley outside Jerusalem and burned it there. He ground it to powder and scattered the dust over the graves of the common people. He also tore down the quarters of the male shrine-prostitutes that were in the temple of the LORD.   (2 Kings 23:1–2, 6–7)

For several generations, evil reigned in Judah. Solomon's temple was in disrepair, Levites no longer led worship to Yahweh, no pilgrims came, no intercessions were offered up, no praises were heard, no gifts and sacrifices received, no forgiveness pronounced. The home where Yahweh dwells among men had become a pagan brothel and a centre for idol worship. If I was God I think I would have taken umbrage and dropped a divine depth-charge on Judah but God's ways are not our ways – he is long-suffering and patient, gracious and merciful; he bides his time and looks to bring revival.

These sons of Abraham might have forsaken the covenant and rejected the God of their forefathers, but God had not rejected them – he is the covenant-keeping God.

Josiah was still a boy when he ascended to David's throne, just eight years old. When he was old enough to truly think and act for himself, as a young man at sixteen, he began seeking the Lord for himself, and at the age of twenty-six he ordered the repair of the dejected-looking Solomon's temple. As the masons are about their business, Hilkiah the High Priest discovers the Book of the Law – Moses' Torah, the first five books of the Old Testament, holding the key to the identity of God's people and his covenant with them. It was the loss of the Bible that led to the ruin of Judah – it was the discovery of the Bible that would bring the recovery of Judah.

As King Josiah reads the law he makes the dreadful discovery of just how far his people have fallen away from God and his statutes. And so he summons the whole nation to gather in Jerusalem and they duly come and stand and listen as he reads the Book of the Law. We do not know if he read the whole Torah or just Deuteronomy – just the latter might have taken three to four hours to read; but if Josiah read the whole Torah, it would have taken about ten to twelve hours to complete.

The official recorder lists in full the groups who came to hear the word of God: the king, all the elders, all the inhabitants of Judah, the priests and prophets and all the people from the least to the greatest (2 Kings 23:2). This law of the Lord is not simply for the ruling elite or religious elite or intellectual elite, just as God is never God for the ruling or religious elite – this is the people's law, this is the people's God. It has never been God's way to speak to the powerful few – he is the God of all and wills his word to be heard by 'the least and the greatest' – note how the text places the 'least' before the 'greatest'. The word of God is to be heard by all – in the king's court, in the temple cloisters, and in the highways and byways.

About five hundred years ago, in what became termed the European Reformation, the people of God rediscovered the Bible that had been figuratively buried for many centuries by the Church – the preserve of clerics, drip-fed to the people via a largely unintelligible liturgy in Latin. As in Josiah's revival, the Bible's discovery and communication in the vernacular fed a widespread desire for the word of God among the general populace. It needed finding, dusting off, translating into the language of the people, printing and disseminating widely, so low-born and high-born alike could hear from God and meet with God in a direct and unmediated way. Tragically, the rediscovery of God's word and the realignment of God's people to it that took place at the Reformation is now being whittled away.

How heartbroken would the Protestant Fathers be if they could see how the Bible they fought to place in the hands of the laity is now left largely unread, lost in the house of the Lord once more, as it were. I was once invited to speak at a conference for worship leaders and song-writers drawn from a particular denomination. After an enthusiastic and creative time of worship, I gave the first of two teaching sessions. I asked the people to turn in their Bibles to the text I intended to expound and apply. To my amazement, only one or two had a Bible to turn to. The rest just sat and stared at me. One or two looked at their phones or laptops and I trusted they were reading the Bible on them rather than resorting to some online shopping. This was a residential conference, so I assumed they had left their Bibles in their rooms and I encouraged them to collect their Bibles at coffee time as I intended to do some detailed textual study in the second session. After the coffee break, I was aware of a couple of folk who had gone to get their Bibles, but most had not. Ironically, we were in a Roman Catholic convent and people were looking through the wall-cupboards to find Catholic Bibles. I was dumbfounded. Luther would have been turning in his grave – let alone those who suffered persecution for seeking to give all people 'small and great' the Bible, martyrs like Wycliffe and Tyndale. The Church today may not be in such disrepair as the temple in Josiah's day, but it's not far off. God's word has been abandoned by many of those who claim to be God's people, and idols have filled the void.

After lunch I went for a stroll in the convent gardens, still troubled by the lack of interest in God's word from those who were church workers and leaders – those responsible for worship. How can we even know how to worship – or who we worship – if we are not people of the Book? Catchy tunes and electric instruments doth not worship make. As I mused, I met a young lady attending the conference – she was carrying a clearly worn and well-loved Bible, personalised with her own cloth cover. Unable to hide my feelings, I said I was glad to see someone with a Bible. She held the Bible to her chest and said how she loved it. I asked her where she was from and it quickly became clear that I had been listening for weeks to a great CD of worship produced by her church worship group. The whole album was great, but there were two songs in particular that I had been listening to over and over in my quiet times for the past month or so. She told me she had written one of the two and was herself enjoying singing the other one. The lesson for me was unmissable – the one who knew and loved her Bible was the one who knew how to really worship and lead others in worship – she was anointed! The year afterwards, I was invited again to address this particular church movement's worship leaders. The theme they set for that second year was 'Worship and the Bible', and I was delighted to see lots of Bibles being used, with one even coming to 'show off' his new Bible to me.

The tragedy is that access to God's word has never been more available, and yet the Church has never been less interested in it. When I consider the humble folk – the 'least' of the 'least and greatest' – who responded to Josiah's call, people who must have left their little agricultural plots and travelled for hours or even days to Jerusalem to hear the law of the Lord, I am reminded of Mary Jones, the young lass from the Welsh valleys who in 1800 walked twenty-five miles to Bala to buy a Bible, having saved up for it for six years. Yes, six years!

Re-Bible is the way of revival

Josiah's revival in Judah was precipitated by a rediscovery of and a return to the law of the Lord. And every successive revival and reform of the Church has always been centred on a rediscovery and realignment with God's word. Whenever God is about to do something through someone, he gets them reading the Bible. George Whitefield was England's greatest evangelist and revivalist, whose ministry, combined with others like the Wesley brothers and Howell Harris and Daniel Rowland, lit fires of revival so that England had a revival instead of a revolution such as the French had. Whitefield records: 'I began to read the Holy Scriptures on my knees, laying aside all other books and praying over if possible every line and word . . .'[1] One biographer said 'he was forged and formed upon the anvil of Scripture'.

The Psalmist boldly celebrated, 'I will not neglect your word' (119:16b), but as with the Judeans in the decades before Josiah, God's people have tragically neglected God's law. Since printing began, the Bible has always been the most printed book in the world – but no longer. Today the IKEA catalogue is the most printed book – approximately 200 million copies a year, versus 100 million Bibles. And it has to be said that some Christians are more familiar with the IKEA catalogue than they are with the Bible. Having said that, you buy your Bible but everything in it is free, whereas you get the IKEA catalogue free and everything in it you need to buy. Many Christians in Britain today know their Bible less well than non-Christians would have done fifty years ago. And as someone who has spent the last two decades inside the charismatic movement, I would say that charismatic Christians certainly know their Bibles less well than devout Roman Catholics, let alone more conservative evangelicals. In recent years I have attended numerous conferences, and while I have benefited from much I have seen and heard and experienced, I have also listened to plenty of gnostic nonsense. It's becoming more and more familiar to listen to a preacher talk for up to an hour yet make no reference to the Bible – just tells stories about himself and his extreme experiences of God. Humour and stories and the gift of the gab are no substitute for God's word. As my colleague Charlie Cleverly firmly impressed on me after a sermon littered with quotes designed to make me sound clever and erudite: 'Simon, it is the Bible that has the power, God's word, not our words.' When preachers move away from Scripture, they lose their power – they end up preaching themselves, not Jesus.

We do not need a diet of conference speakers sharing entertaining illustrations about conversations on aeroplanes – we need God's word. For the past ten years, as an itinerant preacher based at St Aldates, having the privilege to speak in many countries in a wide variety of church contexts and church traditions, I can make two observations: first, Christians are hungry for more of God; and second, Christians do not read or know their Bibles. If only they gave themselves to their Bibles, perhaps they could satisfy their need for God.

When I went to theological college in 1991 to train for the Anglican priesthood, I recall our lecturer Dr John Bimson, in our first Old Testament class, asking the fifty students for a show of hands from those who had read all the Old Testament – perhaps a third put their hands up. These were evangelical ministers-in-training – two-thirds of whom had not read the Bible! While in training I heard a liberal Methodist chaplain say smugly, 'I knew a man once who read the Bible from cover to cover – how dire,' and I thought to myself, how dire for those you minister to, having to endure your godless words! Brian Edwards, a scholar of historic revivals, says God 'will not trust revival to those who won't trust his word . . . It's a matter of historical record that there has never been a revival generated by the Liberal church.'[2] There can be no revival without a return to the Bible. The distinguished Edwardian theologian P.T. Forsyth asked, 'Why do people not read the Bible more?' and then posited an answer, 'Because they have not been in that country – there is no experience to stir and develop.'[3] Tragic but true. Christians who neglect the Bible don't know who they are – they don't know where they have come from, they don't know what they exist for.

God gave this instruction and direction to the people of Israel as they were about to enter the Promised Land:

> Hear, O Israel: the LORD our God, the LORD is one. Love the LORD your God with all your heart and with all your soul and with all your strength. These commandments that I give you today are to be on your hearts. Impress them on your children. Talk about them when you sit at home and when you walk along the road, when you lie down and when you get up. Tie them as symbols on your hands and bind them on your foreheads. Write them on the door-frames of your houses and on your gates.   (Deuteronomy 6:4–9)

God's word was given to instruct and guide and frame the Israelites' life in the land. It was to be in their hearts and on their lips, when alone and when in company. It was bound to their arms so as to direct their actions, it was bound to their foreheads so as to direct all their thoughts. It was on the house door-frame so as to frame all that took place in their home. It was to be on the gates as they left their property to remind them to live out God's law as they went about their work. They were to be a people marked by God's word, marked by God. That was the way they showed and followed through on their love for God with all their heart, soul and strength. And whenever they drifted in this commitment to the law of God, they lost their relationship with the God of the law and ended up whoring after pagan gods and thus inviting all hell to break loose on their nation. Evangelist Luis Palau used to say, 'It's back to the Bible or back to the jungle' and the history of Israel demonstrates this.

'How can a young person stay on the path of purity?' asks the Psalmist, and he answers his own question: 'By living according to your word' (Psalm 119:9). Young men and old men, young women and old women, and all in between find purity by following the law of the Lord. But are we? The prophet Ronald Sider writes exasperatedly about the scandalous behaviour that besets American Christianity: 'Whether the issue is divorce, materialism, sexual promiscuity, racism, physical abuse in marriage, or neglect of a biblical worldview, the polling data point to widespread, blatant disobedience of clear biblical moral demands on the part of people who allegedly are evangelical, born-again Christians. The statistics are devastating.'[4]

I once spoke at an evangelical conference in Holland, and in a talk on holiness referred to the George Barna statistics indicating how Christians in the Evangelical Church in America looked just like non-Christians on most lifestyle criteria. I said that this was exactly the same in England, and suggested it might be so in Holland. The following day a man marched into the leaders' lounge where I was resting after preaching and, saying nothing and staring blankly at me, thrust a carefully typed letter into my hand and marched off.

I was stunned by what I read – it was a broadside against my sermon the previous day, in particular attacking me for using statistics culled from America in Holland. The weight of his complaint was that the Church in America is nothing like the Church in Holland and the Church in Holland had influenced the country for good and for God. There might be a point there – but the irony wasn't missed: his aggressive manner, dishonouring action and self-justifying claims rather proved my point that Christians need to be more Christ-like if non-Christians are to see the point of becoming Christian. Holland was the first

141

country in Europe to legalise euthanasia, prostitution, Marijuana sales and same sex marriage. As in America and in England, God's Church has much work to do in Holland.

The twentieth century's most distinguished Bible teacher, Dr John Stott, in an interview at the age of eighty-six, said there are many themes in the Bible but that there is 'one we have tended to neglect, that is the call to be different from the world around us'. He said this same call to distinction – holiness – is found in all of the four great sections of Scripture – the Law, the Prophets, the Gospels and the Epistles. Stott underlined this by citing the text from Leviticus 18:3–4 where God told Moses to tell the Israelites: 'You must not do as they do in Egypt, where you used to live, and you must not do as they do in the land of Canaan, where I am bringing you. Do not follow their practices. You must obey my laws and be careful to follow my decrees. I am the LORD your God.' Stott then cites the Sermon on the Mount where Jesus, referring to the Pharisees and the pagans, says in just four powerful syllables, 'Do not be like . . .' (Matthew 6:5, 7): do not be like the hypocrites, do not be like the pagans.[5] To the extent that God's people follow Jesus and his standards and his word, they will stand out – a peculiar people, a distinct and markedly different people. Hilkiah, the High Priest, came to Josiah's secretary Shaphan and said, 'I have found the Book of the Law in the temple of the LORD' (2 Chronicles 34:15). The Book, God's Book – God's words for God's people and God's world – needs to be found again in the house of the Lord.

No amount of prayer ministry will help if your Bible is closed

The Church's corporate effectiveness in witness and work and the individual believer's wellbeing is primarily determined by their relationship to God through Scripture, read, studied, proclaimed and applied. I grew up with my father modelling a life of Scripture reading, often in the original languages – he was fluent in biblical Hebrew and competent in New Testament Greek. I never woke up when he hadn't been up for an hour or so already, reading his Bible – every night after the *Nine O'Clock News* (as it was then) he would retire to pray and read his Bible. I once asked him how many times he had read the Bible through – he was reluctant to say, not wanting to appear boastful or to repeat the sin of David's census (1 Chronicles 21), but on being pressed he shared that, during my teens, it had only been once a year, otherwise as many as four times each year – so in fifty years as a Christian, he had read the Bible in excess of one hundred times. And with what result? Well, he is unquestionably the godliest man I have ever met – and I have met and known close up some of the leading church figures of the past twenty years. A life lived immersed in God's word, seeking God, has rubbed off.

The devil wants to shut your Bible

Because God's word is divinely inspired, mediating divine power, exposing and routing evil, it is opposed by the world, the flesh, the devil. Every regime that has seriously attempted to set itself up as a counter-kingdom to Christ's has sought to burn or ban the Bible, for God's word calls all kingdoms and all kings into question. Because of the Bible's power to reveal Christ, to expose evil and to transform lives, the demonic has always sought to attack it, mock it, suppress it. We see this clearly in the persecution and suppression of the Church in ancient Rome up to the conversion of Constantine in the fourth century. We see it with the Communists and the Nazis, as today with extreme Islamists.

To our shame, even some Christian institutions are now embarrassed by their heritage and seek to disassociate themselves from the evangelical faith that gave them birth, downgrading or even sidelining the Bible as their inspiration. The battle for the Bible is going on both within and without the Church. Some years ago, I was asked to speak at a particular university's college chapel – it was Bible Sunday and the theme was the importance of the Bible. As I stood to speak to the arrayed academics, choir, students and guests, I immediately felt my mouth clamped shut, muzzled – I was unable to speak; I could not get a single word out for what seemed like long minutes (though it was probably only a few seconds). The whole room stared at me – beads of sweat rolled down my forehead – in my mind I was calling on Jesus, and finally my mouth opened and words tumbled out. Shaken but not deterred I hammered home the point of the importance of God's word. Afterwards, still wobbly from this bizarre experience, I was told that only that very week the Fellows had debated turning the chapel into a library. No wonder there was a demonic attempt in this place to stop me preaching about the Book of Books. Dark forces were at work trying to remove its voice.

The Bible exposes our idols

At the end of the reading of the law, Josiah covenanted to follow God and his word – and all the people followed – and he removed all the idols in the temple and the land. God's word precipitated a crisis, it demanded a response, and Josiah was quick to act. Christian drama troupe, Riding Lights, once did creative sketches to illustrate sermons. One sketch they did was on Josiah's rediscovery of the Bible. The character playing Josiah when he read the book of the law exclaimed, 'Wonderful [pause] and Terrible.' How wonderful to have God's law – his will, mind, decrees, revelation, direction; but oh how terrible to then see the length we have fallen away from it. God's law exposes our divided heart, it shows the standard God has set and how far from it we are. Immediately upon reading the law of the Lord, King Josiah had the sin in his life and land exposed – and resolved to rightly align himself with the word. Josiah did not merely read God's law, he heeded it.

Baal and Asherah had lain low since the occupation of the land under Joshua, but they awakened and wormed their way into the soul of Judah as she began to wander from the Torah. On reading the law, and seeing God's declared hatred for idolatry, Josiah immediately ordered a 'search and destroy' mission to hunt out everything associated with idolatry. In 2 Kings 23:4, we read that they remove and destroy the vessels and instruments from the Temple of God which have been used for worshipping Baal and Asherah; in verse 5, they remove and destroy the priests who facilitate the worship of Baal and Asherah; in verse 6, they remove and destroy the phallic statues in the house of the Lord – icons of evil; in verse 7 they remove the male temple prostitutes who live in the house of Lord and engage in sexual orgy with the pagan worshippers – and the women who weave tapestries for Asherah – possibly canopies under which the sexual encounter took place (these were the economy and industry of evil); in verse 8 they destroy the altars and idols in high places and sacred groves; while in verse 10 they destroy Topheth (the valley of Hinnom, where the city's waste was burned in a perpetual fire that became a place of worship to the god Molech through child sacrifice).

Let us just pause to consider the fact that the idols and their evil had been set up in the very house of the Lord. The house of the Lord was the temple that God established in Jerusalem in the reign of Solomon, the permanent dwelling of God and the only divinely sanctioned place for offering sacrifices and worship in the manner the Torah prescribed and the Levites facilitated. Idolatry had supplanted Yahweh here. The high places, meanwhile, were self-appointed places to worship in self-ordained ways. An essential aspect of idolatry is refusal to worship Jesus on his terms and his turf. Idolatry is the worshipping of the god you want – where you want, how you want! Much worse than the old high places was the setting up of idols in the house of the Lord, the temple. This was not sin done in secret, this is not the occult, dark arts hidden away and only for the initiated – this was a public supplanting of God, at the heart of the nation's life. The demonic is always seeking to put itself on God's throne and receive the worship due to God. Idols always want to occupy God's place, to receive God's due and to defile the place set apart for God – be it built with human hands or in human hearts.

An infamous example of this is the Greek king Antiochus Epiphanes who defiled the temple in 167 BC by sacrificing a pig on the altar set apart for Yahweh and placing a pagan idol in the Holy of Holies. Later on, in the reign of Herod, when Israel became a province of the Roman Empire, Herod placed a Roman Eagle above the entrance to the temple, an idolatrous image and therefore forbidden. Idols wormed their way into the Jewish temple and they sought to occupy God's place in his temple, and the same is true today for the Church corporately and the

Christian believer individually. Paul wrote to the Corinthian church saying 'flee from idolatry' (1 Corinthians 10:14) – presumably because they were tempted by its all-pervading presence in the surrounding culture. Paul also wrote to the Colossian church saying they needed to put to death various sins, and he lists among them 'sexual immorality, impurity, lust, evil desires and greed, which is idolatry' (Colossians 3:5). St John's final word in his lengthy letter to the church in Ephesus is 'Dear children, keep yourselves from idols' (1 John 5:21) – neither Paul nor John would have needed to exhort the Church in this way if the temptation to idolatry was not a present danger, and through God-inspired Scripture we are warned of the same danger today. I recall reading of an Anglican church where the ordained priest, theologically more pagan than Christian, placed idols from other religions in the sanctuary alongside the communion table and cross. I remember when a popular Christian conference hosted a seminar from a Wiccan witch. I was present at a much-hailed 'Revival' in Florida, to which tens of thousands flocked from around the world, when one speaker led a 'guided trip to the third heaven' that was more New Age than Christian, accompanied by orchestrated animalistic shrieks to scare off the demons and a driving hypnotic drumbeat to help us get into the spirit of the thing. Or was it to get the evil spirit thing into us?

Idols are thieves and liars

They rob God of his glory, and they are liars, never delivering what they offer us. Paul, in his letter to the Romans, says that idolatry is a primal sin – the displacement of God for that which he made – leading to loss of glory and to death. The brilliant G.K. Chesterton described the consequence for those who follow idols: 'they became as wooden as the thing they worshipped'. In the late eighteenth century, travellers discovered Easter Island, where there are hundreds of giant stone statues, idols, objects of ancestor worship associated with the former Polynesian inhabitants. To manufacture and move these idols, the indigenous people had cut down the forests covering the island. However, in doing so it appears that they destroyed the delicate ecosystem. By removing the trees they killed off all the birdlife and wildlife that depended on the trees for the balance of life.[6] The idols consumed everything and gave nothing. After the birds had flown, eventually the inhabitants had to leave as life could no longer thrive. All that was left were the lifeless stone idols, commanders of a lifeless island. Worshipping God brings life, worshipping idols brings death.

What are our idols today?

We are made to worship. If we don't worship God we will find a substitute. An idol is anything that replaces God as the foundation of our life. Secularism drives God out and replaces him with the god of Humanism – this worship of man seeks fulfilment in the three ugly sisters of materialism, hedonism and narcissism. But the search for spirituality cannot easily be stifled and often a DIY paganism is embraced to fill the void.

The devil doesn't come up with anything new – modern idols are the same as Baal and Asherah – they have new names, but represent the same old darkness. Spiritual writer Richard Foster wrote a book saying modern idols focused on one of just three categories: he called the book *Money, Sex and Power*.[7] Not that money, sex and power are bad in themselves; indeed, sex and power were created by God and all three frame human life together, all three can produce great good. But when they become absolutes in themselves, when they are divested of a righteous moral and ethical framework, then they can turn very ugly. Ezekiel speaks of the idols we set up in our hearts (Ezekiel 14:3). Idols are rarely carved statues in shrines – but as the great reformer Luther said, they are anything our heart clings to. John Calvin pointed out that 'every one of us from his mother's womb is a master craftsman of idols' – money, appearance, career, reputation, hobby, success, home – anything, in fact. Tim Keller wisely observed that if we want to discover our idols we need to look at our daydreams.[8]

What do we do with the idols in our heart?

Like Gideon or Samson we must pull them down. In the early centuries of the Church, as the community of Christ sought to integrate converts who had come out of a demonic pagan culture, exorcisms and special rituals became necessary to free them from their entanglement with the occult and idols. Baptismal candidates underwent lengthy preparations and instructions as well as self-examination; then, when they were baptised, the liturgy required them to publicly 'renounce Satan and his *Pompa Diaboli*' – 'all his works', i.e. everything associated with idol festivals. We must ask God to expose the idols in our heart – we must examine ourselves, identifying the idols, repenting of sin, renouncing and ridding ourselves of every trace of idolatry. As with weeds in the garden, they often have deep roots and they will have seeded, so we need to return periodically to examine our souls once more, and root out every trace.

Lenin was the architect of Soviet Communism and his ideology brutalised millions of his 'comrades' for decades. Following the collapse of Communism and the breakup of the former Soviet Union, in recent years statues of Lenin, previously prominently displayed in public squares, have been pulled down. No longer are people willing to give honour to the memory of Lenin. In September 2014 the Ukrainians pulled down a giant statue and the Interior Minister, Arsen Avakov, declared, 'Lenin? Let him fall. As long as nobody suffers under his weight. As long as this . . . communist idol does not take more victims with it when it goes.' On Facebook he commented, 'I ordered the police to protect the people and not the idol.' Idols take victims – they never give what they promise, and they abuse those who serve them. May we identify the idols that have been set up in our own lives, churches, communities and nation, and expose them for what they are and pray for their downfall.

The Bible records the same epitaph for numerous successive kings in Judah and Israel: they 'did evil in the eyes of the LORD'. No one wants to face God with that introduction! But the epitaph the Bible gives for Josiah was different – 'He did what was right in the eyes of the LORD' (2 Kings 22:2). May the Church in our day resolve to do what is right in the sight of the Lord. And that will mean good reading of the Bible – and good riddance to all idols.

Chapter 10

The Lion in Daniel

At this, the chief ministers and the satraps tried to find grounds for charges against Daniel in his conduct of government affairs, but they were unable to do so. They could find no corruption in him, because he was trustworthy and neither corrupt nor negligent.

(Daniel 6:4)

It was probably the seventeenth-century French bishop Jacques-Bénigne Bossuet who set the idea of 'perfidious Albion' running when he wrote of '*L'Angleterre, ah la perfide Angleterre*' ('England, oh treacherous England'). Repeated generations of Germans and French have levelled this charge at the British, not perhaps without some justification. In our political dealings, we are often perceived as duplicitous and double-speaking. Not that we always speak highly of the French and Germans ourselves!

Of course, something is always lost in translation – and while we Brits know what we mean, others may misinterpret that and assume what we never actually intended, or think we were being disingenuous. Below is an oft-shared chart[1] that neatly illustrates the point:

WHAT THE BRITISH SAY	WHAT THE BRITISH MEAN	WHAT OTHERS UNDERSTAND
I hear what you say	I disagree and do not want to discuss it further	He accepts my point of view
With the greatest respect . . .	You are an idiot	He is listening to me
That's not bad	That's good	That's poor
Quite good	A bit disappointing	Quite good
I would suggest . . .	Do it or be prepared to justify yourself	Think about the idea, but do what you like
Oh, incidentally/by the way	The primary purpose of our discussion is . . .	That is not very important
I was a bit disappointed that	I am annoyed that	It doesn't really matter
Very interesting	That is clearly nonsense	They are impressed
I'll bear it in mind	I've forgotten it already	They will probably do it
I'm sure it's my fault	It's your fault	Why do they think it was their fault?
You must come for dinner	It's not an invitation, I'm just being polite	I will get an invitation soon

What an interesting insight this gives. We Brits might think we are merely being polite and not wishing to offend – indeed, we would see such self-deprecation almost as a virtue; however, to others our manner and words are perceived quite differently. We need to say what we mean and mean what we say and make sure those we speak to know what we say and mean – as Jesus said, 'let your "Yes" be "Yes" and your "No," "No"' (Matthew

5:37).[2] Ultimately, to say one thing but to mean another is to lack integrity. And that lack may seem like an interesting character trait for us Brits, but integrity must not be lacking in the people of God. The Psalmist said, 'Because of my integrity you uphold me and set me in your presence for ever' (Psalm 41:12). Only with integrity can we stand in God's presence.

In this chapter I want us to consider 'integrity', its mark and its making, particularly as we see it embodied in Daniel. We are all familiar with the extraordinary story of Daniel in the lions' den; that kind of predicament and that kind of rescue are not exactly an everyday occurrence and historically those Christians who have found themselves entertaining lions, such as in Rome's historic persecutions, generally found themselves eaten by lions. Perhaps the normal part of this story for us is that those who follow God faithfully will face fierce lions of opposition, from the world, the flesh and the devil, encounters that may leave us scarred and scared, and which will both test our faithfulness to God and reveal God's faithfulness to us. However, here I want to focus on the prologue to the story of the lions' den: I want us to look at the lion in Daniel's heart.

The mark of Daniel's integrity

The word integrity, related to the word integrated, comes from the Latin term *integer*, meaning 'whole' or 'complete'. It is the quality of being morally undivided, morally consistent. To have integrity means that your yes means yes and your no means no. The person of integrity has no gulf between what they think, say and do – they are upright, honest, honourable, guileless, without shadows or half-tones. Such was Daniel.

To administrate his vast empire, King Darius appointed 120 'satraps', civil service ministers, who themselves were overseen by three senior governors. Daniel was one of these ruling three. And Daniel so excelled himself in the role that King Darius intended to promote him to the number one job, as prime minister. But Daniel has made enemies – the civil servants and governors are jealous of his promotion. Perhaps the civil servants fear that if Daniel becomes their boss, his integrity and ability will expose their own deficiencies and lack of integrity. Daniel's integrity will make the other governors and satraps look bad. Clearly they fear that Daniel's appointment will not be in their interests – here is a man who cannot be bought or manipulated. So together they conspire to find evidence of Daniel's professional negligence or offence. And Scripture testifies: 'They could find no corruption in him, because he was trustworthy and neither corrupt nor negligent' (Daniel 6:4).

Daniel had no deficiencies; there were no grey areas, no moral weaknesses, no skeletons in the cupboard, no cobwebbed corners to be concealed, no hidden secrets to be ashamed of. So they concluded, 'We will never find any basis for charges against this man Daniel unless it has something to do with the law of his God' (v. 5). What an extraordinary man: the only area of his life they could exploit against him was his evident faith in and faithfulness to God. So they devised a plan: that no one might worship any god but the king for thirty days, on pain of death – and the king, in his vanity, agreed to their plan. They knew Daniel would keep worshipping Yahweh – and of course, he did. Let us not race past this. There are no grounds to find fault in Daniel – he does not have feet of clay; he is morally blameless. An old man, in his eighties, he faithfully served Nebuchadnezzar for forty-two years, briefly King Belshazzar – and now King Darius. Integrity personified, man and boy.

Every sphere of life needs its Daniels – men and women of integrity – politics, economics, the academy, the arts, medicine, industry, sport. We have become so accustomed in our society to a breakdown between professional and private life – little of either integrity or integration. I don't care whether politicians kiss babies, shake hands and smile with beautifully straight white teeth for photographs – I want them to have integrity. Aristotle, the father of moral and political philosophy, believed the necessary quality leaders should possess was 'true virtue', where all parts of the soul are pulling in the same direction to the good.[3] Perhaps nowhere is the disconnect between public and private life, between profession and practice, as stark as in the Church. Unlike politicians we do claim a higher morality, indeed the highest – we claim to have God at work in us: we claim divine agency, possession of the Spirit. And therein lies the problem, as Eberhard Arnold of the Bruderhof Community says: 'So poorly have we Christians lived that the question must be asked: are we Christians at all?'[4]

The words scandal and Church go hand in hand for some these days – the tabloids regularly celebrate the clergyperson caught in adultery or defrocked for indecency. In the powerful movie *Calvary*, an Irish Catholic priest becomes the object of several Sligo townspeople's pain and resentment against abuses they have suffered at the hands of the Church. In one stark scene, the priest is simply having a chat with a young lady when her father arrives, snatches her away quickly and angrily rebukes the priest – the unspoken implication being: these priests are dangerous, don't let your daughters near them. And of course, for the countless victims of abuse, whether mentally, physically or spiritually, many priests have indeed been dangerous! The Church in Ireland and elsewhere cannot easily regain the trust of the people. It is part of a bigger picture no doubt, but in 1984, 90 per cent of Irish Catholics attended Mass weekly, whereas by 2011 only 18 per cent did.[5]

I recall being sickened to my core when a Dutch friend who taught at a theological college in Rwanda, supposedly the most Christian nation in Africa, told me how many of her students were killed during the genocide. The students killed each other. Theologians, ministers, pastors, brothers in Christ, but all of this turned out to be merely superficial – skin-deep, a public religion that couldn't change the heart. Deep down in the dark recesses of their souls, the Spirit of God was shut out as they harboured tribal resentments, allowing demons to dwell and swell. One day they were praying and studying and missioning together, the next hacking each other to pieces with machetes.

In recent years the theological world has been shocked by growing revelations of sexual abuse perpetrated by Professor John Yoder, the world's foremost Christian ethicist. It is alleged that over three decades he sexually abused more than a hundred women. His most famous writing and theological contribution relates to the theme of non-violence – yet he himself is guilty of the sustained sexual harassment of many women over a long period.[6]

These are stark and shocking illustrations – but we Christians reading this need to face up to the fact that many of these people were Christian leaders. They prayed and worshipped, received and even distributed the sacrament, they read their Bibles – but there arose a huge discrepancy between their faith and life. And we must ask, if that is possible for them, what might be true of us? In the summer of 2015 there was a leak of the details of over a million subscribers to an Internet dating club for married people, a site that set up illicit affairs. One Christian commentator claimed that he had evidence that the following Sunday at least 400 church pastors, elders and staff members would be resigning because of being exposed as members of this adultery club![7] I don't know how many actually did, but the very possibility is surely shocking in itself. The renowned Bible teacher Warren Wiersbe wrote prophetically: 'We are facing an integrity crisis. Not only is the conduct of the church in question, but so is the very character of the church.'[8]

Where are the Daniels? Where are the men and women of integrity in whom there is no guile, no shadow life, no fault-lines between claim and reality? People who, when scrutinised however closely, are found to be consistent in every aspect. We must pray that God raises up such men and women, that they are promoted by modern King Dariuses and protected from the machinations of wicked satraps and the mouths of fierce lions.

Few reading this will ever find themselves confronted with the clarity of choice that Daniel was, but we will all many times be faced with a challenge to our faith and called to compromise on integrity. In that moment, may we have lions' hearts.

And in the meantime, let us consider for ourselves: are we so integrated in our culture that we lack integration between our profession and practice?

The making of Daniel's integrity

What created Daniel's lion heart, then?

The integrity of Daniel was grounded on the integrity of God – God the ontologically consistent, the whole and complete, whose yes is yes and no is no, and with whom there is no shadow of turning. It is a life lived looking to the love of God, following in the footsteps of God that creates integrity – as King David prayed: 'Vindicate me, O LORD, for I have walked in my integrity, and I have trusted in the LORD without wavering. Prove me, O LORD, and try me; test my heart and my mind. For your steadfast love is before my eyes, and I walk in your faithfulness' (Psalm 26:1–3).[9]

The discipline of intimacy

'Now when Daniel learned that the decree had been published, he went home to his upstairs room where the windows opened towards Jerusalem. Three times a day he got down on his knees and prayed, giving thanks to his God, just as he had done before' (Daniel 6:10).

Integrity cannot be created in an instant, it is a character trait that has to be cultivated, though it can be lost in an instant. Integrity is not the result of prayer ministry, but a ministry of prayer. Daniel's integrity was created out of his three-times-a-day, year-in and year-out habit. Daniel was shaped by intimacy with God, marinated in God's presence – trusting in God, being searched by God, and always setting the Lord regularly before himself. Daniel's secret history meant that when his faith was put to the test, he did not wobble, he just kept calm and carried on – he simply did as he'd always done.

My dad has more integrity than any man I know. As a rebellious teenager I sometimes wished he'd been different, but over the years I have come to be in awe of the imprint of God on his life. He is a man of absolute consistency and transparency – with family, in church, in friendships. After I left the meat industry and before I went into church ministry, I worked with Dad for twelve months – he was a civil servant with the Law

Society. I got to observe my dad daily at work – and he was the same guileless, kind, godly, gentle man I knew – loved and respected by most of his colleagues, envied by a few. How did my dad become a man of integrity? Just like Daniel, he sought the Lord three times a day – at breakfast, lunch and before bed. Come rain or shine – workdays or holidays – he met with God and prayed. Consistency of intimacy brought about integrity.

The discipline of self-scrutiny

Peter Scazzero pastored a church for seventeen years when, to his great shock, his wife Geri one day simply said, 'I quit.' She refused to attend church any more, refused to be the good little pastor's wife rushing here and there, running this and that church group, filtering out all the gunk coming at her husband, putting on a nice smile and pretending all was glorious when inside she was falling apart and felt all around her was also. She'd had enough of the schizophrenic gap between the front-of-stage show and the backstage reality – the private and public personas – of her marriage and her husband's ministry. She wanted authenticity, integrity, consistency between their private life and public platform, and rather than continue the charade, she came to a point where she precipitated a crisis for her husband by refusing to attend church.

To his credit, Peter didn't try to paper over the cracks. Geri and her husband took time out for a while and underwent counselling and ministry for them as a couple. It led to a total reassessment of how they were to do church. Peter summarises this period:

We finally saw it: Emotional health and spiritual maturity are inseparable. It is not possible to be spiritually mature while remaining emotionally immature. That revelation changed us, and slowly, all of New Life Church. After a sabbatical, we returned in 1996 to slowly begin working this out practically – on all levels of the Church. We began to focus on marriages as part of our discipleship, integrate emotional health skills, and begin confronting the places at New Life where we had placed gifts over character. This was a large, a momentous shift.[10]

In a sermon on the theme of 'The Holy Spirit and Your Integrity'[11] Scazzero asks two searching questions:

1. How much of your life is divided, or involves pretending?
2. How much of your life is about wearing other people's faces?

These are not easy questions – sometimes we don't even know ourselves that well to know our own answers. Maybe we need to ask the person who knows us the longest and deepest in order to answer them. As Christians we need to ask the Holy Spirit, as David did, to 'Prove me, O Lord, and try me; test my heart and my mind.'

When I first reflected on this theme, in preparation for a sermon, I realised I would lack integrity myself if I was to predicate this 'divine spotlight' soul-searching for others without first applying it to myself. So I asked God to test my heart and my mind. The Lord was gentle and tender with me, highlighting no more than a couple of issues at that time – I guess like Colonel Nathan R. Jessup in the military court drama *A Few Good Men*, God knows: 'You can't handle the truth!' But those two little exposures were enough. First, God told me, 'You are *two-faced*.

A hypocrite. You say one thing to people's faces and another behind their backs – you make an effort to portray yourself as nice, interested, attentive, but at home with Tiffany and the boys you can be grumpy, distant, detached, self-occupied.' Ugh – and I knew it was true. It showed I lack integrity: I have two faces, a public and a private persona. That was God's right hook – then came his left. God said, 'You exaggerate – that makes you a liar – you often add an extra 5 per cent for effect – but whether it's 5 per cent or 50 per cent doesn't matter; sometimes what you say is not the whole truth, it's embellished, and therefore it's untrue: a lie.' Seventy-eight times Jesus is recorded in the Gospels as saying, 'I tell you the truth' – but here is my confession: I tell the truth, the whole truth and sometimes more than the truth.

No doubt there is a lot more muck deep down that I am not even aware of – character flaws, hidden shadows, sinful patterns – but the Holy Spirit was too kind to tell me all at once. Just those two insights and highlights were enough for me to feel embarrassed and not a little ashamed – and to realise I had much to repent of and much that I needed to see transformed in my life. But I didn't feel condemned and I was more aware of God's long-suffering and grace and willingness to forgive my sin – I wanted to be a better man, and I will, by the grace of God, as he gives me strength.

The discipline of delighting in the fear of the Lord. This is implicit in all Daniel did. But it is most obvious when he refuses to sin against the Lord by following the king's decree to worship no other god but Darius. Daniel's righteous fear of the Lord trumps his fear of man or the fear of death. Rick Warren, in a leadership address on the importance of integrity, stated, 'I would rather take a knife and stab it in my heart than dishonour God'[12] – little wonder God has so honoured and used this man!

It is prophesied of the Messiah (Isaiah 11:3) that 'he will delight in the fear of the LORD'. Daniel too *delighted* in the fear of the Lord, and he would rather face the man-eating lions – and more quickly go to meet the one in whom his heart delighted – than give worship to a false god just to save his skin. The fear of the Lord rather than the fear of man marked Daniel. And when King Darius sees the fruit of this – seeing Daniel protected from lions by his God – the victory of faith in the lions' den, he issues a new law: 'I issue a decree that in every part of my kingdom people must fear and reverence the God of Daniel' (Daniel 6:26). Daniel's fear of the Lord resulted in others fearing Daniel's Lord.

Closing the mouths of lions

So, what about you? Would your work colleagues recognise the 'church' version of you? Would your church family recognise the 'work' you? If your life were to be scrutinised inside and out, what would you be embarrassed by? How you use your finances? Your social media interactions? Relationships? Things that occupy your mind, or that come out of your mouth? How you treat your pet dog? Where is the breakdown between your private and public personas?

Holiness is integrity and integrity means to be integrated, whole, complete and without side. The popular American Bible teacher Charles Swindoll powerfully challenges us all: 'You want to shock the world? Start here – demonstrating the guts to do what's right when no-one is looking. It takes real guts to stand strong with integrity in a culture weakened by hypocrisy. Start today.'[13]

Chapter 11

Drift and Drown

Watch out that you do not lose what we have worked for,
but that you may be rewarded fully.   (2 John v. 8)

Every year almost four hundred thousand people die by drown-
ing. A number of these tragic deaths involve unsupervised
children on rubber inflatables who have drifted from the shal-
lows by the shore, out into deep waters, only to be capsized by
a large wave, or dragged down by strong undercurrents. We can
only imagine the sorrow of a bereaved parent, wishing they
had taken more care. Yet when it comes to our eternal salvation, we seem to be pretty relaxed about the possibility that we
might 'drift and drown' – it seems to be an apt analogy for
many within the Church who are careless about their belief.
Doctrinally or morally, they allow themselves to be swept out
to sea, where they get sucked down by a strong undertow, or
capsized by a strong wave and – spiritually speaking – drown.

The Psalmist bemoans the loss of those 'with whom I once
enjoyed sweet fellowship at the house of God' (Psalm 55:14)
who then turned against him and away from the Lord. Drift is
nothing new with the people of God. It is a dark thread
throughout Israel's relationship with Yahweh – they constantly
oscillate between faithfulness and prostitution to pagan idols.
In the New Testament, Paul mourns Demas who 'because he

loved this world, has deserted me and has gone to Thessalonica' (2 Timothy 4:10). Many of the apostolic authors wrote their letters to the churches specifically to address the potential for theological or moral 'drift and drown' – viz. the letters to the Corinthians, the Galatians, the Colossians, Hebrews, and the letters of Jude, Peter, the second letter of John, and five of the seven letters to churches in Revelation.

As I look back on my three decades as a Christian, I am gutted to see how many members of my family, how many close friends, how many friends from seminary, how many past colleagues have not paid attention to their lives morally or their faith doctrinally, and have thus severed connection with the hope in Christ as an anchor – so many who have drifted and drowned. The American evangelist and church leader David Wilkerson once said, 'no believer is immune to the sin of drifting from Christ'.[1] By definition, drift does not happen suddenly, but incrementally. Perhaps we fall asleep, as it were, or are distracted and thus unconscious of the undercurrents taking us further from the shore.

There is a clear pattern: spiritual disciplines neglected, cultural norms accepted, indiscretions indulged – and perhaps, if we are challenged, self-justification by alternative readings of Scripture.

Perhaps before you read any further you might pause and consider those whom you know still or whom you once knew, who burned bright with love of Christ, faithfully following their Lord, serving in his Church – but who have drifted and perhaps drowned. Pray for them to be rescued and restored.

John says we need to watch ourselves

John's words in this short letter are not merely advice worth considering; his injunction is not some optional extra for the super-spiritual – it comes with all the force of an anointed apostle writing sacred Scripture, and all the grace of a tender shepherd caring for his flock. The Greek *blepete eautous* literally means 'see yourselves', but can also mean 'take care, watch out, take heed of yourselves'. John is encouraging moral self-scrutiny – a concept found in various ancient traditions, notably in the various Greek schools of philosophy. Socrates exhorted his students to 'Know thyself'; Socrates claimed that 'an unexamined life is not worth living'.

Certainly such a life is precarious. As Saint Paul said, 'Examine yourselves to see whether you are in the faith' (2 Corinthians 13:5). And the writer to the Hebrews says, 'We must pay the most careful attention, therefore, to what we have heard, so that we do not drift away' (Hebrews 2:1) and warns of judgement for those who abandon God's word for sin and disobedience. Tragically, many do abandon God's word; many who once tasted the power of the age to come – the grace of God in the gift of the Spirit – end up rejecting him. Self-scrutiny is not a form of narcissistic self-love, but a challenge to be aware of the state of our soul, the tenor of our basic beliefs and practices – and to discern whether we are still conforming to the character of Christ and the teaching of Christ. If we don't know ourselves, we can end up fooling ourselves and, fooling ourselves, we become fools.

My teenage sons are at that age when they are suddenly taking a great interest in their grooming – spending hours in showers, fortnightly haircuts, various skin treatments: face scrubs, PH balance, zit-zapper, musky aftershaves (when they have barely started shaving) and ice-cool deodorants. Non-stop sit-ups and press-ups and flexing and posing in front of the mirror. Wanting cool kit that enables them to stand out from the crowd and yet fit in at the same time. The attention to detail is impressive – would that they showed the same tenacity in tidying their bedrooms or doing their clothes-washing! Would that we as Christians showed the same tenacity and attention to detail in our spiritual lives!

There are two things we must pay close attention to: our creeds and our deeds. If we don't do this we will end up with doctrinal drift and moral drift: they go hand in hand. Unless we are rock-solid on what we believe, we will let go of things in how we behave. Anyone who has ever relied on a compass to navigate in the mountains or on the moors knows they must keep taking compass readings – making sure they are still going in the same direction, that they have not deviated from the right bearing. If you drift from your bearing you can quickly get seriously lost and find yourself miles from where you're heading – in a bog, or heading for a precipice. With both our personal behaviour and our religious belief we must keep recalibrating and repositioning ourselves according to Christ and his word. The church that John is writing to is being infiltrated by false teachers – they are playing with and preying on the kindness of Christians – leading some astray, encouraging drift. Have we entertained and inculcated a teaching or thinking that is contrary to Scripture? Have we allowed culture more than Scripture to frame our thinking on theological, or ethical and moral issues?

Every year a car must have an MOT, a legal requirement which involves checking numerous features to see if the vehicle is road-worthy. We need to regularly do a spiritual MOT, to see if we are Lord-worthy. John Wesley, with his brother Charles, founded the 'Holy Club' with fellow students in Oxford in the early eighteenth century. This club was committed to seeking God, intercession, personal holiness, almsgiving, preaching in prisons, and living lives to the honour of God. All these were good and important spiritual disciplines. The club's members were young, zealous, enthusiastic, somewhat religious and, influenced by William Law, even rather legalistic, and they needed to encounter the person and power of the Spirit – which they subsequently did. But their earnestness and desire laid a platform for God to meet them and then through them initiate the extraordinary Evangelical Awakening in Britain that also influenced America. At the core of their spiritual disciplines was a daily personal checklist: twenty-two questions they would ask themselves every day that were a plumb-line indicating how they were doing with God:

1. Am I consciously or unconsciously creating the impression that I am better than I really am? In other words, am I a hypocrite?
2. Am I honest in all my acts and words, or do I exaggerate?
3. Do I confidentially pass on to another what was told to me in confidence?
4. Can I be trusted?
5. Am I a slave to dress, friends, work or habits?
6. Am I self-conscious, self-pitying or self-justifying?
7. Did the Bible live in me today?
8. Do I give it time to speak to me every day?
9. Am I enjoying prayer?
10. When did I last speak to someone else about my faith?
11. Do I pray about the money I spend?
12. Do I get to bed on time and get up on time?
13. Do I disobey God in anything?
14. Do I insist upon doing something about which my conscience is uneasy?
15. Am I defeated in any part of my life?
16. Am I jealous, impure, critical, irritable, touchy or distrustful?

17. How do I spend my spare time?
18. Am I proud?
19. Do I thank God that I am not as other people, especially as the Pharisees who despised the publican?
20. Is there anyone whom I fear, dislike, disown, criticise, hold a resentment towards or disregard? If so, what am I doing about it?
21. Do I grumble or complain constantly?
22. Is Christ real to me?

Is it any wonder that men who searched their souls before God in this way would eventually meet him in such a profound way as to bring national revival? Nearly three hundred years later, we still remember and honour these men. And where are their like today?

Reader – could you be such? Will you be inspired by their example? What would our churches look like if we all assessed our lives against such a list – weekly, let alone with daily scrutiny? Having said that, it is so much easier to write such a list than it is to keep it. Ironically, such lists often only serve to show how bad we are at keeping to such lists, and how poor are our attempts at total dependency on the grace of God to transform us. I once worked out ten areas of personal weakness and arranged with a colleague for us to hold each other accountable. We never met again, and I quickly stopped using the list. To be honest, some of those things on the list that I raised as issues of the flesh way back then probably still need resolving in me.

Of course, not only does such an exercise need to be committed to, but those following it need to be brutally honest. A pastor told me how he used to meet with another pastor every month. They held each other accountable and asked searching questions – including, 'Is there anyone that you have become inappropriately attached to emotionally or physically?' They met several times and asked and answered these questions to each other – then, one day, while they were meeting, the husband of a woman who had just owned up to having sex for months with the other minister, turned up at church to vent his anger. The fact was, each month this pastor was asked all the right questions, and each week he had bare-face lied – claiming to be doing all right when, he was in fact having an affair.

Before you go on, imagine God is asking you this question: are you entertaining thoughts or permitting habits or acting in any way that you would be embarrassed telling your spouse or indeed the whole church about? If there is anything that you wouldn't want known, the chances are it's a sin! It's possible to deceive others, it's almost possible to deceive ourselves, but you can't deceive God – 'be sure that your sin will find you out' (Numbers 32:23). In Psalm 139 the writer is confident that, 'You have searched me, LORD, and you know me' (v. 1) – he is aware of God's awareness; nevertheless he welcomes a deeper divine scrutiny: 'Search me, God, and know my heart; test me and know my anxious thoughts' (v. 23). There is no hint at concealment – he is totally transparent, naked before God in spirit. He wants God to show him his sin, so he can confess and be clean. If we can't manage Wesley's twenty-two self-examination questions, maybe we could start by echoing the Psalmist's request that God search, try and know him.

Each autumn, we have a problem with squirrels coming into our attic for the winter. Their favourite spot is just above our bedroom ceiling. They often stay quiet when they hear us wake up in the morning, and only if we lie quiet in bed will we hear them scurrying around, thinking we have gone to work. The thing is, I have become accustomed to these guests in the loft – their noises have become part of my daily routine – and I even prefer their scratching to enduring a visit of the rat-catcher trudging through our house, climbing up ladders and laying traps and carrying off dead squirrels. What once freaked me out and had me on the phone instantly to the pest control man, or lying on my bed praying curses on the vermin, has begun not to bother me! Fortunately for us all, my wife has not become so easily accustomed to housing vermin in the attic, and when we hear them she insists we ring up instantly, remove the offending squirrel family and search out and block the entry holes in our roof. We must never get accustomed to the presence of sin in the attic of our souls. It needs identifying and banishing. It is not enough to confess sin (which is to acknowledge that there are squirrels in the attic); we have got to address sin (we must set traps for it, and block the access points). A.W. Tozer in his book *Five Vows for Spiritual Power* wrote that the first and most important step along the journey to spiritual power is to 'Deal thoroughly with sin'.[2]

In the story of the battle of Rorke's Drift, famously portrayed in the 1970s movie *Zulu*, 150 British soldiers took a stand against a marauding army of 4,000 Zulu warriors. They fought for ten hours, and of the 20,000 rounds of ammunition they began with, all but 900 were spent. They held out, they held the line, they stood their ground – and won the respect of their enemies, as well as the Victoria Cross for eleven men, for showing extreme valour. Rorke's Drift became a byword for courage, tenacity, honour and has been an inspiration to countless soldiers since. At Rorke's Drift the British Army stood their ground. As for us, we all are confronted with many, many opportunities to compromise our Christian belief and our way of life. Watch yourself – do not drift – stand your ground. Win the reward.

Work so as to win

After the initial command to 'Watch out', John goes on, 'that you do not lose what we have worked for, but that you may be rewarded fully.' Drift occurs when we lose our attention, when we fall asleep on our inflatable. The tide will carry us away if we are not alert and active, resisting its pull and directing and controlling our own lives. We have already noted that despite the much-touted 'Protestant work ethic' there is an unease in many Protestants' thinking whenever the word and concept of 'work' is mentioned in relationship to Christianity. Could it be that since the Reformation we have so defended and emphasised the act of faith, of believing, that we have done a disservice to Christ and his cause? We don't work at our salvation, but we do work out our salvation. We don't believe works bring righteousness, but the Bible clearly tells us the mark and responsibility of the righteous is to work. Certainly the gift of salvation is by grace through faith and not of works (Ephesians 2:8) – however, we must also emphasise that we are 'created in Christ Jesus to do good works' (Ephesians 2:10). Jesus said, 'As long as it is day, we must do the works of him who sent me. Night is coming, when no one can work' (John 9:4). Paul echoes this, stating, 'as we have opportunity, let us do good to all people' (Galatians 6:10). There can be no slacking in the task: we must 'work out your salvation with fear and trembling' (Philippians 2:12).

There is no room for passivity when it comes to maturity in the Christian life and conformity to the life Jesus calls us to. To work at, to work out, our salvation involves time and tenacity.

No one can sin easily if they are walking closely to the Lord. No one can sin easily if they are daily reading and applying his word. People drift incrementally – small steps that take them away from God – generally they stop reading their Bible daily, they stop praying, stop meeting together for worship and begin to entertain thoughts and actions they would once have resisted or repented of. Twice the book of Proverbs presents a warning through a picture of a field overgrown with thistles and thorns – 'A little sleep, a little slumber, a little folding of the arms to rest' and . . . ruin (Proverbs 6:10 and 24:33). Little by little by little, and everything is in ruins. C.S. Lewis well understood the power of these small incremental steps into sin. In his masterful *Screwtape Letters*, the senior demon Screwtape instructs his junior, Wormwood, on the destruction wrought by the accumulation of small sins:

> It does not matter how small the sins are provided that their cumulative effect is to edge the man away from the Light and out into the Nothing. Murder is no better than cards if cards can do the trick. Indeed the safest road to hell is the gradual one – the gentle slope, soft underfoot, without sudden turnings, without milestones, without signposts.[3]

Interestingly, St John does not speak of the individual church member drifting and forfeiting what they personally have worked to build – John speaks in the plural, of what *we* have built. One person's drift damages others – it undermines and pulls down what those in the wider Church have built – the wider Church's witness and work is damaged by the individual who self-destructs. The well-known twentieth-century artist, Robert Rauschenberg, deliberately erased a pencil drawing by the much more famous artist Willem de Kooning in 1953. He thought his act was art, but in reality it was vandalism, iconoclasm. When one individual Christian compromises on truth, or gives way on moral issues, they not only lose what they have worked for, but bring into disrepute what other Christians throughout the ages have lived and fought and at times died to hand on to us. Every time a Christian leaves the faith or is involved in public scandal, or modifies the faith for their own ends, the whole Church is damaged.

Paul and the writer to the Hebrews both employ the metaphor of the Christian life as a competition in the athletic arena. Perhaps we can imagine we are a team in a relay race. If I am handed the baton and halfway round I decide to drop it, or carelessly step out of my lane and am disqualified, I not only forfeit the race for myself, I have disappointed and dishonoured the other runners before me and behind me. Just so the Christian who drifts from Christ.

One of the marks of our age is the cult of individualism. One popular women's magazine had an article called 'Nine ways to make relationships work' and the number-one way was 'Put yourself first.'[4] Sin is always selfish – always me, my, I. This is exactly the attitude that leads to drift and drown within the faith – putting ourselves first rather than the desires of Christ or the good of the church community. In the Christian life, the opposite is true – to make a relationship work, with Christ and his family, we must put the other first. In every case I know where friends have left the ministry, or their wives (or too often both), the major driver was putting themselves first – their interests, their benefit, their pleasures – and in doing so they ruined all they had worked for, and the lives of others close to them. John says, 'Watch out' – we need to, for the devil is watching us, biding his time as he schemes for our failure.

God is watching

God is watching us, but wanting to reward us. Indeed, there is a reward to be won or lost. What is that reward? John continues: 'whoever continues in the teaching has both the Father and the Son' (2 John v. 9) – the reward is union with God. Drift and drown – or win the crown. A dear friend lost her brief fierce battle with cancer – but won her reward with God. She had served her dear husband and family, and Christ and the Church faithfully. Her oncologist said he had never seen anyone endure cancer like her. Beth's last words were: 'I and the Father are one.'

Rather than drift and drown we need to watch out, and work out our salvation. Let me conclude this chapter with some sage yet practical advice from C.S. Lewis in his book *Mere Christianity*:

> That is why daily prayers and religious readings and churchgoing are necessary parts of the Christian life. We have to be continually reminded of what we believe. Neither this belief nor any other will automatically remain alive in the mind. It must be fed. And as a matter of fact, if you examined a hundred people who had lost their faith in Christianity, I wonder how many of them would turn out to have been reasoned out of it by honest argument? Do not most people simply drift away?[5]

Chapter 12

Turnings

From that time on Jesus began to preach, 'Repent, for the kingdom of heaven has come near.' (Matthew 4:17)

In the 1990s Brit-pop band Travis produced the rousing anthem 'Turn'. Its lyrics expressed the longing for change. The most memorable part of the song was the repetitive, driving chorus which sang out that 'if we turn, turn, turn . . . we might learn'. The singer longs to see 'the kingdom come' – wanting to belong and live life to the full.

One reviewer called these 'inane lyrics', but people voted with their wallets and the album featuring this song became the best-selling UK album in 1999, with three million sales that year alone – and was shortlisted a while ago as one of the best albums in the past thirty years. 'Turn', more than being just a memorable tune with catchy lyrics, connected with the deep inchoate longing in the human soul for change, for a new song to sing in a new kingdom in which we feel we belong and where we can thrive. And this song understands what we all under-stand at the core of our being: that for there to be true change, there needs to be a turning *from* and a turning *to*.

Jesus came preaching, and his theme was the same: 'Turn'. God has turned to us in favour; we need to turn to him. 'The time has come . . . the kingdom of God has come near. Repent and believe the good news!' (Mark 1:15). There are three key elements here.

The time

The time is now, he said – the Greek word used for 'time' is *kairos*, not the more usual *chronos*, and this conveys the sense of the *now* moment, the crucial, critical crossroads of history and eternity, of humanity and divinity. This moment, Jesus says, has now arrived (the Greek is *pleroou* – literally meaning 'has reached its fullness'). We cannot put off repentance – no waiting for a more convenient time. The long wait is over, the winter is past, the king has come.

The place

'. . . the kingdom has come near', Jesus says – the place where God rules has come to us, it has moved to us, it has sought us out. God's kingdom has made the first move, taken the initiative. We are not in search of a lost mythical kingdom of Shangri-la: the king and his kingdom have come among us.

The response

The 'right here, right now' of God's kingdom precipitates a crisis: something must be done; what are we to do? Jesus says we are to *repent* – to turn and face the king, to align our life with him, and we are to *believe* – to accept and to trust in the good news of the king, and to enter his kingdom. This call to 'repent' is not threat, fear, dread, accusation or intimidation, as sometimes conveyed by caricatured preachers in grubby

176

rain-macs proclaiming 'Repent, for the end of the world is nigh.' This is not so much a condemnation as a universal invitation. As Kierkegaard taught,[1] we turn to the God who has already turned to us in love. Jesus didn't have a growl or a grimace on his face when he called people to 'repent' – it was a loving smile: 'I am come, now is your moment, come to me' – truly, it is the kindness of God that leads us to repentance.

Repentance is entrance into the life of God

The kingdom threshold is very low – anyone may enter it. But there is a bar set: you must repent and believe the gospel. Jesus' call to 'repent' is both invitation and imperative. It is the divine privilege extended to us to receive God's kingdom. But it is also a prerequisite, an inescapable requirement, the precondition for receiving the kingdom of God. What does it mean to repent? The Old Testament concept is conveyed by the Hebrew term *shuv*, meaning simply to turn around – in particular, to turn from sin and to turn towards God. It is a frequent theme, found over a thousand times in the Old Testament – a change of direction and a change of action because of a change of heart. The New Testament word on Jesus' lips in the gospel is the Greek word *metanoia* – a conjunction of two Greek words *meta* meaning change and *noia* from the Greek for mind. *Metanoia*, repentance, here focuses on a change of mind – but a change of mind bringing a change of direction. Repentance conveys a *volte-face*, an about turn, a total rethink.

To repent is to assent to God's assessment of our moral poverty. To repent is to reject all plea-bargaining and accept God's verdict on sin. To repent is to 'surrender' independence and embrace Jesus as supreme Lord of my all. To repent is to die to my old life – hence its close association with baptism, symbolising a dying and burying to the old life and rising to new in, with, for and by Jesus. To repent is to give allegiance to Jesus and align myself to his word, his way.

Why must we repent? Because our lives and thinking are so often going in the opposite direction to the trajectory of God's kingdom – our way is often marked by sin, selfishness and an absence of God. For many years, one of the most requested songs played at funerals has been Frank Sinatra's 'My Way'. A bold and proud exit as the coffin is carried in – the deceased leaving as arrogantly as they lived. How tragic, how foolish – on judgement day we will all be held to divine account, and the criteria will be 'Whose way did you follow?' 'I did it my way' inevitably means we did not do it God's way, and that means there is only one way for us to go at death – away from God (Matthew 7:23)! Most of all, though, we repent because the kingdom of God has come – the king has come. And he is a holy king, his is a kingdom of holiness – and repentance of sin, and the forgiveness God then gives, fits us to receive the king.

'Repent' is the first command Jesus ever uttered in his ministry (Mark 1:15). Jesus put first things first. Repentance is not for the super-spiritual, the seasoned saint – it's the ABC not the PhD of the Christian life. As well as being the first thing Jesus commanded, 'Repent' was part of the last instruction Jesus gave; in Luke's version of the Great Commission, Jesus told them to go and preach 'repentance for the forgiveness for sins' – forgiveness being dependent on repentance. Unsurprisingly, when Peter preached his first sermon at Pentecost about the fulfilment of the ages being found through Jesus, the crowds asked the right question: 'What must we do to be saved?' And Peter replied, 'Repent and be baptised . . . for the forgiveness of your sins' (Acts 2:38). Without repentance there can be no remission of sins – without the remission of sins there can be no admission into the kingdom of God The same pattern is central to Paul's message – speaking to the intellectual elite at the Areopagus on Mars Hill, he declared 'God ... now ... commands all people everywhere to repent' (Acts 17:30).

Repentance encounters resistance

While many are ready to repent, the spirits of the world, the flesh and the devil always put up a resistance to repentance. We employ various forms of subterfuge to avoid facing the truth of our sin and the necessity of our need to turn from it to Jesus.

Some try *pretence*. The term 'cover-up' has a long history ... ever since Adam and Eve's rebellion and sin caused their robing in divine glory to evaporate and exposed their nakedness and shame. They didn't own up, they covered up – they made themselves 'coverings' from fig leaves (Genesis 3:7). King David also attempted a cover-up when he got Bathsheba, the wife of Uriah, pregnant. Neither Adam nor David owned up or faced up to their sin – instead they sought to hide it. Sin that is not faced and confessed, that is swept under the carpet, often multiplies, like maggots under a stone. And the madness of both Adam's action and King David's was that they knew there is no hiding from God. He sees and knows all. Martin Lloyd Jones once wrote, 'Place this text in a prominent position on your desk or on the wall of your house "Thou God seest me" . . . I sometimes feel that there is no better way of living, and trying to live, the holy and sanctified life than just to be constantly reminding ourselves of that.'[2] Had Adam, Eve and David been consciously considerate of the gaze of God they wouldn't have sinned in the first place. And nor would we.

Some try *transference*. When God came and challenged Adam and Eve as they hid behind the leaves in their sin, they tried to pass the buck, to point the blame elsewhere. Adam appears to blame God and Eve ('the woman *you* put here') – he's saying, 'I'm not to blame, this wouldn't have happened if *you* hadn't made *her*.' Eve on the other hand, seeks to evade responsibility by blaming the snake, 'The snake deceived me.' Not my fault – it's his!

In a powerful essay, author, psychiatrist and prison doctor Theodore Dalrymple[3] bemoaned the refusal of the prisoners in his care to take responsibility for their conditions and actions. He notes that they were quick to blame external factors – poor education, poor parenting, the government, their medical condition. What they did wrong was never their fault, but the result of their having been done wrong to. Criminals guilty of extreme violence would blame the fact that their 'brain went off' and request medicine to control their violence. Dalrymple had to explain that the problem was not medical or chemical, but moral – it was them, they were responsible! In an uncomfortable chapter he recalls how one criminal said 'the knife went in' – as if this inanimate object was independent and free-acting, with a mind of its own. But knives don't just go in – they are held in someone's hand and driven in through a violent act, instructed by a darkened mind.

Admittedly this is a very stark example – but I think it highlights a common human response when confronted with our own wrongdoing. We shift the blame, we do not take responsibility: someone or something else must be at fault. A couple of years ago we all joined in enthusiastically with a marvellous worship song about God being our healer, its lyrics made more

poignant because its pastor–author had been battling a debili-
tating cancer for two years. Only he wasn't physically ill at all
and had deceived everyone, including his wife. Yet when the truth
came out, we were all informed that it was his addiction to pornography that made him do it – his faked illness was a symptom
of the guilt and trauma from the porn. And of course the porn
addiction wasn't his fault: he was a victim, as a school chum had
first got him into porn. So two years of deception were blamed
on nearly two decades of secret addiction. Well, while I don't
doubt there was some link between his secret addiction and his
deception, between his false private life and falsified public persona, to suggest porn was to blame is to fail to take responsibility
for his own sin, both the deception and the addiction to porn.
But this pass-the-blame, pass-the-buck, dilute-the-glare-of-guilt
habit is something we have all indulged in – it's as old as Eden: 'It
wasn't really me, it was X [choose your own influencing factor]
affecting me, making me do it – if they hadn't said that, or done
that, or this hadn't happened, then . . .' We want to diminish our
guilt by sharing the culpability with our upbringing or environment or provocation from others or . . . However, there can be
no forgiveness and hence no freedom without repentance, and
there can be no repentance without taking responsibility.

Some try *indulgences*. There are two sorts of indulgence,
very different from each other, but both serve to evade true
repentance and the receiving of grace. The first is the historical
religious indulgence, one factor that precipitated the European
Reformation, that is, the fiction that it is possible to balance
the scales of our wrongdoing by paying up or doing right – a
'buying forgiveness' through our merit and credit. Historically,
parts of the Church have advocated either spiritual acts or
monetary gifts as a means of offsetting sin. Almsgiving,

penances, pilgrimages, self-flagellation, wearing hair-shirts, reciting 'Hail Marys', crawling on one's knees to sacred shrines – attaining credit to balance the scales of justice against sin. Old habits and old heresies die hard. At the heart of true repentance is an acceptance that we bring nothing to God but empty hands to receive his grace.

A second type of indulgence is the personal sort, the indulgences we permit ourselves, sins we say to ourselves are not so bad; no-go areas which we refuse to relinquish to God and give him access to clean up. St Augustine wrote how 'We want to reach the kingdom of God, but we don't want to travel by way of death. And yet there stands Necessity saying: "This way, please."'[4]

This way of death is the way of repentance. Repentance is a death sentence to our old life. We cannot be forgiven if we don't repent – and we are not repenting while we turn a blind eye to our own sin, or make excuses for it, or seek to shrug off the blame for it, or think we can sort it or make amends for it ourselves, or presume on God's grace and keep a little of it by us to come back to later.

Repentance is demonstrated by a transformed life

Nearing the end of his life, Saint Paul summarised his ministry as preaching to the Gentiles that they should 'repent and turn to God and demonstrate their repentance by their deeds' (Acts 26:20). Good deeds are not a substitute for repentance – they don't of themselves merit forgiveness – but true repentance is demonstrated by true change, manifested in good works. I think Peter and the apostles would first laugh and then freak out at today's evangelical 'Sinner's Prayer' – where the listener is encouraged to echo the preacher's pithy penitential prayer, then raise a hand, while every eye is closed and every head bowed, before coming to collect a leaflet from the preacher at the meeting's end. That only became *de rigeur* in the Victorian era. How are we to be sure a new birth has been given, a new life has come into existence? This model seems neither biblical nor truly fruitful – how many whose hands went up incognito became true disciples?

I suggest the major weakness of the above practice is that it does not require repentance. And if there is no repentance there can be no regeneration. In Acts 19:19 we read of the Ephesians who turn to Christ. One evidence of true repentance is that they publicly burned all their costly pagan occult books. A change of life, of allegiance, is seen publicly, and it is both radical and financially significant. Those who become Christians in secret will probably remain Christians in secret and one must ask, how Christian can one really be and keep it a secret? Zacchaeus powerfully illustrates to us an example of real repentance; money had been his god – he paid the Roman occupying forces for the privilege of exacting taxes from his own people, to be free to add on high extras for himself. But once he encountered Jesus and signed up for the kingdom, everything changed – he changed. He declares: 'Here and now I give half of my possessions to the poor, and if I have cheated anybody out of anything, I will pay back four times the amount' (Luke 19:8). Zacchaeus had been eager to see Jesus (and Jesus, seeing Zacchaeus's interest, invited himself to lunch). Having heard the kingdom preached, Zacchaeus was confronted with a choice – and he chose the way of the kingdom, true repentance.

True repentance means walking in the opposite spirit, as we have already seen – Paul said, 'Anyone who has been stealing must steal no longer, but must work, doing something useful with their own hands' (Ephesians 4:28). Have we Protestants so emphasised

Paul's 'justification by faith' that we've lost the kingdom sense of repentance, and good deeds that prove such repentance? Saint John challenges us: 'No one who is born of God will continue to sin, because God's seed remains in them; they cannot go on sinning, because they have been born of God' (1 John 3:9).

This evidently does not take place all at once – 1 John 1:8 presupposes we continue to see sin in us, repenting and receiving God's forgiveness – but there is no doubt that for the apostle, true repentance must show itself, and increasingly so. The Bible assumes instant justification by faith, but not instant sinless perfection. Consequently the Bible requires ongoing repentance and increasing conformity to Christ. True repentance brings obedience to the commands of Christ – true repentance brings conformity to Christ.

Søren Kierkegaard wrote that to repent is to weep for the sins previously committed, and not to commit sins to be wept for.[5] Repentance involves emotion, contrition, confession and action. Remorse is feeling sorry you were caught, repentance is *doing* sorry – and it brings true change. President Richard Nixon was exposed as a crook and a liar in the infamous Watergate Scandal, yet he would not repent – he described it as a tragedy of errors, and was fond of saying 'Watergate was more than a crime, it was a blunder.'[6] That is not repentance – he was sorry he was caught, not sorry he lied. Contrast that with President Bill Clinton after the exposure of his adulterous relations and obstruction of justice in the Monica Lewinsky affair. On 10 September 1998, at the White House Prayer breakfast, he stated:

I don't think there is a fancy way to say I have sinned . . . I believe that to be forgiven, more than sorrow is required – at least two more things. First, genuine repentance, a determination to change and to repair breaches of my own making. I have repented. Second, what my Bible calls a 'broken spirit'; an understanding that I must have God's help to be the person that I want to be; a willingness to give the very forgiveness I seek; a renunciation of the pride and the anger which cloud judgement, lead people to excuse and compare and to blame and complain.

Now that speech understands true repentance. Quite extraordinary! But of course, a transformed life is the real proof of the sincerity of repentance.

Repentance is a constant in the Christian life

Repentance is always a feature of renewal and revival, whether at the personal, church or community level. Frank Bartleman, the founding father of Pentecostalism, who presided over the Azusa Street Awakening in 1906, gave this account of the relationship between revival and repentance: 'I received from God early in 1905 the following keynote to revival: "The depth of revival will be determined exactly by the depth of the spirit of repentance." And this will obtain for all people, at all times.'[7]

The German Martin Luther precipitated the Reformation when he nailed his famous Ninety-Five Theses to the door of Castle Church in Wittenberg. The very first of his theses dealt with repentance: 'When our Lord and Master Jesus Christ said "repent" – he willed that the *entire life* of the believer be one of repentance.' The Vineyard founder, John Wimber, often repeated 'the Way in is the way on' and he applied this specifically to repentance. Repentance is not a rocket booster that launches you into Christian space and then falls away back to earth – repentance is a constant, daily 'Turn, Turn, Turn' – to God. The more we move towards God and keep in step with the Spirit, the more we see him and his ways and understand his word, and the more the Spirit spotlights our own sin and enables us to tackle it. Thus repentance becomes the way on in our way of life.

Every church revival, where a community of believers suddenly bursts into flame and faith breaks out into society at large, advancing the kingdom of Christ, is marked by repentance. Initially by a few Christians, then the wider Church, then whole communities. In the mid-1840s a revival broke out in the Black Forest village of Möttlingen, Germany. It began with a remarkable deliverance of a young lady, Gottlieben, who had been saturated in the occult and was tormented by demons. She had numerous sicknesses, mental, physical and psychic, and the doctors gave up on her. But the village pastor, Johann Christoph Blumhardt, persisted in prayer against these demonic squatters and eventually and dramatically she was set totally free and all her ailments were instantly healed. Word spread like wildfire of this power encounter in which Jesus was victor.

A remarkable awakening began, and the first-fruit was the town tailor Johann Fischer – a mischievous and notorious scoundrel. He visited Blumhardt, and asked if forgiveness and salvation were available for him, too. On being told all his sins could be forgiven by Jesus, he confessed them to Blumhardt, received absolution and accepted Jesus as his Lord and Saviour. His whole being was transformed. The tailor was so overflowing with his new life he immediately became the town evangelist – even gatecrashing a private meeting, preaching to all those in the room, who promptly began to tremble and howl in repentance. The tailor shared the gospel with everyone, and so evident was the new life that he had received that one after another all his friends begin to visit Blumhardt – that they too might confess their sins and receive Christ. This snowballed. Unsolicited, the whole church came one by one and confessed their sins in private to Blumhardt, who absolved them in Jesus' name with the laying on of hands. This awakening was a 'movement of Repentance' as Blumhardt's biographer puts it.[8] The biography records the numbers of penitents: on 8 January, four people came; on 27 January, sixteen; 30 January, thirty-five; in February on one day, sixty-seven; then 156; then 246. Some returned as many as eight times to repent of deeply buried sin until they could find peace. Blumhardt was shocked by some of the stuff he heard people repent of – dark secret sins. The majority of confessions fell into two categories – sexual (adultery, incest, bestiality) and spiritual (magic and occult practices). Though shocked by the sin, Blumhardt was more aware of the power of forgiveness and free grace available.

Now is the time for turning

Ellen G. White, a Victorian apostle, missionary, social activist, writer and mystic, once wrote:

> True confession is always of a *specific* character, and acknowledges *particular* sins. They may be of such a nature as to be brought before God only; they may be wrongs that should be confessed to individuals who have suffered injury through them; or they may be of a public character, and should then be as *publicly* confessed. But

all confession should be definite and to the point, acknowledging the very sins of which you are guilty.

When President Clinton made his famous confession at the White House prayer breakfast, it was specific, particular, public and definite. He drew on a poem by Rabbi Jack Riemer written for the Jewish Day of Atonement, and widely used in the Yom Kippur liturgies of various Jewish traditions:

Now is the time for turning. The leaves are beginning to turn from green to red to orange. The birds are beginning to turn and are heading once more toward the south. The animals are beginning to turn to storing their food for the winter. For leaves, birds and animals, turning comes instinctively. But for us, turning does not come so easily. It takes an act of will for us to make a turn. It means breaking old habits. It means admitting that we have been wrong, and this is never easy. It means losing face. It means starting all over again. And this is always painful. It means saying I am sorry . . . These things are terribly hard to do. But unless we turn, we will be trapped forever in yesterday's ways. Lord help us to turn . . .[9]

And what a gift turning is – no wonder my friend Christy Wimber told me with excitement that when she preached on repentance at her church, the church family received it with a loud cheer. What joy there is in turning from sin, and turning to God.

Epilogue

Christ Formed in You

My dear children, for whom I am in the pains of child-birth until Christ is formed in you.   (Galatians 4:19)

On a regular basis the tabloid press show images of Jesus that people think they have seen in various everyday objects, such as burned cloth on a hot iron; a stain on a window in Florida; a burr on a tree; ivy growing on a telegraph pole; bark on a silver maple tree; or even a rock dug up in a garden. 'Simulacra' is the term for this – an image of someone seen in something else. Food is a common place for people to imagine an image of Jesus – and folk claim to have seen Jesus in their fish fingers, banana peel, sliced oranges, naan bread, a pancake, even crisps. In one of my favourite poems by Gerard Manley Hopkins, 'As Kingfishers Catch Fire', Hopkins says that 'Christ plays in ten thousand places',[1] and that is true – but I doubt if any of these simulacra sightings are true revelations of Christ. People look for Jesus in all the wrong places. They are meant to see him in the Church – they are meant to see him in us.

Paul employs a rather tangled analogy of childbirth – infer-ring that he is like a mother in the agony of birth pains for the Galatian believers, who are like a womb in which Jesus is being spiritually formed and fashioned. This is the burden of the apostle – the burden that occupies his prayers for them and underpins his inspired writing to them: the desire that Christ might be fully formed in them (Galatians 4:19).

You *are* being formed

Spiritual writer and teacher John Ortberg has written, 'Everyone is being spiritually formed all the time. Whether they want to or not. Whether they're Christian or not. The question isn't if someone will sign up for spiritual formation; it's just who and what our spirits will be formed by.'[2] We have already explored how there is a 'biblical binary', if you like – if we are not being formed by our worship of God, other spirits of this world will be working hard to conform us after their image (see Romans 12:2).

In his letter to the Galatian church, Paul develops a spiritual succession: in 1:16 he speaks of Christ being *revealed* to him; in 2:20 he speaks of Christ *living* in him – and in 4:19 he speaks of Christ being *formed* in them. There is a trajectory to the Christian life from seeing Jesus, to Jesus indwelling in us, to becoming like Jesus. We cannot stop at having Jesus revealed to us, or even indwelling in us – we must press on to having him fully formed in us. Paul never resigned himself to the idea of any church he'd founded being half-formed, partly conformed into the likeness of Jesus. His wrestling for this for them suggests that it is not an unattainable goal; were it so his anguish and instructions would be meaningless and cruel. There is more chance of me becoming Christ-like than climbing Everest or winning a Nobel Prize. Becoming like Jesus is the goal of redemption: 'those God foreknew he also predestined to be conformed to the image [the Greek word is actually 'icon'] of his Son' (Romans 8:29). We are to be walking icons of Jesus. So what does it look like for us to look like Jesus, for him to be fully fashioned in us? In Galatians chapter 5 Paul explains what conformity to the spirit of the world looks like and what conformity to the spirit of Jesus looks like. These are polar opposites. He says that the works, outworking, fruit or traits of the sinful nature that are contrary to Christ are self-evident, clearly visible in people's behaviour – and he lists some examples that are representative, rather than definitive: 'sexual immorality, impurity and debauchery; idolatry and witchcraft; hatred, discord, jealousy, fits of rage, selfish ambition, dissensions, factions and envy; drunkenness, orgies, and the like' (5:19–21). If any hint of these is seen in us then Jesus is not fully formed in us. Conversely, if Jesus is being formed in us, then his likeness, character, personality and nature will grow in and flow from us. And what will this look like? Paul describes it in chapter 5, verses 22–23: 'The fruit of the Spirit [the character of Jesus] is love, joy, peace, forbearance, kindness, goodness, faithfulness, gentleness and self-control . . .' This fruit of the Spirit is the character of Jesus fully formed in us.

One way of thinking about the fruit of the Spirit is in terms of WWJD (what would Jesus do) – while the works of the flesh are evident in WWJND (what would Jesus not do). These fruits are not like the categories in personality profiling such as Myers-Briggs, or professional profiling as with Belbin, or even an aesthetic profiling with 'Colour Me Beautiful' where an individual identifies with one or maybe two of the criteria and characteristics highlighted. When Paul speaks of Christ being fully formed in us, he is saying that *all* of these fruits and traits of the Spirit are to be present, and none of the fruits or works of the sinful nature.

If your closest friend was honest and described your character to someone else, what would come first, what would their top-five list look like? I met an old friend for coffee, who had had lunch with Tiffany just before seeing me. He told me he

191

asked Tiffany how I was doing: 'She said one word: "Grumpy".' Grumpiness is not a virtue; it is not the beatitude of mourning. It is the absence of love, joy, peace and patience – it is evidence that Jesus is not fully formed in me. Take a good look at yourself – God is at work in you for good, and you aren't what you were, you are being transformed into the likeness of Jesus. Former sinful patterns of thought and action have diminished and some have disappeared. New fruits from the Spirit are being harvested in your life. But take a good look at Christ – his beautiful perfections – there's still a way to go.

Nonetheless, the gift of the Spirit gives us hope for transformation. As John Piper writes, 'Christianity means change is possible. Deep, fundamental change. It is possible to become tenderhearted when once you were callous and insensitive. It is possible to stop being dominated by bitterness and anger. It is possible to become a loving person no matter what your background has been.'[3]

The world is looking for Christ fashioned in you

What intrigues me is why so many people would be so interested in whether Jesus appeared in bird guano or a window smudge in Florida – a sighting which apparently drew over a million visitors! Few practising Christians would give any credence to such things, so why are non-Christians so interested? Why is this news? I don't think it is merely an unhelpful distraction; I believe that at the core of our beings we are wired for Jesus – that's why people want to see Jesus: they are fascinated by him, drawn to him. In Los Angeles there is a guy called Kevin Lee Light, who has modelled his appearance on iconic perceptions of Jesus: long hair, beard, flowing robe. He now has quite a following on social media with Facebook and Twitter accounts themed around 'IsawJesusinLA'[4] – people upload 'sightings' of him in cafés, the barbers and so on. Again, we see huge interest even though people know this man is not Jesus, yet his caricature of him draws crowds and inspires fascination wherever he goes. People want to see Jesus. And people are meant to see Jesus – in those who are his disciples. Wouldn't it be amazing if we were so transformed and so fully formed into the likeness of Jesus that people who met us in the office or at college or on the train or in the lunch queue, at the supermarket or just in the street, thought to themselves, 'I think I've just seen Jesus.' Can you imagine them tweeting that kind of thing about you, me, us?

One of the most inspiring books I have read in recent years was the autobiographical account of a remarkable man called Jan Karski,[5] who was a leader in the Polish Underground following the German invasion in 1939. With his pre-war diplomatic training, a photographic memory and fluency in several European languages, he was chosen to be smuggled into the infamous Jewish Ghetto in Warsaw and the Belzec concentration camp. With his first-hand experience and further documentary evidence from Jewish leaders he went to the political, military and cultural leaders of the free West to explain that the Nazis were systematically annihilating all of European Jewry. He was received by representatives of the British government and had a private meeting with President Roosevelt, but having discharged his burden of information, he was devastated to see that the Allied governments hardly believed his testimony and did practically nothing about it.

A man of integrity and humility, showing selfless courage in gaining evidence and great conviction in seeking to awaken the West to action on behalf of the Jews, his efforts were like pearls before swine. But what was it that motivated this first witness to the Holocaust? Karski was a devout Catholic – in fact he described himself as a 'Christian Jew', having been made an honorary citizen of Israel and wishing to stand with and for the Jews. Of his witness to the Holocaust he humbly said: 'the Lord assigned me a role . . .' I was moved that he carried a phial of the reserved sacrament around his neck, to be taken as his last grace if death was imminent. I said earlier that we should ask our close friends how Christ-like they think we are. Well, Karski's friend and academic colleague for thirty years, Rabbi Harold White, said in a public tribute to Karski that he was like an Old Testament prophet and yet also 'one of the most humble people I've ever encountered'.[6] Karski survived the war and taught politics for forty years at Georgetown University – one of the students inspired by him was President Bill Clinton. When Karski died, a monument to him was set up at his university – it stated: '*A noble man walked among us and made us better by his presence*'. I believe it was Jesus in him, his Christian faith and the extent to which he had been fashioned into Christlikeness that made him a great man who so inspired others. May Jesus be so formed in us that we make the world better by our presence.

Sadly, as we have noted throughout this book, many are drawn to Jesus, but have given up thinking that the Church is the place to find him. I am a fan of The Proclaimers, a successful pop group from Scotland. A number of their songs have strong religious themes. One has lyrics which I don't think are ironic: 'I want to be a Christian in my heart' and continues, 'Lord I want to be a Christian.' Front man Craig Reid has said, 'I don't see myself as a particularly religious person, and I wouldn't call myself a Christian. I am almost convinced by Christianity, but I have too much doubt to call myself a

Christian.' But what is the source of these doubts? In another of their religious songs, 'The Light', they level a broadside at the Church: 'I believe in God all right – It's folk like you I just can't stand.'[7] How many people have been put off God by those who claim to be God's people!

So much done in the name of Jesus has done damage to the name of Jesus. I recall a sickening image, widely available on the Internet – it is an old photograph of about forty members of the Ku Klux Klan in their bed sheets and pointy hats, holding a meeting in a church, and above them a giant twenty-foot-long painted banner reading, 'JESUS SAVES'. No doubt the Klansmen believed Jesus saved and had even saved them – but their racist allegiances betrayed them. How many in the Church have believed that Jesus saves, but have not allowed Jesus to save them? Singer-songwriter Kevin Max, in his song 'What if I stumble', echoes something once said by Brennan Manning and quoted already in the early pages of this book: 'The greatest single cause of atheism in the world today is Christians who acknowledge Jesus with their lips, walk out the door, and deny him by their lifestyle. This is what an unbelieving world simply finds unbelievable.' And gospel singer Kirk Franklin, in his song 'The Last Jesus', takes the same theme: 'If I say I love Jesus, but you can't see my Jesus / My words are empty, if they can't see Jesus in me. / No more excuses, I give myself away.'

How is Christ formed in me?

Believe it or not, it is now possible to buy a toaster-insert that brands the face of Jesus on your sliced bread![8] Having Christ formed in us, though, is not so quick and easy. First, *Jesus is not formed in us in an instant* – holiness, conformity to Jesus, takes place through process, not a single crisis. Paul uses the metaphor of a child growing in a womb and just as a child takes times to be fashioned and developed, so Christ being formed in us won't happen overnight. This was the claim of the Wesley brothers and the first generation of Methodists; it also influenced the early twentieth-century Keswick Movement and some Pentecostals who spoke of a second blessing, a Spirit baptism, a perfecting love, a crisis event which would crush the patterns of sin in the flesh once and for all and they would be perfected in holiness in one charismatic encounter. Wishful thinking, I'm afraid, rather than biblical thinking. Holiness is a painful process – being confronted with sin, stripped of it, resisting temptation, putting to death the works of flesh. It will not come without a fight. John Ortberg wrote: 'I hate how hard spiritual formation is and how long it takes.'[9]

Second, Jesus is not formed in us by laying down the law. Note Paul's tenderness to the Galatians – he doesn't bark commands like a drill sergeant or rebuke them for their lack of Christ-conformity. Indeed, he speaks in the most intimate terms, calling them 'My dear children'. He presents himself as a mother in agony, bearing children – his tone is maternal and full of winsomeness. Holiness does not come through haranguing people – you can't shout people into holiness. They must be inspired by the example and love of the Jesus they follow. That said, Paul did get quite heavy with them earlier on in the letter when they appeared to have discarded the way of the cross and the Spirit and embraced the legalism of the circumcision group who were seeking to make them holy by obedience to the Mosaic law, by circumcision and the following of kosher rules. That way had been culturally important to identify people as Jewish, but was a dead end as far as constituting true holiness.

Paul is unequivocal: submitting to the Jewish Mosaic law is pointless – it exposes sin but is powerless to help overcome it. It cannot transform the sinful nature and conform one into Christlikeness. Worse still, it actually makes us refugees from grace. The disciple of Jesus who desires holiness must not follow the dead rule of the Mosaic law; instead they are to fulfil the law of Christ (Galatians 6:2), the law of love (5:14) and the law of Spirit (Romans 8:2; Galatians 5:16f.).

Christ formed in us is a work of the Spirit

St Augustine famously prayed, 'command what you will but give what you command',[10] and his prayer truly understood the ways of the Lord. For God does command holiness, repeatedly saying 'Be holy as I am holy' – but the holiness he calls for is the holiness he provides, for by the power of the Spirit he enables us to conform to his commands and decrees and to thus be transformed into the likeness of Jesus. Holiness comes to the extent that we walk with and work with the gift of the Holy Spirit. Christ is fully formed in us by the Spirit – as systematic theologian Louis Berkhof writes: 'The gracious and continual operation of the Holy Spirit by which he delivers the justified sinner from the pollution of sin – renews his whole nature in the image of God and enables him to perform good works.'[11] Willard Erickson defines sanctification as 'The Spirit at work in the believer bringing about the likeness of Christ'.[12] So how does he do this?

First, transformation by the Spirit comes as we live according to God's word. We are not to be conformed but to be transformed, by the renewing of our minds (Romans 12:2). We are what we think – whatever occupies our mind forms our character. If we spend our time meditating on fashion magazines we become vain or insecure. If we spend our time thinking about money we become materialistic and jealous of those with more toys than us. If we spend our time thinking of sex we become dissatisfied and dirty. A transformed life comes by a renewed mind – a renewed mind comes by meditating on Christ's truth revealed in Scripture, inscribed and inspired by the Spirit. It is *de rigeur* for former evangelicals to denigrate and downgrade the Bible; in doing so they can evade a plain reading of its requirements. The Holy Bible is not merely a collection of old stories and letters. It is a collection of works whose calligraphy, content and collation, according to St Paul, were inspired by God, and useful for teaching, for reproof, for correction, and for training in righteousness (2 Timothy 3:16). Scripture tells us the mind of God, the word of God, the truth of God, the story of God; it shows us the power of God and it challenges, corrects, directs and trains us in righteousness, forming us in the likeness of Jesus. There can be no spiritual formation of Christ in us without fashioning our life on the foundation of Scripture. I love the story of Dr David Livingstone, Africa's greatest explorer, missionary and anti-slaver – he was a man made in Scripture. At the age of nine he had memorised all of Psalm 119, the longest chapter in Scripture and grandest meditation on the importance of God's word. During one period of his ministry, he was so wearied by his unstinting efforts, he had a physical breakdown, was covered in ulcers, his teeth fell out, he was confined to his hut for eighty days and could not lift a pen to write a letter. Nevertheless, in that period of enforced rest, he read the Bible through four times. Most Christians won't read the Bible four times through in their lifetime! Is it any wonder that this man, devoted to his God and his God's word, should be used to open up the whole African continent for the gospel?

When the journalist Stanley finally discovered Livingstone in central Africa he spent several weeks with him and later wrote, 'If I had been with him any longer I would have been compelled to be a Christian and he never spoke to me about it at all.'[13] His devotion to the word had transformed him into the likeness of the one the word points to, Jesus. The Bible reveals Jesus into whose likeness we are to be fashioned, the Bible shows us what God required of us to do and not to do, how to live with him, and the Bible is also a means of grace through which the agency of the Spirit operates to shape us into Christlikeness.

Second, transformation comes by the Spirit as we look upon Jesus. The Apostle Paul writes, 'we all, who with unveiled faces contemplate the Lord's glory, are being transformed into his image [like Jesus] with ever-increasing glory, which comes from the Lord, who is the Spirit' (2 Corinthians 3:18). We are to live our lives looking to how Jesus lived his life. And as we continually look on his beauty, we are united with him – it is out of this union with Christ that Christ is fully formed in us. Reformed theologian Sinclair Ferguson notes, 'The Holy Spirit works in the regenerate to unite us to Christ . . . the goal of his activity is transformation into the likeness of Christ.'[14] The American motivational speaker Jim Rohn famously said, 'You are the average of the five people you spend time with.'[15] We must spend more time with Jesus if we are to become like Jesus, so let us set the Lord always before us (Psalm 16:8) through prayer and worship and study and meditation and imitation. Savouring the beauty and majesty and glory of his eternal divinity, his incarnation, humility and humanity, his earthly ministry, his teaching, his example, his crucifixion and penal substitution and glorious resurrection and ascension and accession and preparations for his return and his throne of judgement and his eternal kingship.

Seeing is becoming. In this life we see through a mirror darkly (1 Corinthians 13:12) but when he returns, we will see him face to face, and 'we know that when Christ appears, we shall be like him, for we shall see him as he is' (1 John 3:2).

––––––

Divine alchemy

So we study God's living word and we gaze on Christ and we repent of our sins, and we renounce evil, and we turn and turn again to Christ. And we walk in the opposite spirit to the sin, and we seek to walk in step with the Holy Spirit. And we obey and comply with the instructions of God in his word. And we marinate in God's presence through spiritual disciplines and devotions. And we receive food for the journey through the sacraments. And we do this in the community of the faith. But in and through and over all of this, God's grace received transforms us.

At times in this book I have spoken strong, unsettling, precipitous words. I trust they are not the words of a grumpy middle-aged man, far less words from a sanctimonious prig. I am preaching to myself here, for like Paul I do what I don't want to do and what I want to do I don't do – like all of us, I am a wretched man looking to Jesus to deliver me (Romans 7:19). Christianity is from grace, through grace, and to grace. I love the title of the biography of the flawed saint Brennan Manning, *All is Grace* – from Jesus, indeed, we have all received grace after grace (John 1:16). One of my preaching heroes is the wonderful twentieth-century Edinburgh theologian, James S. Stewart, who referred to grace as 'alchemy'.[16] Yes indeed, like medieval alchemy, the notion of transforming base metal into gold – so God by his grace alchemises us who trust in him and come to him. We turn half-hearted and fickle towards his beauty, and whereas metallic alchemy was a fiction and brass remained brass, God really can and does transform us from base to precious. Yes, it is a work in progress till we see him face to face, but he gives us a promise of progress in the work.

I want to finish with a story of a divine alchemy that has profoundly brought home to me the extravagant grace of God, the saving reach of the gospel and the renewing power of the Spirit. It is rather stark, but it gives me great hope that no one, no matter where they are with God, what they have been into or what they have become, is beyond transformation – even me. Over twenty years ago, I read of two young men aged nineteen who had come to Oxford to re-sit their A levels, aiming to gain better grades to reapply for university entrance. Both young men were from good stable homes, comfortable and upper middle class, financially secure, and both had gone to well-respected public schools. Like many young men, they were inspired by the derring-do of the SAS and both dreamed of one day joining the military Special Forces. On weekends and evenings they energetically committed to fitness regimes and honed their survival techniques in preparation for one day being warriors. But darkness took them over and they became deceived into thinking that to be in the Special Forces they must not just be prepared to kill, but actually have killed someone. And so they planned to commit a murder – going up to London intent on executing a pimp or drug dealer. But the victim they found was just a taxi driver, a family man. As one of the young students held him down the other stabbed him to death. But they were caught, and both sentenced to life imprisonment.

I was appalled by this crime when I read of it and I vividly remember speaking of it in a sermon I preached at a church in

Clevedon in the autumn of 1994 while on deputation from Trinity College. When I came to Oxford as a chaplain in 1998 I often used this terrible story as an illustration of sin when speaking to students. The fact that these two young men were well educated, with a stable family and a good moral upbringing, meant it was an exemplary illustration for numerous evangelistic and Alpha sermons on the biblical truth that evil is located in the human heart, part of fallen nature rather than needing to be nurtured by difficult circumstances. Often when I referred to it I would finish the story with a comment like 'May God have mercy on their souls' – I even recall God's Spirit asking me one day as I was driving along whether I believed they could be transformed and would I pray for it? To be honest, such was the heinous nature of their crime, I wasn't sure I could say yes. But over the years I would half-heartedly pray for God's mercy on them.

And then two years ago a colleague who heads up our prison ministry team came to me: 'You know that student you use as an illustration of evil – the one who killed the taxi driver? He's become a Christian, he's received early parole after eighteen years, and he'll be joining our church.' I could hardly believe it. But it was true. He has repented. He is born again. And every week I see this man sitting in church, reading his Bible, worshipping God, maybe receiving prayer ministry, attentive to and welcoming the stranger. He helps out with our ministry to the poor and ex-offenders and shares his story at churches interested in prison ministries. He returned to formal education and came top of his class in his degree. He is a Christian brother, and a friend, a good and kind man. A life truly transformed. No longer is he a testimony to what evil can do in the human heart – now he is a testimony to the mercy and love of God that saves to the uttermost.

That is the alchemy of grace.

End Notes and Bibliography

Introduction

1 *Luke Skywalker and the Treasure of the Dragonsnakes*, third issue of the *Star Wars* graphic novella series.

2 K. Barth, *Church Dogmatics*, Vol. 1.2: *The Doctrine of the Word of God*, T&T Clark, Edinburgh, p. 868.

3 Abraham Heschel, *Moral Grandeur and Spiritual Audacity*, 1997, p. 67.

4 Heschel, *Moral Grandeur*, p. 147.

5 A.W. Tozer, *The Divine Conquest*, Chapter 8: 'The Holy Spirit as Fire'.

6 From private correspondence with Wimber's daughter-in-law, Christy.

7 http://www.charismanews.com/opinion/heres-the-deal/ 45739–why-are-so-many-middle-aged-men-falling-into-sexual-sin.

8 Hans Küng, *The Church*, Search Press, 1968, p. 319.

9 Often credited to Brennan Manning but source not found.

10 Joakim Garff, *Søren Kierkegaard: A Biography*, translated by Bruce H. Kirmmse, Princeton, Princeton University Press, 2005, p. 773.

11 E. Stanley Jones, *The Christ of the Indian Road*, Abingdon Press, 2010, p. 114.

12 Tearfund survey on church attendance – news.bbc.co.uk/1/
    shared/bsp/hi/pdfs/03.04.07.tearfundchurch.php.

13 http://www.bbc.co.uk/news/uk-32722155.

14 Anne Lamott, *Plan B*, Penguin, 2005, p. 66.

Chapter 1: Sindividual

1 http://www.covenanteyes.com/2013/02/19/pornography
    -statistics/.

2 http://www.covenanteyes.com/2011/09/07/the-connections
    -between-pornography-and-sex-trafficking/.

3 http://character-education.info/Articles/Sommers.pdf.

4 Karl Menninger, *Whatever Became of Sin?* E.P. Dutton, 1973.

5 W. Günther, 'Sin', in Colin Brown, ed., *New International
    Dictionary of New Testament Theology*, Vol. 3, Grand
    Rapids, MI: Zondervan, 1986, p. 578.

6 Quoted in the *Observer*, London, 20 March 1983.

7 https://www.youtube.com/watch?v=NcIWnaXiJLk.

8 Bertrand Russell, *Autobiography*, Routledge, 2010, p. 287.

9 G.K. Chesterton, *Orthodoxy*, London, Bodley Head, 1908, p. 65.

10 Charles Dickens, *A Christmas Carol*, London: Bradbury &
    Evans, 1858, p. 18.

11 C.H. Spurgeon, *Sermon on 8 June 1856, Sermon 84, New Park
    Street*, Day One Publications, 1998.

Chapter 2: New

1 Josephus, *Antiquities of the Jews*, Bk XIII, Ch. X, Sect. 6.

2 C.S. Lewis, *Letter to Malcolm: Chiefly on Prayer*, A Harvest
    Book, 1964, repr. 1992; Harcourt Inc., p. 115.

3 A.W. Tozer, *God's Pursuit of Man*, Wingspread, 2007; (previ-
    ously titled *The Divine Conquest and The Pursuit of Man*),
    3rd page of chapter 9.

4   Leon Morris, *The Gospel According to John*, NICNT, Grand
    Rapids, Eerdmans, 1995, p. 194

5   *Seeing Through the Eye – Malcolm Muggeridge on Faith*, ed.
    Cecil Kuhne, San Francisco, Ignatius Press, 2005, p. 94.

6   C.K. Barrett, *The Gospel According to St John*, 2nd edn,
    London , SPCK, 1978, p. 216.

7   The complete testimony is given in this remarkable video:
    https://vimeo.com/45049349.

Chapter 3: Thy Will – My Will

1   Taken from the New American Standard Bible translation.

2   http://www.truecovenanter.com/truelutheran/luther_bow.
    html.

3   Peter H. Davids, *The Epistle of James*, NIGTC, Eerdmans, 2013.

4   http://billygraham.org/story/billy-graham-on-evil-suffering
    -death/.

5   T.S. Eliot, 'The Love Song of J. Alfred Prufrock' (1920), *The
    Complete Poems and Plays: T.S. Eliot*, London: Faber &
    Faber, 2004.

6   English Standard Version.

7   New American Standard Bible.

8   http://www.religion-online.org/showbook.asp?title=2523.

9   C.S. Lewis, *The Great Divorce*, London, William Collins,
    2012, p. 72.

10 Dante, *The Divine Comedy*, Vol. III: *Paradise*, trans. Dorothy
    L. Sayers, London, Penguin, 1962.

11 'An Account of the Particular Soliloquies and Covenant
    Engagements of Mrs Janet Hamilton', in *Select Biographies*
    Volume 1, edited for the Wodrow Society by the Rev. W.K.
    Tweedie, Edinburgh, 1845, pp. 497–501. I have modestly
    modernised the language by changing Thee and Thou into

'you' and 'yours' and amending the occasional word no longer used in modern speech. I do this to enable the prayer to be more readily used by readers in their own devotion.

Chapter 4: Take Off Your Shoes

1   Matt Redman, *Facedown*, Bethany House Publishers, 2014, Ch. 1. This is the opening line that frames the book.
2   He gave me permission to use this here but I have chosen not to disclose his name.
3   Holman Christian Standard Version.
4   Called *Midrash Rabba* – ten essays of commentary written in Israel, 3rd–5th century; Ch. 2, line 6.
5   See *Desiring God*, 'I Act the Miracle', http://www.desiring-god.org/blog/posts/i-act-the-miracle.
6   Dallas Willard, *The Great Omission*, Oxford, Monarch, 2014.
7   Israel Zangwill, *Children of the Ghetto*, 1892, Bk. 2, Ch. 6.
8   Friedrich Nietzsche, *Philosophical Writings*, trans. Reinhold Grimm and Caroline Molina y Vedia, New York, Continuum, 1997, p. 127.
9   Friedrich Nietzsche, *Thus Spoke Zarathustra*, London, Penguin Classics, 1974.
10 Quoted in Howard Snyder, *The Radical Wesley*, Wipf and Stock Publishers, 1996, p. 14.
11 Gordon Wenham, 'Holiness', in *The Dictionary of Biblical Tradition in English Literature*, ed. David Jeffrey, pp. 353–4.
12 http://news.bbc.co.uk/1/shared/bsp/hi/pdfs/03_04_07_tear-fundchurch.pdf.
13 http://www.christiantoday.co.in/article/mahatma.gandhi.and.christianity/2837.htm.
14 E. Stanley Jones, *The Christ of the Indian Road*, Abingdon, 1925.

Chapter 5: Religion is Nuts

1   See 'Ethelothreskia', in W. Bauer, F.W. Gingrich, W.F. Arndt and F.W. Danker, *A Greek-English Lexicon of the New Testament and Other Early Christian Literature*.

2   http://www.catholicsforchoice.org/conscience/archives/c2002 spring_abuseofpowercomesasnosurprise.asp.

3   I have written on the place of food in the Christian faith in my study on Romans, *God is For Us*, Monarch, 2013, Chs 45 and 47.

4   http://www.lewissociety.org/innerring.php.

Chapter 6: Even Tigger Needs a Hug

1   Frederick Beuchner, *Secrets in the Dark*, San Francisco, HarperCollins, 2006.

2   'Taken from A.A. Milne, *The House at Pooh Corner* (1928), p. 35.

3   CNN news report, 5 May 1991, http://www.chabad.org/ therebbe/livingtorah/player_cdo/aid/490071/jewish/Acts-of -Goodness-and-Kindness.htm.

4   *Remplis de tendresse* – 'filled with tenderness' – a term used by Corrie ten Boom.

5   For further reading on this topic, see Simon Ponsonby, *Loving Mercy*, Monarch, 2012.

6   Philip Kitcher, *Living With Darwin*, Oxford University Press, 2009, p. 124.

7   'Letter to Diognetus' 5.6–7, http://www.christian-history.org/ letter-to-diognetus.html.

8   Based in part on the translation of Edward J. Chinnock, *A Few Notes on Julian and a Translation of His Public Letter*, (London, David Nutt, 1901, pp. 75–8, as quoted in D. Brendan Nagle and Stanley M. Burstein, *The Ancient World: Readings*

in *Social and Cultural History*, Englewood Cliffs, NJ, Prentice Hall, 1995, pp. 314–15.

9   http://www.dogonews.com/2013/10/27/pay-it-forward-the-random-act-of-kindness-fever-that-is-spreading-across-america.

10   While not a smoker myself, I was intrigued by a friend, himself not a smoker, who would buy cigarettes just to be able to offer them to homeless folk on the streets and get into conversation.

11   Abraham Heschel, *The Ineffable Name of God: Man* Continuum, 2005, p. 39.

Chapter 7: Baal and Asherah

1   https://www.youtube.com/watch?v=DDepuej0LSI.

2   'The American Way of Sex', *Muggeridge Through the Microphone*, BBC1 broadcast, 21 October 1965.

3   Interview in the *Guardian*, 13 March 2012.

4   http://www.bbc.co.uk/news/technology-23030090.

5   Michel Foucault, *Power/Knowledge: Selected Interviews and Other Writings 1972–1977*, ed. Colin Gordon, New York, Pantheon, 1980, p. 57.

6   Charles Taylor, *Philosophy and the Human Sciences*, Philosophical Papers 2, Cambridge University Press, 1985, p. 162.

7   *The Encyclopedic Dictionary of Religion*, Vol. F–N, Catholic University of America Press, 1984, p. 1343.

8   *Encyclopaedia Judaica*, Jerusalem, Keter Publishing House, 1st edition, Vol. 11, p. 144.

9   Leanne Payne, The Healing Presence, 1995, p. 240, Baker Publishintg, Grand Rapids.

10   C.S. Lewis, *Mere Christianity*, Macmillan, 1960, pp. 38–9.

Chapter 8: Porn Free

1 Joyce Huggett, *Dating, Sex & Friendship*, Downers Grove, IVP, 1985, p. 31.

2 *Oxford English Dictionary*, online.

3 http://www.safefamilies.org/sfStats.php; http://www.covenant-eyes.com/2013/02/19/pornography-statistics/; http://www.getintolife.org/SolutionsResources/Statistics/PornographyStatistics/tabid/2662/Default.aspx.

4 http://www.ted.com/talks/zimchallenge/transcript?language=en.

5 http://www.catholicculture.com/jp2_on_l&r.pdf.

6 https://stoptheonlinetraffick.wordpress.com/2015/02/16/the-facts-and-figures/.

7 *Sunday Telegraph Stella Magazine* supplement, 27 November 2011.

8 Dr Jill Manning, Senate Testimony 2004, citing J. Dedmon, 'Is the Internet bad for your marriage? Online affairs, pornographic sites playing greater role in divorces', 2002 press release from The Dilenschneider Group, Inc.; http://www.psychologytoday.com/blog/inside-porn-addiction/201112/is-porn-really-destroying-500000–marriages-annually.

9 C.S. Lewis, *The Four Loves*, William Collins, 2012, p. 94.

10 https://www.psychologytoday.com/blog/hope-relationships/201501/is-porn-the-most-prevalent-drug.

11 http://www.everydayhealth.com/sexual-health/internet-porn.aspx.

12 Cited in *Why We Whisper: Restoring Our Right to Say It's Wrong*, Senator Jim DeMint and J. David Woodard, Rowman & Littlefield, 2008, p. 140.

13 Tim Challies, *Sexual Detox* (ebook), http://www.challies.com/sexual-detox.

14 http://www.3ad.com/history/wwll/feature.pages/d.day.letters.
htm.

Chapter 9: Idols or Bibles

1 George Whitefield, *Journals*, ed. Arnold Dallimore, George Whitfield's Journals, Banner of Truth, 1986, p. 60.

2 Brian Edwards, *Revival: A People Saturated with God*, Evangelical Press, 1990, p. 64.

3 P.T. Forsyth, *Work of Christ*, Independent Press, 1910.

4 Ronald J. Sider, *The Scandal of the Evangelical Conscience: Why don't Christians live what they preach?* http://www.christianitytoday.com/bc/2005/001/3.8.html.

5 John Stott, *Principles for Whole Life Discipleship*, https://www.youtube.com/watch?v=vs64yiwOulc.

6 http://rainforests.mongabay.com/09easter_island.htm.

7 Richard Foster, Money. Sex and Power: The challenge of the disciplined life, Hodder & Stoughton, 2009

8 Timothy Keller, *Counterfeit Gods*, Hodder & Stoughton, 2010 – highly recommended for further reading on this crucial issue of contemporary idolatry.

Chapter 10: The Lion in Daniel

1 http://greatbritishmag.co.uk/lifestyle/what-the-british-say---and-what-they-actually-mean.

2 New King James Version.

3 Scott LaBarge, Prof in Philosophy/Classics, Santa Clara University; http://www.scu.edu/ethics/publications/ethicsoutlook/2005/heroes.html.

4 Eberhard Arnold, *God's Revolution*, Robertsbridge, England, The Plough Publishing House, 1997, p. x.

5 http://theweek.com/articles/445823/everything-need-know

-about-irelands-disaffected-catholics. For analysis in the American context see Paul R. Dokecki, *The Clergy Sexual Abuse Crisis: Reform and Renewal in the Catholic Community*, Georgetown University Press, 2004.

6   http://ncronline.org/news/accountability/mennonite-seminary -apologizes-victims-famed-theologian-john-howard-yoder.

7   http://www.christianitytoday.com/edstetzer/2015/august/my -pastor-is-on-ashley-madison-list.html.

8   Warren W. Wiersbe, *The Integrity Crisis*, Nashville, Oliver-Nelson, 1988, p. 171.

9   English Standard Version.

10   http://newlifefellowship.org/about-us/about-new-life/new-lifes -history/.

11   http://www.youtube.com/watch?v=B7OqO9ylMI4.

12   https://www.youtube.com/watch?v=vIFNPIrm1fw.

13   Charles Swindoll, 'A Battle for Integrity', *Insights*, March 2003, pp. 1–2.

Chapter 11: Drift and Drown

1   David Wilkerson, sermon entitled 'Drifting Away from Christ', 6 July 1992, http://www.tscpulpitseries.org/english/ 1990s/ts920706.html.

2   A.W. Tozer, *Five Vows for Spiritual Power*, Christian Publications Incorporated, 1990.

3   C.S. Lewis, *The Screwtape Letters*, HarperCollins, 1996, pp. 49–52.

4   http://www.marieclaire.com/sex-love/advice/g1136/new-couple -rules/?slide=1.

5   C.S. Lewis, *Mere Christianity*, New York, HarperCollins, 1952, Ch. 11, p. 141.

Chapter 12: Turnings

1 Kierkegaard's Second Prayer, 'You have loved us first' – http://www.thewords.com/articles/soren1.htm.

2 Martin Lloyd Jones, *Studies in the Sermon on the Mount*, p. 15.

3 Theodore Dalrymple, *Life at the Bottom*, Ivan R. Dee, 2003, Ch. 1.

4 St Augustine, 'Exposition II, Sermon I on Psalm 30', in *Expositions on the Book of Psalms*, Vol. I, Oxford, Parker, 1847, pp. 248–9.

5 Søren Kierkegaard, *Provocations: Spiritual Writings of Kierkegaard*, New York, Plough Publishing, 1999, pp. 363–5.

6 Richard Nixon, *In The Arena*, Simon & Schuster, 1991, p. 31.

7 Frank Bartleman, *Azusa Street*, Bridge-Logos, 1980, Ch. 2.

8 Dieter Ising, *Johann Christoph Blumhardt: Life and Work*, Wipf and Stock, 2009, p. 201.

9 http://www.washingtonpost.com/wp-srv/politics/special/clinton/stories/clintontext091198.htm.

Epilogue

1 http://www.bartleby.com/122/34.html.

2 Essay in *Christianity Today* titled 'Seven Things I Hate about Spiritual Formation', http://www.christianitytoday.com/le/2013/april-online-only/seven-things-i-hate-about-spiritual-formation.html.

3 http://www.desiringgod.org/articles/all-gods-commands-are-possible-with-god.

4 https://www.facebook.com/isawjesusinla.

5 Jan Karski, *Story of a Secret State*, Penguin Classics, 2012.

6 http://cdn.jankarski.net/files/tribute.pdf.

7 http://www.stmungos.org/malcolms-blog/sunshine-on-leith-the-proclaimers-film/.

8 http://www.amazon.com/Burnt-Impressions-The-Jesus
   -Toaster/dp/B0042QRYO8.

9 Ortberg, http://www.christianitytoday.com/le/2013/april
   -online-only/seven-things-i-hate-about-spiritual-formation.
   html.

10 *The Confessions of St Augustine*, Book 9, Ch. 29.

11 Louis Berkhof, *Systematic Theology*, Banner of Truth, 1939,
    p. 532.

12 Millard J. Erickson, *Christian Theology* (three vols in one),
    2nd edn, Baker Academic, 1998, p. 971.

13 William Barclay, *The Acts of the Apostles*, The New Daily
    Study Bible, Edinburgh, St Andrews Press, 2003, p. 13.

14 Sinclair B. Ferguson, *The Holy Spirit*, IVP, 1996, p. 139. For
    further reflection on the Spirit's role in sanctifying the believer,
    see the chapter in *The Pursuit of The Holy*, Simon Ponsonby,
    2010.

15 Jim Rohn, *The Law of Average*, video clip based on a rather
    idiosyncratic take on the Parable of the Sower, but with some
    insights on influence: https://www.youtube.com/
    watch?v=DMmz-_MLudQ.

16 James S. Stewart, *Heralds of God*, James Scribner and Sons,
    1948, p. 160.

Acknowledgements

Once again I am reminded how graced I am by my church family, St Aldates Oxford, who allow me to work out my theology on them through my preaching. I am forever grateful to my colleagues, especially Charlie and Anita Cleverly who have encouraged, nurtured and released me in my teaching ministry. Bringing a book to birth is always a joint effort and I want to thank the Hodder editorial team, especially Director of Publishing Ian Metcalfe for his confidence in this project, patience with me, and brilliance in landscaping and editing my manuscript. Thanks to also to my colleagues and friends Dr Frank Curry, Revd Mark Brickman, Aidan Hampton and Rose Hunter for their careful reading and constructive insights on the manuscript. This book was written in Zappi's Coffee Shop – their energising flat whites, weight-gaining banana bread, inspiring academic community and all round good banter have provided me with the perfect setting to write as well as generating numerous anecdotes for this book. The Bike Zone crew have repeatedly challenged me not to be 'holier than thou' while also encouraging me to live out what the boss, Neil Johnson, once defined me as having, 'a God-based life.' My father, as always, has prayed my book into being, and my wife Tiffany has been the perfect model of all that holiness means. I am a blessed man.

Do you wish this wasn't the end?
Are you hungry for more great teaching, inspiring
testimonies, ideas to challenge your faith?

Join us at www.hodderfaith.com, follow us on Twitter
or find us on Facebook to make sure you get the latest from
your favourite authors.

Including interviews, videos, articles, competitions
and opportunities to tell us just what you thought about
our latest releases.

www.hodderfaith.com

 HodderFaith

 @HodderFaith

 HodderFaithVideo

HODDER
WHERE FAITH IS INSPIRED

Angels

How to connect with heavenly
guardians of light

Emily Anderson

ARCTURUS

To all those connecting with the angels, right now.
May they bring peace and harmony to humanity.
And to my mum, shining your loving light from
the angelic realm.

All images courtesy of Shutterstock.

ARCTURUS

This edition published in 2022 by Arcturus Publishing Limited
26/27 Bickels Yard, 151–153 Bermondsey Street,
London SE1 3HA

ISBN: 978-1-83857-395-9
AD007831UK

Printed in China

Contents

ARCHANGELS & ARCHEIAI

Introduction

A ngels watch over you, whether you know it or not. In some form or another, they have been around at least as long as humanity. There are Aboriginal paintings on the walls of caves depicting creatures with halos of light around their heads while, in Buddhism and Shintoism, beings of compassion and grace can be called on to help rise above fear and suffering.

Statue of an angel in front of Castel Sant'Angelo, Rome.

Angels are sung about in Christmas carols and pop songs, appear yearly in school nativity plays, and are mentioned in the holy books including the *Bible*, *Qur'an*, *Zohar* and *Kabbalah*. They are also described in many other ancient texts such as *The Book of Enoch* and *The Book of Tobit*.

You can see their cherubic or giant-winged images in art through the centuries, from the Renaissance painters Michelangelo and Raphael, and many Old Masters, to Paul Klee and Kandinsky. Modern British sculptor Anthony Gormley even created the colossal cast iron *Angel of the North* in Gateshead. Literature features angels, too, in famous poems by William Blake and John Milton's *Paradise Lost*, among other great works.

There's no denying that angels have a strong presence in many cultures and eras right up to the present day. A survey of 2000 British people, in 2016, showed a third believed in angels and one in ten had experienced them directly. In the US, as many as eight out of ten people believe in them and have often seen signs that they're around, such as white feathers or repeating numbers.

But what exactly are angels, how can you tell when they're near, and what can they help you with?

What are angels?

Angels are divine beings of light vibrating at a higher frequency than humans. This is why many people can't see them, in the three-dimensional world we live in, but some can if they tune into their energy. Fundamentally, they are a gift from God, Source or Creator, to guide, awaken or assist us on our journey through life.

The word *angel* comes from the Greek word *angelos*, which in Hebrew is *malach*, and means messenger of God. They communicate love, guidance and important news in a variety of ways, most famously by heralding the births of Jesus and John the Baptist, as Archangel Gabriel did in the *Bible*. This same Archangel also revealed the Islamic scripture to the prophet Muhammad.

One of the oldest written records of angels is in the early Hebrew Scriptures, over 3000 years old. The story of three angels visiting Abraham, the father of religion, would have been passed on in Jewish oral traditions prior to that and led to the formation of Judaism, Christianity and Islam.

The Archangels

Archangels are the chief messengers, who appear at times of great change or when asked to help with specific things, as detailed in this book. All religions mention them, but you don't have to be religious to believe in them or work with them.

Muslim traditions talk about Archangels Michael, Raphael and Azrael, while Gabriel and Michael – "one of the great princes" (Daniel 10:13) – are named in the Christian holy book. In the *Kabbalah*, it is Archangel Metatron who led the children of Israel through the wilderness after the Exodus. The non-canonical *Book of Tobit* is the account of Archangel Raphael guiding the travelling Tobias, helping him make healing potions for his ill father Tobit. The second book of Esdras calls Archangel Uriel, the "angel of salvation".

Due to such abundant mention of Archangels in these ancient texts, there have been many scholars on the subject, including fifth century Christian monk Dionysius and the great philosopher Thomas Aquinas, in the Middle Ages, who wrote a treatise on these purely spiritual creatures exploring many facets of their non-physical, but nevertheless genuine, existence. This era saw a huge interest in angels, and they are heavily represented in the art, literature and cathedral architecture from this period.

There have been sightings of angels at various times in the past, such as in the First World War when the heavenly hosts were seen in the trenches, and a rumour spread about an angel bowman defending the

British troops at Mons. Archangel Michael, protector of the military, is believed to have helped with the victories of Emperor Constantine and appeared to him in his newly taken city of Constantinople. Famously, 12-year-old Joan of Arc had a vision of Archangel Michael who told her to clear the English out of France. Four years later, dressed in man's clothing, she joined the French army and brought them great success with her skilful strategy, until she was captured and killed by the English.

THE ARCHEIAI ARRIVE

In the 21st Century, interest in angels has surged, due predominantly to the work of two major angel healers: Diana Cooper, in England, and Doreen Virtue, from the US (although Virtue has subsequently converted to a sect of Christianity that rejects all aspects of the New Age and she has, as a consequence, denounced all her previous work). Both have written a great many books, created angel cards, and given talks about the different aspects of angels, including the Archangels, ascension, and healing. Kyle Gray is a younger, male angel expert, from Scotland, who had a connection with the angels at a very young age, denied it, and then had to share it with the world – to great success.

These experts explain that, as well as our Guardian Angel who has been with us since birth and through all of our times on Earth and can be called upon for help, we each also have an overlighting Archangel. Usually this is Metatron, Michael, Gabriel, Raphael or Uriel, but other Archangels can work with us when asked, to help on issues including healing relationships, finding our purpose, clearing clutter and teaching us about self-love.

Since 2020, a whole new side to the Archangels is being written about and explored by angel experts Calista, from Scotland, and Claire Stone, from Merseyside, England, in their books, both entitled *The Female Archangels*. These angel communicators are revealing knowledge of the female Archangels, or Archeiai, as they are called, who are making their presence and powers known on Earth now, to help with the rise in the divine feminine energy that our out-of-balance planet needs.

Despite traditionally being thought of as androgynous beings, the patriarchal culture of the last few centuries has always presented Archangels as male, sometimes with swords and armour in the case of Archangel Michael, and usually with typical masculine traits of protection, strength and bravery. But Calista and Stone have discovered, through direct experiences with the Archeiai for over a decade already, that each of the "male" Archangels has an equally powerful "female" side. A bit like twin flames of the angel realm, but divine reflections of each other, the Archangels and Archeiai work miracles together, but also separately, to bring their uniquely magical transformations into our lives and the world.

Most of their names are high vibrational virtues – Hope, Faith, Clarity, Purity. Calling them into your awareness raises your frequency to unite with theirs, waking you up to your own divinity that can be accessed all the time. The Archeiai are here to encourage compassion, kindness and nurturing of our spiritual development to help us ascend into a life of unconditional love and happiness. To get there, they shine their light on your shadows to make real and lasting positive change. A helpful exercise is included with each Archeia entry to assist you with your ascension, some of which were first revealed to the world in Calista's and Claire Stone's books and have been adapted for use here.

Prepare to transform your traumas, break through blocks and reprogramme limiting beliefs, so you can live your best, most fulfilling, and joyful life. Feelings of not being worthy of a blessed life can be transmuted with the Archeiai's assistance and bring us into alignment with the true love, bliss and abundance that is our divine birthright.

In this book, fifteen cosmic couples of Archangels and Archeiai are explored in detail, revealing the specific things they can help with and how to work with their powers to maximum effect. You'll find out how to see the signs, colours and coincidences that they're around and connect to them each through guided meditations and exercises to expand your mind, body and spirit.

So, let's get started by tuning in to these incredible beings of light and love.

TUNING IN

When you take the time to tune into the angelic realm, and ask for guidance from the Archangels and Archeiai, your life will expand in new and exciting ways. All you have to do is be still and silent regularly and start a conversation with the cosmic couples that will enrich, enlighten and evolve your awareness of the magic and miracles around you.

Making an Angel Altar

Find an area in your home where you won't be disturbed and choose that as your angel space where you can put together a special altar to sit at and call in their presence.

First, smudge the area with white sage, or another cleansing herb native to your part of world, to cleanse it of all energy ready for it to become your sacred space.

Find a small table or shelf as something on which to place various items. Cover it with a piece of fabric in the colour of the angel's energy that you wish to tune into. Or something more generic, to start with, such as white or silver.

Choose coloured candles in the same way, to ignite the fire energy and focus on bringing in the light. Any fragrant, uplifting incense, such as frankincense, rose, bergamot or white sage will also add an angelic aroma.

Next add some sparkle. See the secton on page 150 about the various crystals connected to each Archangel and Archeia (the singular term for the plural Archeiai). Seek those gems that resonate most with you and whatever your purpose is for connecting with the angels.

Place them on your angel altar alongside any other items that help you tune into your angelic guides, such as feathers, photos, flowers, stones or ornaments.

Make the place comfortable with cushions, a kneeler or straight-backed chair. You want to be able to sit upright, for ideally 20 minutes or more, to connect best with your higher consciousness and the cosmic realms.

Now you are ready to sit quietly and meditate in this special place and see what manifests for you from now on.

How to meditate

* First, get comfy. Wriggle and stretch a little to smooth out any discomfort.

* Now, be still. Close your eyes, gently.

* Become aware of your breath. Just your breath, moving in and out. Relax your mind and body into a state of calm presence.

* Ask to connect to Source, Gaia, the Goddess, God, whatever your deity is, or simply the Universe, if you prefer. Keep breathing. Clear your mind. Open your being to a higher consciousness.

* Ground yourself equally to Mother Earth, for balance and stability as you climb to lofty new spiritual heights. Feel your body touching the ground and imagine roots growing into the earth.

* Ask the angels, Archangels, Archeiai or any particular one or pairing, described in this book, to come to you. Don't expect anything, just stay open to experiencing something new, a brightness of being, a deeper

presence, a sense of well-being. You don't have to name the feeling, just stay open.

* Perhaps you see a colour, an outline, even some details, or maybe you simply feel an extra incoming of love, warmth, comfort, balance and calm.

* The angels are here to support you, to help you raise your frequency, and to live a richer, more fulfilling life and ascend to higher states of consciousness.

* Pray to them to assist you in any way you wish.

✳ Then trust. Feel into what resonates most with you. What keeps drawing your attention, capturing your mind and, most importantly, your heart? Your heart wants you to do what feels good, so seek for and do whatever brings you joy. If you follow your passions, your bliss, then you cannot go wrong.

✳ Pay close attention to the urges and inspirations you have, as these will steer you on your path of ascension. This means ascending to higher vibrations of being, following a path of love and expanding your radiant self to be the best version of you, in this incarnation, at this time.

PROTECTION TIP

You are always safe when working with the angels as they have your best interest at heart and only ever share love. But if you want some extra protection from other possible negative influences, you can ask Archangel Michael to shield you with his protective blue light or drape his big blue cloak around you to repel any bad vibes.

Signs the angels
are near

Once you start tuning into angels regularly, you might start to feel or even see their presence. Remember, they will only help you if you ask as they know we humans have free will overall – unless an urgent situation means they need to intervene, such as if your life is threatened when you still have a mission to complete on Earth. Just don't rely on them to step in for you unless you ask them to.

When you do call upon the Archangels and Archeiai, and communicate your hopes and dreams, receive their wisdom and grow with their encouragement; their loving input will expand your life in miraculous ways. But if you're still unsure they are there for you, ask them to show you a sign. They may appear to you in one of many different ways. The most important thing is to tune into the message at the time of the sign appearing for reassurance or the guidance you need.

Feathers

One of the most common signs from the angels is the appearance of white feathers. You may be thinking about a lost loved one or wondering if angels really do watch over you and suddenly a single, white feather floats down from the sky or appears right on the path in front of you or in an unusual place. Take it as a message that you are loved and guided by those in the angelic realm.

Music

Deep in meditation with the angels, many people hear celestial sounds of strings or angelic voices singing. But signs from our Archangel or Archeia can come from popular music, too.

Perhaps you're thinking of a loved one recently deceased and suddenly you hear the song that was played at their funeral. That's the angels letting you know your beloved watches over you, and that they are here to help bring you comfort, closure and compassion.

If still doubting divine beings exist, simply say, "Dear Archangels and Archeiai, show me a clear sign that you exist". You may turn on the radio and there's Beyonce singing 'Halo' or 'Angels' by Robbie Williams is playing. Nothing could be a clearer sign than that!

Voices or smells coming from nowhere

Out of the blue, you suddenly smell roses or lilies, that could be the Archeiai in particular, making you aware of their presence around you. Be still and listen, awaiting any guidance that you may sense, see or hear.

You may hear voices, clearly and loudly, guiding or warning you. Author Doreen Virtue's awakening to the angelic realm came in this way, in 1995. While parking her car on her drive one day, she heard a clear voice telling her to stay in the car and drive. She questioned it, and heard the same urgent message again but chose to ignore it, only to be the victim of a car-jacking. The same voice shouted at her to scream, which she did, and the startled thief ran away. Had Virtue not acted on what angel experts believe to be the voice of Archangel Micheal, she would have lost her car and may have been injured or even killed.

Strange people appearing at the right time – or with the name of the Archangel you were asking about.

Celestial creatures may come to you in different guises at different times – sometimes in apparent human form. In the Bible, apostle Paul declares that, "some people have entertained angels unawares." This suggests that angels appear as humans to help us. A great many people have experienced a tall stranger with unusually bright eyes, sometimes smart, sometimes shabby, who arrives to help or to comfort at the perfect time. Often he says his name is Michael before disappearing as quickly as he arrived, never to be seen again.

OTHER LIGHT BEINGS TO LOOK OUT FOR
Orbs

In the Hebrew Bible, angels were called "spheres of fire" presumably because the ancient people saw fire as light. We know now that orbs of light – often appearing around people in photographs, if not to the naked eye – are seen as our guardian angels looking out for us.

Unicorns

Unicorns are fully enlightened beings of light from a higher dimension who come to earth as a great gift to assist with our ascension. The horns seen on their foreheads are in fact spiralling, white, healing energy beaming out of their third eye. As well as being guides for children, unicorns go to people who radiate light and want to help humanity awaken to its divine essence. Much like the Archeiai and Archangels, they can give us strength, faith and the ability to manifest our visions of a new earth. Ask for their help for healing your mind, body and soul, as well as clearing karmic wounds and balancing your chakras while you sleep.

Fairies and Elementals

Fairies and other elementals are smaller beings of light that appear more in powerful places in nature, such as the ocean or forests. You can ask them to work with plants to help them grow healthy and abundant. One of the founders of the Findhorn Foundation spiritual retreat in Scotland, Eileen Caddy, famously communed with the elementals in the garden to help their allotment grow well. It worked as the place had a more vibrant, succulent and sizeable produce than was expected to grow in the nutrient-depleted soil there.

Numbers

Repeating numbers, either on a digital clock face, or elsewhere in your life, such as on transport times or bus numbers, shopping bills or television, are often a message from the angels. Different digit sequences mean specific things, some of which are explained in more detail in the Archangel and Archeia descriptions. But here are a few common magic numbers – all of which can reveal a connection with the angels.

11:11

Probably the most often seen magic number, which signifies that we are all one, connected with the Creator, the angels, and the Universe. If you keep spotting this number, particularly on a clock, it's a call to action to align yourself with all that is and feel the loving vibration of the divine within us and in the angelic realm.

Many people around the world purposely stop and sit in meditation at 11:11, am or pm, and set the intention to hold the light of this higher frequency to help humanity ascend.

22:22

Twos are all about connection with others and healing relationships with the love you radiate naturally. You have the ability to light up the world, especially if you focus on the highest good and keep shining your intentions brightly.

3:33

Threes bring in the optimistic and creative energy of Archeia Hope as well as the ascended masters, great spiritual teachers who lived on earth but now share their wisdom from the celestial realms. You are being guided by great power; allow the esoteric knowledge to help you expand your spiritual awareness.

4:44

Fours encourage you to have faith in higher powers. Know that your prayers to the angels are being heard and they are with you now, particularly Archeia Faith whose number this is.

5, 55, 555

Fives mean Archangel Uriel and Archeia Grace are working together to support you through a time of change or to greater freedom. Act according to your intuition and guidance from them to get through any challenges.

6

Six is the symbol of Venus, love and the divine feminine, and says Archeia Charity is here for you now to bring balance and harmony to all you love and value.

7:77

Archeia Christine reveals that you are on the right path towards living out your true purpose. Magic will manifest for you when following divine inspiration from the angels.

888
Archangel Ariel shows you this number to tell you that abundance is yours as you grow spiritually and learn the lessons of your past before releasing those patterns and moving forward.

9
This signifies connection with the divine feminine, Archeia Purity in particular, who urges you to 'keep going, you're nearly there'. Seeing a sequence of nines highlights unity with your higher self to help you master your spiritual skills.

12:34
A sequence of numbers says the angels are helping you move toward your best life. You are expanding your awareness and aligning with love. Let the angels help you tap into this loving frequency and encourage you on an enlightened journey.

12:21
Mirrored numbers are a message to reflect more on what you were thinking about at the time, so that you receive what you need for growth. 12:21 suggests self-care is needed more so that you can support others through their ascension process.

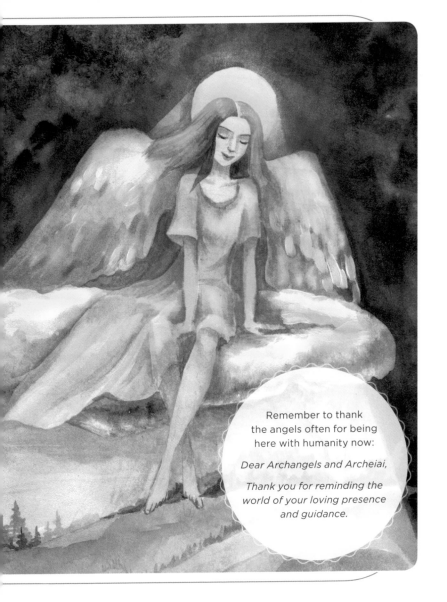

Remember to thank
the angels often for being
here with humanity now:

Dear Archangels and Archeiai,

*Thank you for reminding the
world of your loving presence
and guidance.*

The colours connected to the angels

Energy vibrates at different frequencies creating the appearance of different colours, so it makes sense that beings of light such as angels will emit different colours depending on their frequency. If you suddenly see a colour during meditation, experience flashes or sparkles of certain shades around you, or are suddenly attracted to things of a certain tone, it could be an angel's presence. The following colours specifically relate to the different angels.

Archeia Faith	bright sapphire blue
Archangel Michael	rich royal purple or royal blue
Archeia Virtue	gold, violet and emerald green
Archangel Raphael	green
Archeia Hope	white with gold and green sparkles
Archangel Gabriel	mother-of-pearl with copper/orange

Archeia Grace	warm red and pink
Archangel Uriel	soft golden glow with ruby red
Archeia Charity	radiant white with a hint of pink
Archangel Chamual	sparkling pink or pale green
Archeia Clarity	golden yellow
Archangel Jophiel	bright white with fuchsia sparks
Archeia Constance	purple, indigo, or sparkly silver and gold
Archangel Metatron	violet and dark green
Archeia Patience	vibrant rainbow
Archangel Sandalphon	turquoise and platinum / sometimes black and white
Archeia Mercy	magenta and copper making rose gold
Archangel Azrael	black and creamy white

Archeia Ariel	cool pink with sparkling gold, flashing with all the colors of the rainbow,
Archangel Raziel	indigo and gold plus rainbow
Archeia Freedom	rich warm orange
Archangel Jeremiel	rich warm orange
Archeia Haniel	pale blue with silver flashes
Archangel Nathaniel	bright turquoise, red and orange flashes
Archeia Purity	amethyst purple
Archangel Zadkiel	white and purple amethyst colour
Archeia Serenity	pearlescent silver
Archangel Cassiel	silver with hints of purple, pink or bronze
Archeia Radiant	shining blueish white light
Archangel Haniel	light turquoise and silver

ARCHANGELS & ARCHEIAI

On the following pages, you
will meet the pairs of 15 archangels
and 15 archeiai who will help you
with different aspects of your life.
You will learn how to connect with
their healing energy and move
into a place of light and joy.

I Archeia Faith

Also known as
Lady Faith, Mikaela

Helps with
Trusting in your powers of light, protection and clear communication, dispelling doubt on your path.

Affirmation
"*I am ready to remember and reclaim the truth of my soul's existence. I trust in divine guidance and the best outcome.*"

Twin flame
Archangel Michael

Appearance: Archeia Faith wears a sapphire crystal at her third eye to connect her with her Archangel counterpart Michael. She often appears in a royal blue cloak radiating a cobalt-blue light, while carrying a shield and the sword of truth, like her armour-wearing warrior twin Archangel Michael. Connecting with Archeia Faith brings the glowing gold light of 'Christ consciousness' into your energy field to bless everything around you.

Guidance: Archeia Faith helps us move on from painful situations and regain our sovereignty if we've given away or lost our power. She especially likes healing female relationships and the painful 'witch wound' that all women inherit after the witch trials of old.

Her blue light heals the throat chakra, to enable clearer communication of your truth, and aligns the heart and third eye to connect you to her warrior-goddess guidance.

Have the courage to be authentic, as this integrity makes you powerful. Focus on the fullness of who you are at a Source level and life will expand beautifully. This is what ascension is, and what Faith encourages most. As we make a conscious choice to connect with her, we bring in more of our light, our strength and our decisive leadership qualities, raising our vibration and attracting ever more blessings into our lives.

She wants you to cultivate an inner knowing that all will be well, both personally and globally. Believe in yourself and have confidence everything will work out well, for you and for humanity. Trust that the Law of Karma *will* re-balance the scales. You have all it takes to get through any challenges, especially if you learn to protect yourself.

Protecting your aura with Archeia Faith

First, arrange your meditation altar to refect Archeia's Faith's energy, by adding a dark blue cloth, blue and white candles, and incense of cedarwood or frankincense. If you have any of the relevant crystals (see pages 150–5), add those too.

Sitting or kneeling in your meditation space, take some deep breaths, in and out, to come fully into the present moment. When fully relaxed, ask for Archeia Faith's help with learning how to protect your energy and she will guide you through this process.

First, ask all energy that is not yours to go back to where it came from. Feel your whole body, your chakras and aura being cleansed of all residual energy that isn't your own. Tune in to how you feel when your aura is sparkling clean.

Next ask that all your energy come back to you from wherever it may be, passing through a filter so it is cleansed. See this as golden light filling you up from head to toe and expanding outwards into your aura and as far out as you feel comfortable with. Feel the fullness of light, loving energy for as long as you wish.

Now, bring your glowing light back in towards your body, and ask it to be surrounded by a bright indigo protective energy to bring you balance, nourishment and protection. Again, sit within this light, feeling it supporting you.

This indigo energy can be called into action any time you feel yourself out of balance and in need of strength. It is your psychic protective shield. Thank Archeia Faith for this gift.

II Archangel Michael

Also known as
Prince of Angels, Mika'il, Sabbathiel. His name means "Who is like God?"

Helps with
Protection, strength, courage and truth, cutting cords, balancing your energy field.

Affirmation
"I am safe and protected from harm. I am ready to speak my truth with courage."

Twin flame
Archeia Faith

Appearance: The most military of the angels, Archangel Michael is usually depicted clad in full armour, holding a golden shield of light and a blazing blue or white sword of truth. But this might not be how he appears to many. Instead, you may see royal blue or purple during meditation or in things around you if he is near, as his energy field shines with these colours and he is said to wear a royal blue cloak of protection.

Guidance: Archangel Michael is helping to raise the frequency of humanity by giving us all the strength, courage, vision and love to get through the darkest of times. He can be trusted to protect your energy from any negativity coming your way. Much like his female counterpart, he encourages you to develop your own strong, inner light of self-protection through self-belief and trust.

With support from Archeia Faith, Archangel Michael helps you discover your life purpose and know what action to take next. Get clear on your desires then ask him for guidance. When sitting quietly in meditation or before you go to sleep, ask Archangel Micheal clear questions and note down any answers that come to mind or in your dreams.

His royal blue energy invigorates the throat chakra

Start every day thanking Archangel Michael for his protection and strength. Tell him how good it feels to know he's got your back.

enabling you to be bold and honest with your words, inspiring others to stand in their full power and blaze their light brightly. Request that he rebalances your energy field when people's vibes have swamped you, or do the cord-cutting exercise below to release you from karmic ties with any people or places.

Ask for Michael's protection any time, for yourself, your family, even your home. Pay attention to any messages or strong intuition you receive while driving or taking any transport. His voice can often be heard very clearly, especially in an emergency.

Archangel Michael's cord-cutting exercise:

You can ask for Archangel Michael's help to cut any cords binding you to negative energy, emotional upsets, past life trauma or any other blockages.

Sitting comfortably at your angel altar, with hints of his purple or royal blue aura connecting you to him, breathe in and out calmly to relax your mind and body.

First, see yourself surrounded by Michael's golden protective light as it runs into your crown chakra and down your whole body, filling your aura with light.

Now, let your mind present any blockages or restrictions you have on following your life path in peace. Imagine each situation, person or place is a white ribbon wrapping itself around you, as you stay relaxed in your meditation.

See Archangel Michael with his bright blue light and sparkling sword shimmering behind you. As he touches each ribbon restriction with his sword, it unravels and disappears. See his magical sword cutting all cords entangling you and stopping you from moving forward in your life. Feel the release of these blockages from your being.

You are now free. Sit with this feeling of freedom for as long as you can. Feel its power. You are ready to take that into your life.

Open your eyes and go about your day.

Say, "Thank you, Archangel Michael, for cutting these cords and setting me free. And so it is!"

III Archeia Virtue

Also known as

Lady Virtue, Mareia, Mother Mary as Archeia Virtue was one of the spirit guides of Christ's mother and helped Jesus to realise his divinity.

Helps with

Healing, dispelling dis-ease, forgiveness, mothering – of others and yourself.

Affirmation

"I am ready to forgive all that has harmed me and feel good once again. I am fully healed and aligned with my radiant inner being."

Twin flame

Archangel Raphael

Appearance: Feminine and motherly, glowing with her healing pink light, Archeia Virtue exudes compassion and understanding. She shines gold and violet rays into your awareness or the emerald green colour that links her to Archangel Raphael.

When you see white doves, that's Archeia Virtue's symbol of peace and forgiveness giving you a sign that all is well.

Guidance: Angels help us embody our divinity in human form, enabling us to enjoy the vibrant physical, mental and emotional well-being that we all deserve and are capable of. Archeia Virtue wants you to heal any *dis-ease* you feel through the freedom of forgiveness and honesty with yourself. If we deny or avoid our feelings, without taking the time to really look at them, we're missing any chance for growth. Virtue guides you to allow suffering from past or present events, or from people in your life, to come to the surface and be properly felt and acknowledged.

She guides you to ask these questions:

* Who or what do I need to forgive?
* Is it me, other people, a situation or place?
* Am I ready to let go of these feelings and stories that make me feel less than I am?
* Am I ready to feel better in every way and to work with the angels to create the well-being that is my birthright?

Spend some time thinking about and feeling what perfect mental, physical and spiritual health would be like for you. Know that this is possible if you allow yourself to connect with the perpetual stream of love that you came from and can connect with in every moment.

Forgiving with Archeia Virtue

The best way to connect with Archeia Virtue is by tuning into your heart and realising that even painful experiences bring wisdom and expand your capacity to understand and grow. Try this meditation to delve deeper into forgiveness.

As you sit comfortably in your quiet space, inhale and exhale deeply and slowly to stay in a relaxed, centred state.

Imagine your heart centre is full of the bright pink healing light of Archeia Virtue. As you breathe in and out, allow this pink light to expand until it surrounds you with a large circle of healing energy.

Ask Archeia Virtue to be with you and make you aware of anyone or anything that needs to be forgiven.

Let all the feelings fully arise with the memories of any past wrongs, without getting too attached to any of it.

Keep breathing deeply and sitting in the healing pink light as everything comes forward to be felt, seen and cleared from you now.

It's time to let go of all the negative emotions that have been making you feel less than your true loving self.

Say: "I choose to forgive on all levels of being, all timelines, all realities. I choose vibrant health and pure love. And so it is."

See all that has arisen enveloped in loving kindness. Bathe in Archeia Virtue's healing frequency as together you transmute all into love.

When you feel ready, thank Archeia Virtue and all that came forth, then send all energy that is not yours back to where it came from. Feel renewed as you open your eyes.

IV Archangel Raphael

Also known as
Labbiel, Raphael's original name.

Helps with
Healing yourself and others, clearing the third eye to bring about enlightenment, travel.

Affirmation

"I clear my mind, body and spirit to allow true healing to occur. I am radiant with good health. I am safe and well."

Twin flame
Archeia Virtue

Appearance: Archangel Raphael's energy sparkles an emerald green radiance from his halo. He is one of the angels often depicted in famous art, including paintings by Rembrandt, Titian and Botticini, holding either a pilgrim's staff or a fish; as the "sociable angel" in *Paradise Lost*; and as one of the "seven angels of the presence" described by Blake in his epic poem *Milton*.

Guidance: Archangel Raphael hopes to liberate your mind from what you've already learned so you can become an empty vessel for spiritual truths and healing wisdom. He encourages positive thoughts to raise your frequency and enable your own healing. With his help, you can even use the power of your mind to minimize pain and bring comfort through any physical treatment or therapy, such as counselling, Reiki, or massage.

Archangel Raphael activates the third eye chakra, to bring a clearer vision of ideal health and encourage you to imagine better well-being for yourself and others as you move into alignment with your Source-created self.

You can also help others heal by asking for Archangel Raphael's assistance. He will never go against another person's free will so if they don't want to be healed, for whatever reason, he won't override this. But he will watch over and guide the person you send his healing energy to, so they will feel his positive effects.

In a similar way, Archangel Raphael can look after and heal pets and other animals if you ask him to. Try requesting his assistance for healing any animal's injuries quickly and to find lost pets. Due to his journey with Tobias, as described in the ancient scripture *The Book of Tobit*, later rediscovered as a Dead Sea Scroll in 1952, Archangel Raphael is also believed to look after travellers and help make any journey smooth, if you ask for his guidance.

Healing with Archangel Raphael:

Feel full of vitality and send healing to others and Mother Earth with this powerful meditation.

Sit quietly at your angel altar, to which you've added touches of green, such as candles, fabric and relevant crystals. Close your eyes and take some deep breaths to bring you into a relaxed state.

Focus on the third eye area between your eyebrows. Imagine there is a bright green, spinning sphere full of Archangel Raphael's healing energy, right at this point on your forehead.

See that emerald healing light fill your whole body. See yourself glowing and feel your body vibrating with health, strength and a deep feeling of well-being.

Now, ask Archangel Raphael to send his healing blessings to everyone you love.

Next, do the same for anyone in need of his help.

Visualize his powerful healing energy moving to a person or pet, group of people or animals that need it most. Imagine them filled with his emerald healing light and manifesting full health and vitality.

Send the same healing green light all around the planet to heal the whole population of the Earth, including all the creatures of the seas, land and air, and Gaia herself.

Thank Archangel Raphael for his healing work.

Bring all your awareness back into your body, clearing all energy that is not yours, and take a few deep breaths before opening your eyes. Be sure to drink plenty of water to ground you through the day after your healing session.

V Archeia Hope

Also known as
Lady Hope, Annunciata.

Helps with
creativity, manifestation, fertility, birthing new ideas and projects.

Affirmation
"*I am birthing the new. I am filled with positive energy and inspiring ideas. Miracles come my way.*"

Twin flame
Archangel Gabriel

Appearance: Archeia Hope has one of the highest vibrations of all the Archeiai so often appears in a pure light, gossamer cloak. She has a brilliant white aura that sparkles with gold and green. Her flower is the lily, long seen as a symbol of angel communication and depicted in angel paintings, such as Da Vinci's *Annunciation*, next to Archeia Hope's twin flame Archangel Gabriel.

Guidance: Bring more hope and optimism into your life with Archeia Hope. Connecting to her sparks the inspiration to begin new creative projects that push you forwards on your path. She brings a healthy dose of self-belief and the chance to break through mental blocks or stuck habitual patterns to help you ensure your wishes are joyfully fulfilled.

Linked to water and fertility, Archeia Hope helps women with their moon cycles, sexuality and pregnancies. She also brings forth child-like curiosity and openness in us all to help us sail through life more smoothly.

Archeia Hope encourages positive thinking to help you manifest your best life. Trust in her to bring magic and miracles into your world and she will always support you, even if you're feeling alone, struggling with debt or relationship issues. If you let her pure light fill all of your being, she will transform your fears into positive inspiration.

Manifest the best with Archeia Hope:

If you want to birth a new business, relationship or creative project, set up your angel altar to connect deeply with Archeia Hope's powerful positive energy.

Use an orange cloth to cover your altar to represent creativity and inspiration.

Choose some of the crystals linked to Archeia Hope on page 152. Light an orange candle and burn some oils or incense of neroli or orange blossom.

To bring even more power to your wishes, a crystal egg is a great addition to this manifestion meditation because eggs represent new life, abundance and fertility.

Choose the right colour for what you'd like to see manifest:

* pink for romance
* red for more energy
* yellow for increased
  happiness
* purple for deeper
  spirituality
* blue for clearer communication
* orange to bring inspirational ideas.

Smudge your crystal egg with sage or another cleansing herb before you use it to clear it of past energies.

As you sit quietly, breathing deeply, hold your cleansed crystal egg in your hands.

Now see the brilliant white and golden sparkly light of Archeia Hope surround you with her positive energy. This can often be felt from the sacral chakra, with a tingling sensation moving upwards through your body. Feel her optimism and enthusiasm fill your whole being.

Now imagine whatever it is you want to manifest into your life. Really conjur up the details and the feelings it would bring. Sit with this vision for as long as you wish. Take note of any ideas for action that pop into your mind.

Now imagine sending all that positive feeling and the details of your dreams into the crystal egg. Place your egg in the centre of your altar to remind you of your future vision whenever you see it. Spend time every day meditating holding this crystal egg and imagining your wishes coming true. And so it is.

Thank Archeia Hope for bringing life to your desires and manifesting all you dream of.

VI Archangel Gabriel

Also known as
Jibril, Gabriel means "mighty man of God".

Helps with
communication, good news, fertility and children.

Affirmation
"I communicate clearly and kindly. I bring peace and harmony with my words."

Twin flame
Archeia Hope

Appearance: In Jewish scriptures, the Christian New Testament and Muslim Qu'ran, Archangel Gabriel appears as the messenger bringing the good news from God, usually of births, including John the Baptist's and Jesus Christ's. He is celebrated on the feast day of the annunciation, 25th March, when he appeared to Mary and told her about the birth of Jesus.

Often seen with a copper-coloured trumpet symbolising his communications from Source, his mother-of-pearl-coloured aura sparkles with the same metallic shade. In Renaissance artwork, Gabriel has more feminine features, long flowing hair and gown, probably due to his connection with birth and child-raising, spheres that were historically seen as more female than male concerns. He exudes a gentle but strong, nurturing power.

Guidance: As the main messenger of God, Archangel Gabriel is the heavenly guide for anyone working in the arts and communications of any kind, including postal workers, teachers, counsellors, coaches, writers and actors, helping these professionals hone their presentation skills. He may bring you messages through these industries, or via connecting with him directly in meditation or appearing to you in dreams, where his information will be crystal-clear.

Similarly, Archangel Gabriel will help you communicate with others in a clear and positive way. Whether you're writing an article, filming a video to share on social media or about to have a difficult conversation, request that Gabriel help you express yourself calmly and cooperatively.

Ask him to help you break through any fears of self-expression or performance anxiety, as well as overcome procrastination.

Archangel Gabriel's soft strength and child-like innocence guides and protects the youngest of humanity and mentors parents and anyone who looks after, or works with, children. Ask him simply to protect any children in your care and trust that he is there for them. He will also help you heal your wounded inner child by shining his light on any pain or trauma experienced as a child so it can be fully acknowledged and released. This way Gabriel can help your thoughts and feelings be purer, smoothing your spiritual development.

Asking for clarity with Archangel Gabriel

If you are seeking clarity on a decision, or wondering about your career path, ask Archangel Gabriel to show you the simplest, most effortless way forward, in this meditation.

At your angel altar, light a white candle, for purity, anointed with uplifting orange blossom or neroli oils. Alternatively, a Himalayan salt candle would work well here, as they give off a lovely, warm, glowing light. Salt lamps also purify the air around you by creating a negative ion-rich environment making your long, refreshing, deep breaths even more beneficial for your well-being.

Imagine yourself surrounded by a bright white light with orange-copper twinkles. Feel Gabriel's sweet, innocent energy fill up your entire being.

Ask Archangel Gabriel to clear your mind of chatter around a situation or person, enabling you to see and work towards the highest outcome. Feel the situation resolving peacefully.

Say, "Archangel Gabriel, please show me clear signs that you are guiding me in the right direction."

Now, when you go about your day, look out for any signs that Archangel Gabriel is nudging you. These could include messages from anyone out of the blue, interesting job opportunities presenting themselves, or symbols, such as seeing copper coins or anything copper-coloured, bright flashes of light, lilies or any other trumpet-shaped flower, or even a trumpet itself, signifying an important message is about to come your way.

VII Archeia Grace

Also known as

Lady Grace or Aurora. The word grace comes from the French for "to thank".

Helps with

accepting and moving through change with ease and determination, also rebirth, intuition and inspiration.

Affirmation

"*I am in sync with the flow of life and filled with grace. Everything works out perfectly, at the right time, to bring me bliss.*"

Twin flame

Archangel Uriel

Appearance: Ruby tones of red and pink are Archeia Grace's colours that you may see in meditation or around you in daily life. She rarely appears in a physical-like form but shows herself through eye-catching aspects of nature, such as abundant autumn leaves, an uplifting sunrise or striking sunset. These natural reflections of Grace connect you to the power of natural cycles of death and rebirth.

Guidance: Archeia Grace brings us the awareness that we are one with all life. Through this connection with Source we can feel the joy of life as a sovereign soul having a human experience. Living in this state of grace means we can stop limiting our lives by holding ourselves back with negative self-beliefs or old patterns of behaviour. Feelings of abandonment or of not being enough, come from a place of lack and are disempowering, false and only serve to hinder us on our path to a joyful existence. Archeia Grace reminds us that we are all worthy of a wonderful, fulfilling life.

When unpleasant situations or feelings keep repeating and causing you pain, ask Grace to shine her light of divine alchemy to help you see the blessing within the turmoil, and transform the issue into the chance to change and grow. Allow Archeia Grace to help you realise the incredible, magical being you truly are, to see the light that shines within you, even when it appears lost.

From the perspective of infinite bliss, life flows with purpose and everything works out perfectly. Archeia Grace encourages you to expect miracles, so that events occur and people appear at exactly the right time, with the very lesson you need, to help you on your path. Synchronize with this natural stream of abundance and well-being by trusting your intuition and following the guidance of your higher consciousness, through any inspired ideas and creative urges.

Realising Grace through your loved ones

Connecting to the natural flow of life brings a deeper awareness of death, not as the end but as a new stage in the path of the eternal soul. Even after the body is no more, there is a connection to something deeper and more profound.

When you see, sense or hear from your loved ones in spirit, either in your dreams or in meditation, they are offering you love from Source. Any messages from loved ones, such as a certain smell coming out of the blue or favourite animals appearing when you think of the deceased person, show that their love and support from the spirit realm never fades and will always guide you if you ask.

Through this connection know that you are never alone, are always supported, guided and loved. If in doubt, ask for help from Archeia Grace by saying: "Dear Archeia Grace, help me to flow as creative source energy, synchronized with all life, so my actions are inspired by your elegance and grace. What is the highest guidance for me right now so that my path unfolds with ease and joy?"

Listen for the first answers that come to mind, knowing that they will always come from a place of love and make you feel good.

VIII Archangel Uriel

Also known as
Auriel, Nuriel or Phanuel, his name means "fire of God".

Helps with
intellectual ideas and insights, finding answers, speaking and writing wisdom, spiritual development.

Affirmation
"I am grateful for being given the information and insight I need to bring peace and happiness into my life. I share with confidence, kindness and strength."

Twin flame
Archeia Grace

Appearance: Archangel Uriel features in Christian Gnostic scriptures where he shares esoteric information and metaphysical teachings with the prophet Ezra. He also guided John the Baptist to escape the massacre of the innocents and leave Egypt.

In Christian theology and various art, Uriel is depicted as a cherub, often carrying a glowing, pale yellow lantern to light the way ahead. You know he is guiding you if you see rose garlands, lotus blossoms or lilies of the valley.

Archangel Uriel's energy is a soft, golden colour mixed with ruby crystal, like his twin flame Archeia Grace, emanating tones of red for his powerful, inspiring strength of conviction and royal blue for clear communication of inspired ideas.

Guidance: Allow Archangel Uriel to illuminate your mind with the information and insight you need to guide your intellectual pursuits. If you are studying or sitting an exam, ask him to help focus your mind on the knowledge you need. He can help you find the right words in personal conversations, business meetings or public speeches so you come across with confidence, kindness and tact.

Archangel Uriel holds the blueprint for world peace by guiding people to align with their soul path and experience more self-worth and satisfaction. This deeply contented energy will then ripple out around the planet. Call on Uriel to help your community to work together for the highest good or send him to work his magic in areas around the world that need healing.

With his fire energy, he is the Archangel of creative inspiration and new beginnings, especially if they are in harmony with the rising divine feminine energy, needed so much at this time of imbalanced masculine power.

Develop your spiritual wisdom with Archangel Uriel

Sit quietly in your meditation space, feeling relaxed. See yourself surrounded by a white light and know that you are safe.

Now, focus on your solar plexus chakra in the centre of your body. See this area as a ruby-red rose, with its petals starting to fan outwards.

Say out loud: "Archangel Uriel, I ask you to fill me with your golden energy, emanating from my ruby-red solar plexus, to bring wisdom, insight and epiphanies to me."

See Uriel's golden energy shining out from the rose at your solar plexus. As the ruby-red petals fan out more, see this golden glow fill your entire body and aura with Archangel Uriel's light of clear insight and infinite wisdom.

Know that as this stream of knowledge fills you, it strengthens and emboldens you to stand in your true power, ready to receive whatever information you need.

Sit and breathe in this powerful energy for as long as you wish.

When ready, send all energy back that is not yours, allow your aura to settle and your awareness to come back into the room. Visualize roots growing from your body into the earth, to ground you, before opening your eyes.

Note down any enlightening ideas or information that emerged, and follow the urges to explore areas of spiritual development further.

IX Archeia Charity

Also known as
Lady Charity, Seraphina.

Helps with
self-care, loving yourself unconditionally, strengthening relationships.

Affirmation
"I choose to look after and love myself. I trust that love will lift me up to my best life."

Twin flame
Archangel Chamuel

Appearance: Archeia Charity's aura glows with a warm pink and radiant white light. She may appear as more petite or curvaceous than other Archeiai, and is adorned with heart motifs or the rose of Venus symbol expressing the everlasting, pure love she has for you.

Guidance: Both Archeia Charity and Archangel Chamuel are powerful expressions of light and love, and inspire you to act selflessly by being charitable and giving whenever you can. They help you see the beauty in everything and the good in everyone, even those that provoke us. Ask yourself often: "How can I bring more love into this situation?" and listen to your heart's response.

Archeia Charity helps you to open your heart chakra, to allow more love into your life, and to express your authentic, unfiltered self to the world. To do this, she guides you to love and accept yourself un-conditionally by realising that you are already perfect just as you are. The angels see you as flawless sparks of divinity, so Charity urges you to stop comparing yourself to others or using negative self-talk, which makes you feel bad about yourself.

Instead, Charity guides you to make time for serious self-care. This includes talking to yourself in a loving, uplifting way, saying yes to whatever inspires you and no to anything – or anyone – that drains you. De-clutter your home, meditate regularly, rest and eat well, and stay active by doing things you love, such as dancing, running or swimming. Make time for pleasure and for people you enjoy being with. Then you'll keep your vibration high and, in turn, see that positive energy ripple out into your other relationships, including attracting the right kind of romantic partnership if you're single.

Loving yourself with a bathing ritual

First, turn your bathroom into a sacred space by playing some gentle music and lighting candles, ideally white or pink like the colour of Archeia Charity's energy.

Run a warm bath and add rose oil and rose petals or even some gold leaf for added angelic sparkle, to really wallow in Charity's gift of beauty and self-love.

Before stepping into your beauty bath, ask Archeia Charity to channel her warm pink positive light through you and into the water so you can bathe in her pure energy of love.

As you get in the water, say, "Assist me, Archeia Charity, in softening fully into loving myself. Please dissolve anything stopping this right now. Thank you."

Now lay down in your sumptuous bath and let the nourishing energy of Archeia Charity wash over you as you breathe in loving thoughts and breathe out gratitude for this time for yourself. Let every long, deep breath relax you more and more.

Allow any past experiences where you have felt unworthy of love or hurt pass over to Archeia Charity for her to transmute into love.

Lay your hands on your heart and affirm: "I am lovable and I am loved. I am worthy of love," as many times as you need to really feel it.

Soak in the splendour of this moment of true love for as long as you wish. And when you leave your bath and release the water, bless it with love as it travels around the world.

X Archangel Chamuel

Also known as
Camael, Khamael, means "he who sees God", his name comes from the Hebrew word meaning compassion.

Helps with
smoothing relationships, manifesting peace, finding solutions and lost items.

Affirmation
"I love unconditionally. Solutions to my problems are now clear and everything I seek, I find."

Twin flame
Archeia Charity

Appearance: In Druid mythology Camael was the god of war, ruler of planet Mars, while in Jewish legend he wrestled with Jacob. In the mystical tradition of Kabbalah, he is one of the ten archangels who oversee the pathway of love on the Tree of Life.

His gentle-giant energy emits a sparkling pink, the same as the heart chakra he helps open. When around, you will feel intense love pouring from his heart, hands and eyes into you. He and his twin flame are symbolised by the rose, so add these to your angel altar to connect more deeply to them, along with Archangel Chamuel's other blooms of lavender, violet and chamomile.

Guidance: Archangel Chamuel has an omnipresent vision of all, enabling him to see the best solution to problems. He helps smooth turbulent relationships and bring peace and harmony, personally and globally, when called upon. Ask him to protect you from others' anger and jealousy to avoid getting into conflict.

As the archangel of unconditional love, Chamuel will help you find friends and attract a true soulmate. Ask him to open your heart chakra, raise your energy and allow a deeper, spiritual love and contentment to grow in your life. Say, "Archangel Chamuel, please open my heart so I can give and receive love."

Chamuel knows what Source has in store for you so can steer you towards your soul's purpose, into a better career or a new place to live. Ask for his help and pay attention to the signs he will show you through your inspiration, creative urges or practical desires.

If you feel scared or lost, anxious or in despair, ask for Archangel Chamuel to guide you until your fear dissipates and the way forward is shown. Try saying the following invocation a few times if you're still worried or dreading what may happen: "Archangel Chamuel, please use your loving power to banish all forces that are against love, now!"

Finding lost items with Archangel Chamuel

If you're missing something in your life, such as a partner or special place to live, or you've lost your phone or car keys, ask Archangel Chamuel to help find what you are looking for.

Sit quietly at your angel altar, with a piece of amber, rose quartz or amethyst in the centre to help you tune into Chamuel's energy.

Light a rose pink candle anointed with rose oil ideally, to bring in the loving energy of Archangel Chamuel.

Breathe in and out slowly and deeply, until you feel relaxed. Now say, "I call upon Archangel Chamuel, to bring forth your unconditional loving, rose pink energy and open my heart with your divine presence."

Sit for a while in his love-filled field. Then ask: "Please assist me in finding …. [what you are looking for]."

Pay attention to any feelings or thoughts that arise, any visions or ideas you receive during this meditation and afterwards. They will point you towards what you are searching for, which he may highlight with some angelic light. The inspiration breathed into you by Chamuel will help you connect more deeply to divine love so you are no longer lonely or longing for anything but restored to full divine glory, ready to attract whatever it is you need.

XI Archeia Christine

Also known as
Archeia Clarity, Lady Clarity, Christophina.

Helps with
present moment awareness, spiritual enlightenment, concentration.

Affirmation
"I trust the wisdom of my soul to guide me towards the light. I keep my energy bright and balanced."

Twin flame
Archangel Jophiel

Appearance: With her Archangel counterpart, Archeia Christine represents the Christ energy, the sun that is essential to all life. She radiates an intense and powerful energy and beaming golden yellow aura. Wearing a bright yellow crown to denote her ability to heal the crown chakra, she connects you to higher dimensions and the universe.

Powerful birds of prey, such as eagles, are symbols of Christine, so whenever you see or tune into them, she is around you.

Guidance: Archeia Christine reminds us that we are all made of Source energy, connected to all that is. She wants you to meditate every day so you know you are more than just your physical body or beliefs, you are an infinite being on a path to spiritual enlightenment.

Earth and its inhabitants are ascending into a new age of inter-connectedness, deeper awareness and peace, but we must raise our frequencies to get there. Ask for Archeia Christine's help accessing your higher mind, to boost your mental powers and aid concentration. Becoming aware of the present moment through mindfulness is her special gift to you, for it creates contentment, clarity and calm.

Archeia Christine brings illumination and determination in even the darkest of times. Allow her to guide you to the truth underlying all, to bring wisdom to confusion, and positive, practical insight to get you through fear, negativity and control. She also balances the divine feminine and divine masculine within and outside of us – the soft, nurturing yin and more determined, dynamic yang energy – as both are needed for a fulfilling life.

Meditating with Archeia Christine enables your kundalini energy to rise from the base of your spine, up through your chakras to your crown, which may feel warm or tingley. She heals your crown chakra, syncs it to your higher self and connects you with other dimensions to raise your frequency higher.

Quicken your ascension by appreciating everything in your life – including yourself. Make your self-talk positive by saying uplifting affirmations, such as: "*I am so blessed,*" "*I love my life,*" or "*I can do this!*"

Connect to the sun every day

Help the divine masculine rise as well as the divine feminine by connecting to both the Earth and the Sun every day.

Go outside, stand firmly barefoot on the ground, and imagine roots growing from the soles of your feet. Thank Mother Earth for supporting and guiding you.

Now raise your face to the sun, feel the warmth on your skin, heating every bit of your body. If it is not sunny, remember how wonderful it feels when the sun warms your skin and makes you smile inside and out.

Now take all that warmth into your heart. See it as a golden ball glowing and growing bigger and bigger until it fills your whole aura.

From the golden ball at your heart chakra see a column of bright white light running up through your body to your crown chakra, and up into the cosmos.

Say: "Archeia Christine, please connect me to my higher mind, to divine intelligence, and guide my spiritual ascension. Thank you for everything in my life."

When you're finished, bring all your energy back into yourself cleansed, and feel your feet connect firmly to the floor. Open your eyes and have a drink of water to refresh.

XII Archangel Jophiel

Also known as
Iofiel, Zophiel, his name means "beauty of God".

Helps with
beautifying you and your surroundings, positivity, teaching wisdom.

Affirmation
"I am beautiful. I beautify my surroundings to make myself feel happy. I have a strong connection to nature which increases my well-being."

Twin flame
Archeia Christine and companion of Archangel Metatron.

Appearance: The most feminine-looking of all the archangels, Jophiel is delicate and beautiful, with a sweet and gentle energy that will slowly but surely come in when called for. His halo can appear bright white with fuchsia pink sparks, so if you're attracted to this colour suddenly, he is guiding you.

Guidance: Like Archeia Christine, Archangel Jophiel carries the Christ light and wants us to feel as bright throughout our lives. He suggests we get out in nature more, to walk among trees and alongside rivers, to boost our mood in beautiful surroundings. Children especially thrive with outdoor exploration and play.

Jophiel wants everyone to learn about the universal laws, of attraction and karma, for example, and about the ascension process so humanity can raise to even greater spiritual heights. He helps us develop our individual gifts, talents and ideas so we can feel fulfilled.

In his wish to beautify our lives, he can help clear out clutter, give your pad a re-paint and adorn your home with incredible art and fragrant flowers, such as lilies or sweetpeas. Follow his inspiration to make your house a calming sanctuary away from the bustle of life outside. Remember to take the time to appreciate it as this raises your vibration even higher.

If you want assistance shopping for clothes or changing your image, ask Archangel Jophiel to push you towards the perfect outfit, haircut, or make-up style. Don't assume it's trivial or that you're taking the angels away from greater issues, they are infinite beings of light whose purpose is to help uplift us. As they see it, what could be more important than making you feel happy with how you look, and raising your frequency?

Activate your crown chakra to allow in Christ light

Sitting comfortably in your meditation space, light a white candle for the Christ light of Jophiel and Christine. If you have some frankincense oil anoint the candle with that, or burn incense of the same heavenly fragrance.

Breathe deeply to relax. Ask Archangel Michael to drape his big blue cloak around you so you are protected throughout this meditation.

See yourself sitting inside a thousand-petalled lotus flower, with its flowers spread open all around you sparkling white and pink light into your aura. Ask Archangel Jophiel to fill your entire being with his Christ light.

Focus your attention on your crown chakra on the top of your head, Imagine it, too, is a thousand-petalled lotus flower, but with golden petals fanning out around your head.

Archeia Christine steps forward now to pull a golden thread of light from the centre of your crown chakra lotus flower up into other dimensions on stars far away. Safely accessing these higher realms though this golden light beam you can receive downloads to help with your ascension. Let the visual images come to you and feel the bliss of this universal light connection for as long as you wish.

When finished, pull the golden thread back into your crown, fold up the many petals of the lotus flower and thank the angels for their wisdom and knowledge.

Take some time to come back into the room, feel your body touching the ground, and then note down what you experienced.

XIII Archeia Constance

Also known as
Lady Constance, Sophia.

Helps with
ascension, balancing the chakras, aligning with your path, feeling motivated and getting organised.

Affirmation
"*I am ready to rise. I trust the guidance of my soul. I relax and allow life to unfold.*"

Twin flame
Archangel Metatron

Appearance: Archeia Constance has a powerful, regal beauty, standing strong and brave in her vital feminine energy. Her aura colours are purple, indigo, or sparkly silver and gold. Bees and stars are her symbols, representing the interconnected constancy of life.

Both Archangel Metatron and Archeia Constance help us connect with the ancient wisdom of sacred geometric shapes, so are often depicted holding powerful symbols, such as Metatron's cube or the *Vesica Piscis*. These two over-lapping circles represent a portal for pure feminine creation energy to manifest in physical form.

Guidance: Archeia Constance awakens us from self-limiting beliefs and blocks to rise in harmony with Mother Earth. She wants to simplify the process of ascension from our three-dimensional, desire-led, material life to a more expanded and expressive experience of the love that we are.

She reminds us to stay present to every moment and trust we are always in the right place at the right time. Relax and allow the natural flow of life and the urges of your soul to carry you in the right direction, fully appreciating all that is happening is for your highest good.

Take some time to imagine your ideal self and then let it unfold in your life. Constance will help you see the synchronicities and signs that show your dreams are unfolding as they should, and give you strength, determination and motivation to keep going. Connecting with her will prompt you to be more organised and build a better life for yourself, step by step.

Archeia Constance encourages us to do more of what makes us happy as this will help manifest our desires by raising our frequency. So if you feel like taking a long bath, a yoga class or having a massage, enjoy it to the full. You don't have to be busy or productive all the time. Let your pleasure become your path and your ascension journey will be a lot smoother – even more so if you sing! Angels love hearing happy, melodic voices. Singing connects you to Source energy, clears the aura and expands the chakras, all of which boosts your intuition and connection to divine guidance.

Connecting to Constance

Sitting comfortably at your angel altar, close your eyes and sense yourself in a column of sparkling diamond light. As you breathe in and out let this magical energy fill your body and aura. See it stretching into a column connecting you up to heaven and down into the earth. Know you are protected and filled with love by your guardian angels who stand beside you.

To connect with Archeia Constance say out loud: "Dear Archeia Constance, please attune me to your vibration so that I may channel your uplifting energy in everything I do. Help me stand strong in my power, to express all that I am and can be. Support me to ascend my consciousness by knowing when and how to act, and when to rest and allow. With gratitude for your guidance. And so it is."

Feel her presence with you as you ask what the best action is for you to take. Sit quietly and receive her wisdom. Thank her again before opening your eyes and carrying on with your day, following all of your soul's messages for happiness.

XIV Archangel Metatron

Also known as
The Angel of Empowerment.

Helps with
healing, spiritual development, confidence, cleansing negative energy and ascension.

Affirmation
"I am a being of light. I vibrate at a higher frequency from now on and ascend into a brighter realm to help humanity raise its consciousness."

Twin flame
Archeia Constance

Appearance: Metatron and his spiritual brother Sandalphon are archangels who are believed to have lived as humans. Metatron was the biblical scholar and scribe Enoch, and was so pure and good that he was rewarded with ascension to the angelic realm.

Archangel Metatron has a violet and dark green aura and carries the Merkabah, the sacred geometric cube with the "flower of life" symbol and all the shapes of all God's creations contained within it. This magical cube is used for healing and astral travel to other dimensions to explore the deeper meaning of life.

His powerful energy comes through even stronger than the likes of Archangel Michael, so prepare to feel his high vibration blast in when you connect to him. When you see the master number 11:11, this is Metatron trying to make you aware of your higher spiritual purpose.

Guidance: Metatron is the go-to Archangel for empowering your spiritual abilities and encouraging ascension, whether alone in meditation or together with other light-workers. Asking Metatron to guide you brings a deeper understanding of your true self and innate powers as well as golden opportunities for planetary service to help humanity rise from our 3D world. Working with his intense, direct energy will give you confidence in your esoteric abilities and clear your chakras so that kundalini energy can rise freely, boosting your ascension process.

He is the keeper of the Akashic Records, where everything that has happened and will unfold is recorded. He knows how negative thoughts lead to bad situations in life. Working with Archangel Metatron motivates you to choose positive thoughts, words and actions instead, to ensure you have a fulfilling and happy life.

Archangel Metatron is an excellent teacher of mystical subjects and their practical uses. He especially loves sharing his wisdom with the indigo and crystal children, highly sensitive youngsters with intuitive gifts that they may not fully understand. He will help them utilize their spiritual skills and give them the courage to follow their purpose, as well as to fit in better at school and cope with the world's harsher energies.

Healing your energy with Metatron's cube

Lie down somewhere comfortable for this meditation. Close your eyes and focus on your breathing. Ask Archangel Metatron to prepare his light bath for you.

Relaxing deeply, you may hear or feel the vibration of a gentle light current running through your body.

Say: "Archangel Metatron, please surround me with your light bath."

See yourself lying inside Metatron's cube with all its powerful cleansing, cosmic connection. With his hands gently upon you, he pours his high-vibration frequency through your entire being. Imagine your whole body turning into a pure golden liquid light.

Ask Archangel Metatron to dissolve any negativity within you, any energetic, emotional or physical issue that has been holding you back.

Feel or see the honey-golden light flow up your spine, through your chakras, cleansing and opening them fully so they can spin at a higher frequency of pure love.

Ask that Archangel Metatron keep your body and aura at this higher level of light and clarity at all times, from now on.

Say aloud: "Thank you Archangel Metatron. And so it is."

Relax for a while in this newly enlightened state. When you're ready, open your eyes and drink some water to ground and rehydrate.

XV Archeia Patience

Also known as
Lady Patience or Shekinah.

Helps with
manifesting prosperity, connecting with Mother Earth, healing money blocks.

Affirmation
"I am ready to live a prosperous life. There is an abundance of love and money for everyone. I am friends with money and am ready to receive more of it now."

Twin flame
Archangel Sandalphon

Appearance: Archeia Patience has a vibrant rainbow aura, sparkling all colours in all directions. She often appears covered in flowers, in particular the tiny, but perfect, daisy to remind us to have pure intentions and stay rooted in innocence as we tune into our desires.

She is represented by Mother Earth herself, abundant with fruits and teeming with life, symbolizing the infinite potential within us all. Her name comes from the Latin word *patientia* which means endurance. Harness this aspect of her to keep faith that all you desire will come to you.

Guidance: Archeia Patience reminds us that prosperity is all around us, as seen in nature's abundance. As on Mother Earth, where things don't happen all at once but according to their season, you must be patient and let everything happen according to divine timing or natural flow. Trust that the reality you want will come to you in time, without getting hung up on when or how.

Patience reminds us that manifestation isn't about simply asking the universe for something to come to us, it's about being a vibrational match for that reality. Feeling wealthy and worthy inside attracts your desires to you. So ask for Archeia Patience's guidance to feel open to the love and abundance within you, and to help you ditch the negative beliefs around attracting money, in particular.

If you ever feel frustrated that your dreams haven't emerged quite yet, Archeia Patience suggests standing outside with your arms outstretched, palms and fingers facing up towards the sky. Visualise your heart space glowing brightly with all the colours of the rainbow as it expands to fill your whole being with love and abundance. Breathe pure prana energy in and out, reminding yourself of this most natural of flowing cycles.

Healing your negative money beliefs

Archeia Patience gives us permission to receive prosperity. But first, release any old beliefs and feelings of unworthiness that you have, by answering these questions honestly and from the heart:

* What one word sums up your relationship with money?
* Growing up, what did you believe money was?
* What do you believe about money now?
* What would feeling fully aligned with the abundant flow of money mean for you?

Now, really feel the energy of poverty in your body. Breathe into where this focus on poverty feels most strongly – your heart or throat chakra, for example.

Ask what is this energy giving me? Listen to your soul's response without judgement. Perhaps it creates an excuse to hold yourself back or brings you some attention. As you explore the root of these feelings of lack, allow yourself to transform your limiting, old beliefs into expansive, new thoughts and feelings on living an abundant life.

Ask Archeia Patience to shine her rainbow light into all your shadows around money so you can release the blocks, beliefs and contracts your soul may have made to keep you in poverty.

Say out loud: "I activate the energy of prosperity in my life now. I am able to give and receive easily because I am abundance itself. I know there is more than enough for everyone. Thank you Archeia Patience for your blessings. And so it is."

XVI Archangel Sandalphon

Also known as
Sandolfon or Ophan, his name means "brother" in Greek.

Helps with
musicality, present moment awareness, strengthening connection to Source and ascension.

Affirmation
"*I raise my frequency to the fifth dimension and all magical, spiritual possibilities unfold.*"

Twin flame
Archeia Patience but also Archangel Metatron

Appearance: At the end of his life on earth, the Biblical prophet Elijah ascended to become Sandalphon, brother of Metatron. Known as master of heavenly song and the patron of musicians, he is often depicted with a musical instrument.

One of the tallest in the celestial realms, his height is said to span from heaven to earth. He emits a calming turquoise shade of blue from his aura with flashes of platinum, in tune with his gentle, soothing yet powerful presence. Alternatively, he may come across as black and white, like his symbol the yin/yang circle representing the perfect balance between masculine and feminine energies that he assists with.

Guidance: Archangel Sandalphon delivers prayers from earth to heaven, making the esoteric understandable and the spiritual more practical for us humans to comprehend.

As master of musicians, you can ask for Archangel Sandalphon's help to improve your singing, songwriting or instrument-playing. When your favourite track comes on the radio and cheers you up or when you feel the urge to play a certain artist's album and dance around the house, that's Sandalphon showing you how music lights up your life.

Anyone sensitive to loud, jarring noises can ask Archangel Sandalphon to rid their environment of irritating sounds. Simply imagine the soundwaves going into the ground right underneath you and Sandalphon will take it from there. This is because he, along with Archeia Patience, heal the earth star chakra which spins at the very bottom of your aura, about 20 centimetres below your feet. The earth star chakra is especially important, right now, as it's the foundation for humanity as we rise into the next Golden Age. During this prophesied time, said to start in 2032, we will have evolved into a more crystalline form so we can hold more light in our bodies, access knowledge from other dimensions including the angelic realm, and develop increased spiritual talents and abilities.

Raising your aura to the fifth dimension with Sandalphon's magic sphere

Sitting comfortably at your angel altar, light a silver candle if you can.

Imagine you have roots growing into the ground beneath you to anchor you and keep you safe.

Now, ask Archangel Sandalphon to activate your earth star chakra, 20 cms below you, until it is shining silver. See him make a fifth-dimensional sphere starting from this silver chakra and encompassing your whole energy field including all your other chakras so your aura becomes reflective silver.

Take some time to feel this new 5-D aura and the higher vibration within it. Every cell of your body is raising its frequency now.

Focus back to your grounded connection to Mother Earth before feeling her flow her energy into you making your aura get bigger. Imagine this ball of high-frequency energy expanding out into your street, town, country and all around the world. Feel the harmonious resonance of all beings united in one joyful song.

When you are ready to finish, bring your aura back in to your body. Send away any energy that is not yours and thank Archangel Sandalphon for his blessing.

XVII Archeia Mercy

Also known as
Lady Mercy, Magdalena. The word *mercy* comes from the old French word *mercit*, which means kindness.

Helps with
self-acceptance, kindness, rebirth and selfless service.

Affirmation
"*I embrace the gorgeous goddess within me and empower my body as well as my soul. I release any repression of my true loving self and reclaim my true divinity.*"

Twin flame
Archangel Azrael

Appearance: Archeia Mercy was the angelic influencer of Jesus' Christ's soulmate Mary of Bethany, named Mary Magdalene when she ascended as master of compassion and kindness.

Roses are her flower, so you may see more of these in your meditations or around you in your life to show that Archeia Mercy is with you. Place them on your angel altar to work with her energy.

Her aura shines with magenta and copper rays, which together make a rose-gold light, combining her ancient goddess wisdom with new Golden Age energy to heal the throat, heart and base chakras.

Guidance: Archeia Mercy guides you to fully love your body. Our flesh and bones are not just a vehicle for our spirit but are how we experience the world and express ourselves, through our creativity, sensuality and feelings. But sometimes we bury our emotions, and shame or blame our appearance for attracting the wrong kind of attention. Negative feelings need acknowledging to move beyond them and appreciate all your body has been through. When we love our bodies we can have more fun with them through movement, sound and tender love-making to raise our vibration.

Women carry the 2000-year-old wound of body shame and persecution pushed by the patriarchy to keep us from living in our full glory. Now it is time to reclaim ourselves from this conditioning, and rebirth our pure, purposeful, passionate, loving essence.

Allow Archeia Mercy to help you empower your divine feminine consciousness and find your true soul's purpose through kindness and compassion towards yourself and others. Take back your gentle, feminine power, oppressed for so long, and help humanity's rebirth into a nurturing, caring and supportive society.

Body love bathing ritual

Run a warm bath with a few drops of rose oil and some rose petals. Before stepping in, invoke Archeia Mercy by saying: "Loving Archeia Mercy, please help me to love my body and relinquish any negative acts, thoughts or feelings I've had towards my appearance. Guide me to fully accept and appreciate myself from now on. Thank you."

Sinking into this blissful bath, breathe deeply and imagine Archeia Mercy's rose-gold energy filling your body, aura and the bathwater as it envelopes you in her kind, loving embrace.

Start to touch your body tenderly, stroking every part of it, in turn, from your feet which walk you through every day and connect you to Mother Earth, all the way up to your head, containing your intelligent, creative mind, rich with ideas and dreams.

Think about all the things your body does for you, including how your ankles, legs, hips, spine, joints, bones and muscles help you move every day. Thank all your internal organs for keeping you alive, enabling you to have children, to breathe, detoxify and heal. All your curves contain you, your scars show your story, your textures create a work of art. Appreciate how your hands touch and hold, your arms move and hug, and the various incredible parts of your face that see, hear, speak and smile at the world.

What a magical miracle of nature you are, full of aliveness and love.

Feel every cell and sinew renewed, your whole self rebirthed as you thank Archeia Mercy for her rejuvenating blessing.

XVIII Archangel Azrael

Also known as

Azriel, Izrail or variations on the same name which means "whom God helps".

Helps with

birth, death, transitions, major life events and grief.

Affirmation

"I glide through transitions with ease, knowing that as I raise my frequency I have nothing to fear. All will be well."

Twin flame

Archeia Mercy

Appearance: As the angel of birth and death, Archangel Azrael is often seen as black, but in a creamy-white cocoon of angelic energy or carrying his light within him.

Ravens, rooks or crows are Azrael's birds and often appear at times of transition to remind people to raise their frequency for a smoother journey through the turbulence.

Guidance: Archangel Azrael oversees the start and end of a human or animal's life. He greets each soul when it leaves the earth plane and lovingly guides it back to the spiritual plane. Then he consoles all those left behind, bereaved, and helps them overcome their loss.

Archangel Azrael is expert at soothing people's grief whether due to death, relationship breakdown, or any of life's big changes. Call on him for help if you feel sadness and he will show you signs of his being with you, such as sending his birds or bringing you healing visions in your dreams or meditations.

If you are a counsellor and aware of how unrecognized grief can turn into further psychological problems, such as addictions to numb the pain of loss, then ask Azrael to join you in your work with others to give them the best guidance for each individual.

This angel of light will dispel any fear you may have of any of life's changes. He will help you realize and cope with all endings and new beginnings, knowing that they are a natural part of life and nothing to be scared of, especially if you have the strength and wisdom of Archangel Azrael on your side.

Connecting to Archangel Azrael through prayer

Whenever you need Azrael to help you through a tricky transition, at a birth or at a loved one's death, he will automatically be with you. But it can help in times such as this to pray to him, as follows, to bring calm reassurance and peace.

Loving Archangel Azrael,

I pray for all souls currently being born. May their births be smooth and trauma-free. Please assist them and their mothers in this time of great initiation. Guide the whole family to open their hearts, strengthen their relationships and be supportive to mother and child.

Please comfort all those going through any big transitions and losses in their lives, including house and location moves, career changes, partnership breakdown, or anyone grieving the loss of a friend, family member or beloved animal companion.

I ask you to go to those who are leaving the earthly plane so they may be comforted in your presence and reassured that higher, heavenly dimensions await when they pass over. Help them know there is nothing to fear, they can feel safe as you take their soul home to the infinite consciousness from which they came. Please open your cocoon of welcoming light and encourage them to step in beside you for the celebrated journey to the other side, where loving light, jubilant angels and other passed loved ones will meet them.

Thank you Archangel Azrael. And so it is. Amen.

XIX Archeia Ariel

Also known as
Lady Ariel, Lioness Goddess.

Helps with
courage, strength in adversity, protection of the planet and all its creatures.

Affirmation
"I stand in my power, with confidence to be my true self and help protect our planet and all its creatures."

Twin flame
Archangel Raziel

Appearance: Archeia Ariel's aura is a cool pink with sparkling gold, flashing with all the colours of the rainbow, much like her counterpart Archangel Raziel's. She changes colour to give you the strength required in different areas of life, for example, if you need confidence her aura will glow red, if you want help communicating, it'll be blue. Her energy is vibrant and revitalising.

In meditations or dreams, Archeia Ariel may appear with the head of a lion, to denote her strength and courage, or bring you her animal symbol of cats to show she is near.

Her angel number is 888, so if you see 8 repeated anywhere she is guiding you towards growth.

Guidance: A natural, wise leader and peaceful, warrior goddess, Archeia Ariel knows it's better to show strength through gentle warmth and kindness rather than force. She'll help you stand in your power and not let anyone push you around, enabling you to become your true, authentic self. Archeia Ariel works on healing your root chakra to give you the confidence to go for your dreams, say no to things you don't want, and point the way to practical, financial support. Ariel's love and care extends to all of Mother Earth's bounty, encouraging us to look after our planet by reusing and recycling, using natural beauty products, with nourishing essential oils, and by being loving to all the world's creatures. If you feel drawn to donating or volunteering with environmental or animal welfare charities, especially if they get you outside in nature, that's Archeia Ariel working her magic. Ask for her help to heal sick animals, whether your beloved pet or all the fish in the polluted seas.

As protective guardian of all that exists on Gaia, Archeia Ariel also works with the elemental energies of the trees, plants and minerals. So you can ask for her help to bring you earth energy to plant seeds of intention; to give you the fire energy of inspiration; air to encourage clear thinking and connection to Source; and water to cleanse and connect to your feminine intuition.

Water element blessing of love

Giving your love generously with blessings such as this is always appreciated by Archeia Ariel.

We know from the work of Masaru Emoto that water carries a memory that can be enhanced with our positive thoughts and emotions. So, whenever you have a glass of water to drink, hold your hand over it, focusing your full attention on the wonder of the liquid of life, and say: "I bless this water and fill it full of love."

When you drink it, the molecules of water will be imprinted with the energy of love and fill your cells with this loving vibration.

Whenever you have a bath or a shower, say the same prayer of love to the water you wash in. When that water goes down the drain and into the water system, travelling around the planet, it will transport that energy of love everywhere it goes.

When you visit the sea, a river or any other body of water, call on Archeia Ariel to purify and rebalance all the water of the world. Say, "May this water be blessed with love, filling everything it touches with loving vibration, healing all water everywhere. And so it is."

XX Archangel Raziel

Also known as
Ratziel, Suriel, Angel of Mysteries, Secrets of God.

Helps with
past-life learning, esoteric knowledge and intuitive gifts.

Affirmation
"*I am reawakening my spiritual powers and intuitive abilities. I trust that I will be given all the wisdom I can cope with to expand my consciousness.*"

Twin flame
Archeia Ariel

Appearance: Archangel Raziel appears as tall and wizard-like, think Gandolf or Merlin, who was one of the physical incarnations of Raziel.

His indigo and gold aura shimmers with all the colours of the rainbow.

Guidance: This divine magician brings you sudden gifts of creative inspiration or deep esoteric insight to help you transform your life for the better. Even if matters appear chaotic and confusing, trust Raziel is bringing you the experience for a deeper purpose. Follow his guidance, particularly in your dreams, to know the right way through turmoil.

If you want to boost your psychic or clairvoyant skills, call on Archangel Raziel to help develop a solid spiritual practice, such as regular meditation. His perfectly timed messages will encourage you to trust your innate powers of telepathy, channelling and remote viewing.

Another Archangel keeper of the Akashic Records, where everything is recorded, Raziel knows all of your past lives and the patterns and preferences stemming from them. Let him help you tap into these memories to heal from problems they may be causing in your present life.

Past-life regression meditation

Lie comfortably, breathing deeply, with your eyes closed.

Ask Archangel Raziel to surround you with his protective indigo

cloak and fill your aura with the colours of
the rainbow. Ask for his guidance in taking
you back to the right past life for you to
discover the root of the issue you need help
with right now.

Imagine you are in a welcoming forest of ancient
trees. Walk down the path taking in all the sights,
sounds and smells of the woods. In one of the trees there
is a door. As you move closer, it opens and you walk inside to see
a black and white staircase going down into the earth. Walk down the
steps, one by one, knowing you are safe and protected.

At the bottom of the stairs you reach another door. Archangel Raziel
takes you through it, into a vast, high-ceilinged room lined with rows
of shelves of different kinds of books. Walk around the room looking
at all the past-life tomes on the shelves until one jumps out at you or
attracts your attention. Allow that book to open and reveal its contents
as you merge with the stories inside it.

Now look down at yourself. What are you wearing? Where are you?
What is surrounding you or attracting your attention? Are there any
people you know with you? What era are you in, what country? Are
you male or female? Are you feeling any strong emotions? What's
about to happen?

Really look into this life for as long as you can, noticing every detail. Don't second guess yourself, just relax and follow wherever these memories lead. What resonates with the issues you are having in your present life?

When you feel you have explored this past life enough, ask Archangel Raziel to cut any bonds you have made to poverty or self-sacrifice so you can be free to live your best life.

Now, close the book and put it back on the shelf. Thank Archangel Raziel for his help and leave the Akashic library, head back up the stairs, through the doorway and back into the forest. Walk out of the woods into the light clearing ahead and slowly open your eyes.

Take a few moments to recall and write down what you experienced.

XXI Archeia Freedom

Also known as

Lady Freedom or Annacea. Her name comes from the old Norse word *frja* which means "to love".

Helps with

healing inner feminine wounds, reconnecting with pleasure, our body, and finding respect.

Affirmation

"I release any restrictions to my sexual self and allow my sensuality to unfold with light and joy."

Twin flame

Archangel Jeremiel

Appearance: Archeia Freedom glows with the same warm orange ray of her twin flame Archangel Jeremiel. Her presence is subtle and ethereal, so you're more likely to feel her accepting and comforting embrace, or sense healing energy from her hands, rather than see her in great detail.

Guidance: Archeia Freedom helps heal any inner goddess wounds so we can stop holding ourselves back out of fear, shame or judgement over who we are and how we express our womanhood, whether mother, grandmother or sensual maiden. If we have stifled our sexual selves after unwanted attention or painful pasts, Archeia Freedom will liberate us from limitation and reconnect us with greater pleasure.

She shines her love on any shame or guilt inside us over past sexual experiences. Her light will help overcome any wounding by realizing the hidden blessings and enlightenment that can come out of difficult situations. Acknowledge how you feel and then ask that your woes be dissolved in your sleep. Then choose not to settle for suffering or hang onto ties that hold you back and bring no joy. Freedom is within you, it's time to express it outwardly. Let Archeia Freedom help you kick any numbing habits you have when feeling discomfort in your life, such as consuming too much alcohol or drugs, compulsive shopping or any other addictions that dull your sparkle. These 'quick fixes' may provide instant relief if negative emotions are triggered but Freedom urges you to choose a more empowering activity that boosts your well-being for the longer term. You deserve it.

Enjoy your body

Many of us have been taught that self-pleasure is dirty or shameful but it's a natural, enjoyable expression of your sexual self. So, let Archeia Freedom help you find the fun at your fingertips and feel your sensual self return.

Take some undisturbed time to yourself for this sexual ceremony. Set the erotic mood with soft lighting or candles, aromas and music that turns you on.

Lie naked on your bed, breathing love in and out as you tune into your body and its connection to Source.

Focus your loving attention on your navel area and ask Archeia Freedom to bathe this area and your whole body with her warm orange light.

Now, turn your attention to your pelvic area and feel your sexual energy building inside you. You may want to visualize it as a sparkling ball of light, growing in intensity as you start to stroke your stomach and your thighs.

If you wish, rub some massage oil, mixed with a few drops of sensual essential oil, such as patchouli or bergamot, into your hands so they can glide more smoothly over your skin.

Gently caress your whole body, in particular your sensitive and sexual areas, feeling your touch, whether gentle or firm, all over. Take time to focus on areas of particular pleasure. Let the sensations intensify, and feel yourself glowing with sexual energy, safe and warm in Archeia Freedom's loving light.

Give thanks for this time to reconnect with your sexual self. Allow the glowing sensuality to stay with you as you go about your day, or drift off into a deeply satisfied sleep.

XXII Archangel Jeremiel

Also known as

Ramiel, in the *Book of Enoch*, one of the seven Archangels. Also known as the Angel of Hope or the Angel of Dreams and Visions, Jeremiel translates as "mercy of God".

Helps with

examining emotions, life review, solving problems and unblocking intuition.

Affirmation

"I look back on my life and know everything happened for a reason. Solutions to my problems will manifest at the right time. It is safe to be connected to my intuition."

Twin flame

Archeia Freedom

Appearance: Archangel Jeremiel is more likely to come through in dreams or visions, or make his presence known through repetitive angel numbers, such as those listed on pages 24–6, rather than be seen in any physical form.

His colour is the same warm, comforting orange as Freedom, his Archeia counterpart.

Guidance: Archangel Jeremiel is another angel said to look after souls as they depart for heaven, as he did with those dying after the Great Flood, written about in the Bible. He brings hope as well as visions of the future for you to translate into meaning in your own life. Call on him to give you inspiration in finding your purpose and seeing why you came to earth at this time, in this incarnation.

Compassionate Archangel Jeremiel helps us look back and do an inventory of past emotions and persistant thoughts to enable us to change them into something more positive. Ask for his powers of reflection while in meditation and you may see past events and feelings come back to you like scenes in a movie. This gives you the chance to reflect and adjust your outlook to help you move forward on your path in a new and peaceful way, realizing that everything happened for a reason, to bring you to where you are now.

If any past experience has led you to switch off your spiritual side or block any psychic gifts you have, let Archangel Jeremiel reassure you that it's safe to be in touch with your intuition. Ask for his guidance to enable you to develop your clairvoyant skills so you can know the best way forward for yourself and others. Pay close attention to any visions in meditation or messages in dreams that you have, especially regarding this untapped aspect of your life.

Decoding your dreams

Before you go to sleep, pray to Archangel Jeremiel to give you answers to your questions in your dreams.

Then, as soon as you wake up, write down everything you dreamed about. The imagery might not make sense immediately but let the visions percolate through your awareness during the day and revisit your notes later to see if anything makes more sense. It may be more of a feeling you got when something happened in your dream. If it was a positive feeling, this is Archangel Jeremiel's way of telling you that you are on the right path. If negative, re-adjust where you're heading.

XXIII Archeia Haniel

Also known as
Lady Haniel, Goddess of Grace.

Helps with
living in tune with natural cycles, menstrual problems, fertility, birthing and releasing.

Affirmation
"I am in tune with the lunar cycles and it empowers me to live a natural life, tapping into my intuition and strong feminine side."

Twin flame
Archangel Nathaniel

Appearance: Not to be confused with Archangel Haniel, Archeia Haniel is a being in her own right but also with a strong connection to the moon. She has a pale blue aura with silver flashes and bright-white wings.

She's connected to another mystical being, the unicorn, so expect to see these in symbolism, meditations or dreams, which become extra powerful when you tune into this Archeia.

Guidance: Archeia Haniel shares the wisdom from the witches and all wise women of the past to encourage our compassionate, intuitive and nurturing sides. She wants you to tune into the power of the moon, with its regular rhythm of releasing and starting afresh, to birth new ways of being and shed the old. Start women's circles to share the wisdom of your natural cycle and empower each other.

Make the most of the lunar phases for attracting what you want, whether it's plants, people or projects. Different plants grow best according to certain phases of the moon, so research thoroughly. For goals, think about what you want to attract at the new moon. As the moon grows bigger (waxes), write down your intention. Take action when half the moon is visible in the sky, and as the moon gets fuller refine your plans and overcome any obstacles. At the full moon, harvest the blessings, deciding what you need to release as the moon wanes (grows smaller).

If you have crystals, cleanse and charge them by laying them outside under a full moon. Similarly, you can refresh your energy by being outside with the full moon, or 'moon-bathing'. As you look up towards the moon, imagine Archeia Haniel's bright white and silver rays shining down on you and filling you up with her spiritual powers.

Releasing ritual with the new moon
Place some items connected to Archeia Haniel on your angel altar, such as a silver cloth, moonstone crystal, white or silver candles.

Have a pen and paper near, but spend a few moments sitting in silence, during the waxing moon phase, to collect your throughts.

Now, write down the answer to these questions, if relevant. Don't over-think the answers, often the first to come to mind is the one to focus on.
* Has anyone or anything upset you or angered you this month?
* Are you holding on to any negative feelings?
* Has anyone criticised you in any way?
* Is anyone draining your energy?
* What would you like to release from your energy field, thoughts and emotions?

Light a white candle to purify these negative aspects of your life.

Say: "Dear Archeia Haniel, please bathe me with your calming, silver-white light. Align me with the moon phase, with the powers of women and with the cycles of nature. I am now ready to release [whatever you want to let go of] and any negativity I carry. And so it is."

Now, carefully burn your piece of paper in the flame of the candle. As it disappears so do the issues written down. Allow the candle to burn down and then get rid of it outside your home, ideally by burying it in soil.

Thank Archeia Haniel and the powers of the moon.

XXIV Archangel Nathaniel

Also known as
the Angel of Fire, Angel of Purpose or Angel of Energy. His name means "Gift of God" or "God has given".

Helps with
motivation, transformation and support for men in particular.

Affirmation
"*I use the power of movement to transform harsh emotions into a lighter state of being. I clear the way for the new to enter my life.*"

Twin flame
Archeia Haniel

Appearance: Archangel Nathaniel wears a white and gold robe, and his aura shimmers a bright turquoise, beaming out the red and orange flames of passion and inspiration.

He is said to have lived as John the Baptist, when he used the power of water to cleanse and rebirth. You may feel his presence stronger near waterfalls or rivers, especially since 2012 when he has been appearing to help with humanity's ascension.

Guidance: As the patron of lightworkers, Archangel Nathaniel encourages healers and sensitives to fully shine their light to help people with their awakenings and transition into the New Age. Archangel Nathaniel urges you to gather with like-minded others to heal and empower humanity. He supports men, especially, to share their emotions and move away from toxic masculine ideas.

After delving into deep feelings with Archeia Haniel, Archangel Nathaniel helps you release them by moving your body, in whatever activity brings you most pleasure. He will uplift your spirits and ignite your enthusiasm for your life's purpose.

Call on Archangel Nathaniel to keep you grounded in meditation and expand your heart chakra so you can know and share your true desires with the world.

Allow him to ignite your motivation and confidence to combat any concerns about not being good enough, and instead start living your life joyfully, now. Let him inspire you to stop procrastinating and work hard on your passions.

Clear clutter to welcome in the new

Ask Archangel Nathaniel to help you clear any clutter in your home to ensure you can swiftly and smoothly bring in new opportunities and experiences.

Focus some time and effort on working out what to get rid of in any area you need a good clearout, whether it's your wardobe, kitchen cupboards or garage. Anything you do not use regularly or really love, Nathaniel will help you release with gratitude for it being in your life.

When doing substantial clutter-clearing at home, expect to release emotions, and even relationships, that no longer serve you.

This Archangel can work rapidly to bring about change, so once you've asked for his help, prepare to say goodbye to the old and welcome in fresh, exciting times.

XXV Archeia Purity

Also known as
Lady Purity or Holy Amethyst.

Helps with
protecting your energy field, clearing drama and negativity, transformation.

Affirmation

"I am empathic while maintaining my own boundaries. I clear my energy whenever needed and transform darkness into light."

Twin flame
Archangel Zadkiel

Appearance: Carrying the violet flame of transmutation energy, Archeia Purity appears in all shades of purple and often wears an amethyst crystal. This highly spiritual stone connects her to her counterpart Archangel Zadkiel and shares her enigmatic energy of sobriety and pure connection to Source. She exudes a fiery, warrior-like presence.

Guidance: Archeia Purity helps clear your energy field of anything unwanted, whether that's people, situations or limiting beliefs and behaviours. Let Purity assist you in living life more consciously, to break free of anything dragging you down.

Having clear boundaries about what you will and will not allow in to your energy field is a gift from Archeia Purity. Only let in that which serves you – from the most nutritious foods to the most beneficial and joyful relationships – and protect yourself from anything detrimental. Learn to discern the density of others as they enter your aura, then honour yourself by only connecting deeply with whatever and whoever inspires and uplifts.

Archeia Purity gives strength to empaths, healers or carers who struggle with letting others' negativity, dramas or dis-ease take over their mood. As an empath, you have a big heart and want to help, but picking up people's vibes or the atmosphere in a room can weigh heavy on a sensitive soul. If you find yourself regularly drained, Archeia Purity encourages you to clear your energy field often. Simply sit or stand quietly, take a few deep breaths, and ask Archeia Purity's powerful violet flame to swirl around you, working its cleansing magic for as long as you need to feel like yourself again.

Archeia Purity can also help cleanse the energy of items in your home, or things you use regularly, which have a lot of human contact. For example, when you receive money it has already passed through many hands, so ask Purity to energetically cleanse it and then reprogramme it to bring you the highest blessings from Source. Do the same if you use a massage table or chair for treatments, so each person's energy is cleared from it before the next session.

Cleansing an object with Archeia Purity

If you feel a favourite object, such as a crystal, or anything you buy secondhand, needs its energy cleansing, hold it in your hands or place your hands upon it and take a few deep breaths to tune into it.

Ask Archeia Purity to remove all past events, emotions and stories connected to this item, and surrender these energies to Source for energetic purification.

To reprogramme something, such as a favourite piece of jewellery, or crystal pendant, hold it close to your heart and say out loud: "Dear Archeia Purity, please charge up this item with your loving light and help it protect my energy from anything that isn't for my highest good. Assist it in keeping my energy pure and strong. Thank you. And so it is."

Now tune into the energy of the item to sense the difference between before and after this ritual so you know when it needs repeating.

XXVI Archangel Zadkiel

Also known as
the angel of benevolence, mercy and memory, his name means "righteousness of God".

Helps with
decision-making, willpower, organisation and bringing magic into your life.

Affirmation
"I clear all ties to past trauma and events to soar higher in my vibration. I shine my light clearly out into the world."

Twin flame
Archeia Purity

Appearance: Look out for amethyst crystals in visions or in your reality, as these are a sign Archangel Zadkiel is watching over you. He may appear to you in your dreams or meditations wearing bright white and purple, along with a necklace of this very spiritual crystal.

Guidance: As a cosmic couple, Archangel Zadkiel and Archeia Purity help with your spiritual ascension by giving you an energetic upgrade. Another angelic keeper of the Akashic records, Archangel Zadkiel knows your ancestral and past life patterns and can help free you from all ties with them, enabling you to soar to higher vibrations in this lifetime. His main aim is to help you forgive past wrongs, clear past trauma and bring greater clarity, so you can make more positive and empowering choices.

Archangel Zadkiel keeps you disciplined in your spiritual quest, helping you turn away from too many indulgences and any addictions. Treating yourself is one thing, but not when you feel guilt or regret afterwards. These emotions bring you down and you are here to rise up and be your best self. So call on Zadkiel to help cease any cravings. Then you can be a clearer conduit for the magic that will then come into your life via this Archangel.

If you ever feel unsure, anxious, or withdrawn from your radiant, luminous self, pray to beloved Archangel Zadkiel, asking him to fill your intentions and actions with his light. See your heart centre and all your chakras, from bottom to top, shining crystal clear and beaming ultra-violet healing energy out into the world.

Archangel Zadkiel and the Violet Flame:

Working also with the Violet Flame, Archangel Zadkiel can send this transformational energy down into areas in order to clear and raise their frequency.

Whether in your own home or neighbourhood, or in the wider world's trouble spots, such as hospitals or prisons, ask Zadkiel to flow the violet flame into portals in these areas continually.

The Violet Flame

This transformational energy, which can be called upon to bring healing to any situation, has been shared by Ascended Master Saint Germain for centuries.

This legendary spiritual master worked on earth in various impressive incarnations. According to the Theosophical Society he was: a high priest in Atlantis; Samuel, the 11th Century BCE religious leader and last of the Hebrew judges; Greek philosopher Plato; English philosophers Roger and Francis Bacon; and the explorer Christopher Columbus, among others.

Now channelling his powerful energy from the spirit realm, he is credited with bringing about the New Age of esoteric wisdom and magic that humanity has been slowly progressing towards since the 1960s.

Archangel Zadkiel and Archeia Purity are also keepers of the violet flame and can assist you in bringing about healing anyone and anywhere by transmuting negative energy into positive, and raising the vibration of all who ask or are sent this miraculous blast of beneficial light.

All you have to do is ask for the violet flame to be present and visualise it around you whenever you need it, or wherever in the world you send it to work its high-vibrational magic.

XXVII Archeia Serenity

Also known as
Lady Serenity and Cassibella.

Helps with
bringing balance, fear-busting, breaking through limitations and dualistic thinking.

Affirmation

"I am courageous and ready to conquer my fears. I am determined to shine my full light out into the world."

Twin flame
Archangel Cassiel

Appearance: Archeia Serenity peacefully shines a pearlescent silver light, and often appears with a symbol of balance, such as the black and white yin and yang symbol. This shows there is more to life than black and white, good and bad: there is everything in between and all is Source energy.

Guidance: Archeia Serenity guides us to face our fears, shining the light of awareness on them so we can understand and accept them. By exploring why something scares us, and moving towards accepting it or doing it, we illuminate and flow with our fears to bring a greater confidence in ourselves. Think of all the times you have been scared about something, such as before trying a new experience or taking a test, but you did it, and felt amazing afterwards. Or maybe you failed, but you learned from your mistakes. Either way, as you master your fears, you empower yourself even more.

Instead of focusing on limitations or problems, playing the victim or repeating the same dramas, stay in the energy of love and see everything as a blessing. Even the seemingly negative parts of our lives serve as opportunities to explore our shadows and transform them to bring harmony. Archeia Serenity wants to hear you sharing what *is* working in your world, and giving thanks for it, so that from this place of gratitude your life expands positively.

As we develop our spiritual side and become more aware of other dimensions, new fears may arise, perhaps to do with ghostly or other-worldly presences, or dark energy. But these worries are unnecessary as everything comes from Source, and even troubled spirits usually just need understanding and compassion to return to the light. Trust that Archeia Serenity will protect you by guiding you to live more from a state of love. Then, as your heart centre grows, it will protect you with its radiant glow.

Catching your fears

If you are still anxious about something, ask Archeia Serenity and her counterpart Archangel Cassiel to protect you with their powerful web of light.

At your angel altar, place shungite or hematite for protection, as well as a silver candle and any other ornaments to help you stay calm in the face of fear.

Breathe deeply and see yourself sitting in a column of pearlescent silver light. Ask Archeia Serenity to shine her healing energy into you, and Archangel Cassiel to watch over and clear away any residue of fear.

See them standing either side of you. Watch them cast a shimmering iridescent net between them and over you, as it falls to the ground beneath you. This magical web catches all that isn't love in your energy field, thoughts and surroundings, and transmutes all that fear into soothing peace.

See or sense this cosmic couple slowly moving this silvery mesh up your body and your energy field, capturing anything that doesn't resonate with the vibration of love.

Ask Archeia Serenity to take these fears into the light and transform them into inspiration to act differently and more positively. All fears and negativity are now caught in this web as it is gathered up, above your crown chakra. Archeia Serenity now dissolves this net of fears into liquid love and peace, which rains down on you now, revitalizing your energy completely.

XXVIII Archangel Cassiel

Also known as

The Archangel of Duality or the Archangel of Tears, Cassiel's name means "speed of god". Along with Metatron and Sandalphon, Cassiel is said to have lived a human life on earth before ascending to the angelic realm.

Helps with

balancing duality within you, strengthening your aura, manifesting positive, new realities.

Affirmation

"I am connected to my deeper self, the angelic realm and Source energy. I know I am always supported."

Twin flame

Archeia Serenity

Appearance: Sometimes seen or depicted with a beard, a crown and a long black cloak, carrying a scythe, or riding a dragon carrying a spear, Archangel Cassiel is not the angel of death, as it may appear, but one who guides souls to God after they have passed on from the physical realm. His aura shines white or silver with hints of purple, pink or bronze.

Guidance: With more of a supportive, watchful, rather than active, presence, Archangel Cassiel can help you find harmony and hope when you're feeling down. If your world looks bleak, he will remind you of your powerful, creative self and boost your aura so you can magnetize more upbeat situations into your life.

He primarily looks after anyone feeling lonely or genuinely alone, whispering the truth that they are never really on their own, the angels are always with them. Try to enjoy times of solitude knowing Archangel Cassiel is with you, encouraging you to connect deeper with your lost self and giving you strength and resilience in your independence.

Even if surrounded by friends or in a relationship, you can still feel isolated and as if no one understands the real you. But Archangel Cassiel is here to sift out the fake friends, back-stabbing colleagues or unsupportive partners by showing you who has really got your back. Allow him to bring peace and balance back to your life.

Meditate more

Archangel Cassiel guides you to meditate more often, so you can feel the divine within and around you.

Make the time every day, ideally for twenty minutes or more, to sit in stillness at your angel altar.

Simply become aware of your breathing, watching any thoughts come and go, not getting attached to any of them.

Breathe love in and out, letting it fill your whole body and aura around you.

Then say the following prayer to call Cassiel close:

"Beloved Archangel Cassiel, please come into my aura now. Help me feel the love inside my heart, healing it of any wounding holding back love's true expression. Help me to trust in others again and appreciate the love I receive. Protect me from hurt and betrayal. Enable me to see that I am love incarnated so that I can attract more love. Thank you for your strength and wisdom. And so it is."

Archangel Cassiel has a strong connection to dolphins with an ability to understand their wisdom and share it with those tuned in enough. Call upon Cassiel's connection to the sea to protect you if sailing or living by the coast.

XXIX Archeia Radiant

Also known as
Lady Radiance or Maryllisa.

Helps with
seeing the beauty in everything, stopping judgement of yourself and others, sharing your love with the world.

Affirmation
"I drop all judgement towards myself and others, starting each day full of love."

Twin flame
Archangel Haniel

Appearance: Archeia Radiant is the brightest, most luminescent of all the Archeia. You may see nothing but a shining white light or feel the comforting, warm embrace of her loving energy as you call her towards you.

Her flower is the amaryllis so any time you see this variety of lily, it is Lady Radiant making her presence known. Put this flower onto your angel altar as often as you can to bring in her power of constant, unconditional love.

Guidance: Archeia Radiant wants you to remember your brilliant radiance and let it shine. Let your eyes sparkle with the truth of your inner light and reveal to the world the love you are. Share your brilliance with everyone, everywhere you go. Smile at strangers, appreciate the beauty in all of humanity, let your love touch everyone you meet.

She shares the wisdom that Source's unconditional love is always there for you, pure and perfect, you just have to allow it to steer your life and let the magic unfold. Connect to Creator energy regularly to feel an increased sense of self-worth, trust and confidence that things will work out well if you move in the direction of love.

Go forward towards your dreams and goals instead of complaining that they haven't materialised yet. Start the day without a judgement of what may happen or what has gone on in the past. Ask Archeia Radiant to take away any negativity from your life. Be free from running a habitual commentary inside your head. Instead, begin the day with a clear, calm mind coming from a place of gratitude for everything in your life, and see more joy and blessings manifest. If judgements still arise, delve deeply into where they come from in your past and face the negative imprinting of your upbringing as part of someone else's programming. Forgive yourself and others for making these judgements, then you can release and replace them with loving thoughts, and move forward positively. Peace, tranquility and contentment are yours when you allow your light to shine brightly.

Mirror gazing magic

Start each day with love and gratitude for yourself by looking in the mirror at your reflection and seeing the beauty within you.

Look deeply into your eyes and say, "I love you," three times, slowly.

Acknowledge yourself by saying: "I am a being of love and light. My radiance shines for all to see and experience. In shining my light brightly I allow others to do the same. Together we are luminescent beings of love. Thank you Archeia Radiant for showing me my true radiance."

Now, close your eyes, and for at least ten minutes, really feel the love in your heart space shining brightly, growing outwardly, filling your whole being and aura. Sit in this loving presence as it permeates every area of your life.

Rub the palms of your hands together and place over your closed eyes, before opening your eyes behind your palms. Remove your hands and gaze at yourself in the mirror again. Repeat the affirmation:

I am love.

Now go about your day remembering your connection to your divinity. Talk less and listen more to love's nudgings. Worry less, smile more. Judge no more and feel free to act with love. And so it is.

XXX Archangel Haniel

Also known as
the Archangel of Joy or Angel of Intuition.

Helps with
experiencing more joy, happiness, balance and harmony.

Affirmation

"I follow my intuition to develop my spirituality and know I am one with Source energy. I am happy and fulfilled knowing more about the divine."

Twin flame
Archeia Radiant

Appearance: Archangel Haniel's aura shines a bright, turquoise light and he is often seen with silver wings, whether in your dreams, meditations or supernatural vision. Alternatively, you may feel Haniel as an energy buzz at your crown or third eye chakra. Of all the Archangels, Haniel has the most feminine energy, with connections to the Moon and to eternity, as written about in the Kabbalah.

Guidance: Much like his spiritual partner Archeia Radiant, Archangel Haniel wants you to have a strong connection to Source so you can know that you are not only deeply loved, but are love energy in motion. Then you can live a life of true joy and wonder as you carry out all Source has planned for you.

However, if you often feel depressed or your emotions fluctuate wildly, pray to Archangel Haniel to bring back balance and show you the way to well-being. He will then guide you towards the best information, teachers and mentors to help you realize this loving connection and broaden your spirituality. If a certain esoteric book keeps coming to your awareness, or you keep feeling the urge to develop your psychic side, follow these nudges in the direction of your spiritual expansion, as it is Archangel Haniel guiding you forward.

Enjoy learning about and mastering all the spiritual techniques you need to reconnect you with the divine, from praying and meditation to yoga and conscious dance. You will then attract more of the right people and situations to spur you on and bring you a deeper happiness and connectedness with the flow of life.

Ask for help from Archangel Haniel if you are starting something new in your life, such as a different job or relationship, or moving house. He will ensure you have the best of luck and support in this fresh chapter, and enable you to see the change as exciting rather than destabilizing. From new shoots grow beautiful flowers, such as amaryllis, flower of Archeia Radiant who joins Haniel in wanting you to shine with positivity and love so you can be a blessing to the world.

Pray for love

If you are looking for love or are not getting on with your partner right now, ask Archangel Haniel for help.

At your angel altar, light a pink or red candle to represent your desire for true love to come to you.

Take some time to settle your mind before praying out loud as follows:

"Dear loving Archangel Haniel, please shower me with your bright, joyful energy. Help me to experience inner happiness so that it may shine out into the world and attract the same to me. Bring harmony into my life in all my existing relationships, releasing those that dull my sparkle, and helping me meet new, healthy, balanced, supportive souls [add any description of the kind of people you would like in your life]. Please give me abundant opportunities to appreciate beauty in life, to laugh and have fun, so that I can add joy and jubilation to the world. Thank you."

Connecting with the Archangels and Archeiai using crystals

C rystals are a great way to connect with the Archangels and Archeiai and bring their energy into your life. Keep a look out for crystals crafted into angel shapes as these make a lovely addition to your angel altar. To bring the energy of a particular Archangel or Archeia into your meditations

add the specific gem below. Simply sit holding the crystal, place it on your body, or wear it in jewellery to have your favourite angel's divine presence with you all the time.

The following crystals are good for connecting generally with the angelic realm as well as increasing your abilty to tune into them.

Amethyst: A very spiritual stone to meditate with as it surrounds you with a protective light as you expand your higher mind into magical realms.

Angelite: This light blue stone of compressed celestite will increase your ability to see, hear or sense the angels' presence, as well as bring them to you in your dreams.

Selenite: This wand-shaped crystal opens up your crown chakra so you can connect to the higher realms. It will also bring you deep peace and tranquility.

Celestite: These light blue clusters help you float deeper into meditation and enable you to clearly pick up messages from the Archangels and Archeiai.

To connect with...

Archangel Michael and Archeia Faith: With his halo emitting gold, royal blue or royal purple, Archangel Michael is connected with crystals of the same colour, such as sugilite or sapphire, while Archeia Faith is associated with celestite, sodalite, blue lace agate, lapis lazuli and labradorite.

Archangel Raphael and Archeia Virtue: Archangel Raphael emits a bright green healing light so he is often linked with gems such as emerald and malachite. On your meditation altar, add sapphire, aquamarine and rhodochrosite for Archeia Virtue to bring forth her healing heart energy.

Archangel Gabriel and Archeia Hope: Archangel Gabriel's halo is a vibrant copper colour, so any crystal with orange flashes, such as tiger's eye or jasper will help tune into his energy. Archeia Hope appears as bright white with twinkles of gold or green, reflected in quartz, herkimer diamond and orange calcite.

Archangel Uriel and Archeia Grace: Often depicted holding a lantern shining its pale yellow candlelight, Archangel Uriel's amber and citrine crystals share that same uplifting golden glow. A similar warm energy exudes from Archeia Grace's fire opal and yellow tourmaline gems.

Archangel Chamuel and Archeia Charity: Down-to-earth Archangel Chamuel often appears in a light green shade so use fluorite or amazonite to vibe with his energy. Compassionate Archeia Charity resonates with crystals connected to the heart incuding rose quartz, petalite and pink rhodochrosite.

Archangel Jophiel and Archeia Christine: Archangel Jophiel with a deep fuscia halo brings beauty into life especially if you meditate with pink tourmaline or rubellite to harness this energy. Use citrine, azurite, aquamarine or healer's gold to tune into Archeia Christine's illuminating presence.

Archangel Metatron and Archeia Constance: Archangel Metatron is associated with the sacred geometry of the merkabah so multi-faceted diamond is his crystal along with watermelon tourmaline to reflect his green and violet light. Connect with Archeia Constance through these gems, as well as angel aura andara and the rare quartz azeztulite.

Archangel Sandalphon and Archeia Patience: Archangel Sandalphon shines a clear turquoise light, so the gemstone of the same name is the best for linking in to his powerful energy. His Archeia counterpart Patience exudes her trust through smoky quartz, amber or rainbow moonstone.

Archangel Azrael and Archeia Mercy: These two angels of kindness manifest in a blend of copper and magenta rays making shimmering rose gold. Meditate with yellow calcite to connect deeply with Archangel Azrael or garnet to feel the benevelent energy of Archeia Mercy.

Archangel Raziel and Archeia Ariel: Archangel Raziel has a multi-coloured halo so harness his power by sittting quietly with titanium rainbow quartz or clear quartz, which turns sunbeams into a colourful arc. Choose rainbow moonstone, ruby or tiger's eye to connect with the courageous energy of Archeia Ariel.

Archangel Jeremiel and Archeia Freedom: Amethyst is the best crystal to help tune into Archangel Jeremiel's higher guidance. While the rich orange gems of carnelian and orange calcite will help you harness Archeia Freedom's sexual liberation and healing.

Archangel Nathaniel and Archeia Haniel: Bring in inspiration for abundance through Archangel Nathaniel by meditating with carnelian, orange calcite, garnet and rutilated quartz. Archeia Grace, goddess of the moon, is activated and connected to through moonstone and selenite.

Archangel Zadkiel and Archeia Purity: Archeia Purity wears a sacred amethyst crystal to connect her with Archangel Zadkiel. Use amethyst, aquamarine, or clear quartz for a stronger connection to Archangel Zadkiel, and sugilite, lapis lazuli and violet flame opal to bring Archeia Purity into your life.

Archangel Cassiel and Archeia Serenity: Tune into your third eye, which Archangel Cassiel represents, by meditating with blue topaz or jet, plus silvery gems such as hematite. His counterpart Archeia Serenity inspires fearlessness through these crystals plus shungite, larimar and shimmering angelinite.

Archangel Haniel and Archeia Radiant: Archangel Haniel has a radiating halo of blueish white for purity and truth. Tune into this energy with moonstone and blue lace agate. Haniel and his twin flame Archeia Radiant help you shine your beauty from within by connecting with iridescent gems.

Angels at a glance

Archangel or Archeia	Helps with	How they help
Archeia Faith I	Protection, clarity, trusting yourself	Aura clear and shield technique
Archangel Michael II	Protection, strength, balance	Energetic cord-cutting exercise
Archeia Virtue III	Forgiveness, healing, mothering	Forgiveness and healing pink light meditation
Archangel Raphael IV	Travelling, animal healing, overcoming pain	Healing meditation
Archeia Hope V	Creativity, raising vibration, manifesting new ideas and projects	Manifesting the best
Archangel Gabriel VI	Communication, children	Asking for clarity and signs
Archeia Grace VII	Seeing blessings as miracles, intuition, rebirth	Connecting to deceased loved ones
Archangel Uriel VIII	Wisdom, spiritual development and insight	Developing spiritual wisdom

Archeia Charity	Self-love and self-care	Self-love bathing ritual
Archangel Chamuel	Giving and finding love	Finding lost items or what is missing in your life
Archeia Christine	Ascension, higher consciousness, shining your light	Connect to the earth and the sun daily practise
Archangel Jophiel	Beauty, positivity and wellbeing	Activating crown chakra for higher consciousness
Archeia Constance	Ascension through joy	Knowing when to act and when to rest
Archangel Metatron	Ascension and healing with Metatron's cube	Frequency-raising light bath
Archeia Patience	Abundance and prosperity	Healing negative money blocks
Archangel Sandalphon	Balancing the masculine and feminine, musicality, ascension	Raising frequency meditation
Archeia Mercy	Loving ourselves, especially our bodies	Body love bathing ritual

Archeia Azrael	Grief, death, changes	Prayer to help all those in life transitions
Archangel Ariel	Courage to be yourself, strength, animal and plant protection and healing	Water love blessing
Archeia Raziel	Psychic development and past lives recognition	Past-life regression meditation
Archeia Freedom	Releasing shame or addiction, returning to pleasure	Enjoy your body ritual
Archangel Jeremiel	Intuition, psychic skills, dreams	Decoding your dreams
Archeia Haniel	Tuning into the moon and natural cycles, women's wisdom	Releasing with the moon ritual
Archangel Nathanial	Awakening, new beginnings, motivation, inspiration	Clutter-clearing to bring in new experiences
Archeia Purity	Clearing energy field, sobriety, boundaries	Object cleansing
Archangel Zadkiel	Forgiveness, healing the past, addictions	Healing with the Violet Flame
Archeia Serenity	Tranforming fears and shadows	Catch fears and turn them into peace

Archangel Cassiel	Manifesting positivity, sorting out relationships, boosting love	Meditate more
Archeia Radiant	Unconditional love, radiating love into the world	Mirror-gazing love-in
Archangel Haniel	Knowing you are love, bringing joy, harmony	Prayer for romantic love

Further Reading

BOOKS

Angel Numbers, Kyle Gray (Hay House, 2019)

Angels: A Very Short Introduction, David Albert Jones (Oxford University Press, 2011)

Archangels 101, Doreen Virtue (Hay House, 2010)

The Archangel Guide to Ascension, Diana Cooper and Tim Whild (Hay House, 2015)

Connecting with the Angels Made Easy, Kyle Gray (Hay House 2015)

A Dictionary of Angels, Gustav Davidon (The Free Press, 1967 and 1971)

The Female Archangels, Calista (That Guy's House, 2020)

The Female Archangels, Claire Stone (Hay House, 2020)

ONLINE RESOURCES

www.archeiaiguidance.com

www.archangelsecrets.com

www.archangelsigns.com

www.alurasangels.com

www.anow.org/archangels-and-archaia

www.theangelwhispers.org

www.beliefnet.com/inspiration/angels

www.heartscenter.org

www.innerlightworkers.co.uk

www.summitlighthouse.org

www.thesecretofthetarot.com

www.theblackfeatherintuitive.com

soundofheart.org/galacticfreepress

www.unifycosmos.com